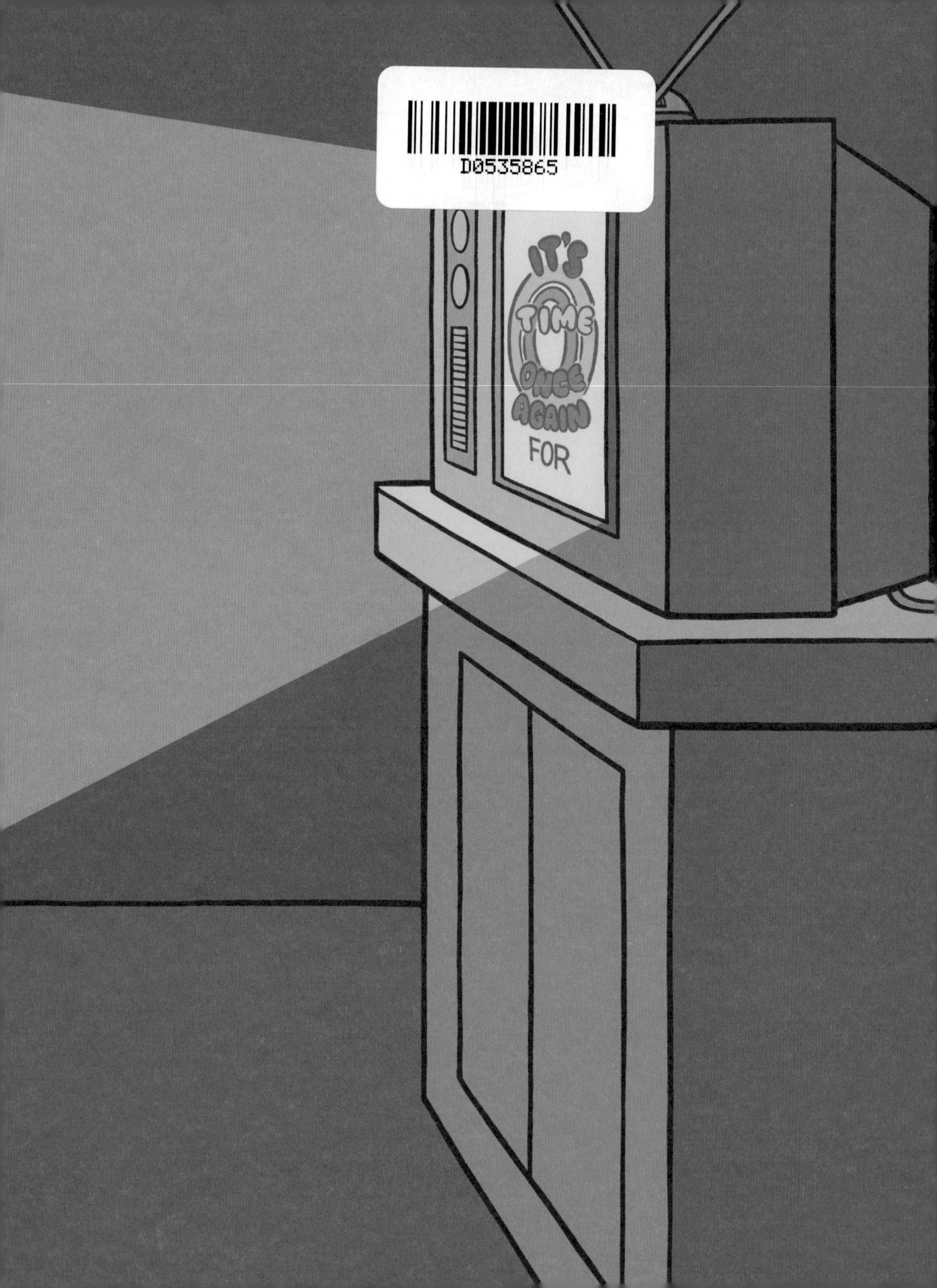
IT'S
TIME
ONCE
AGAIN
FOR

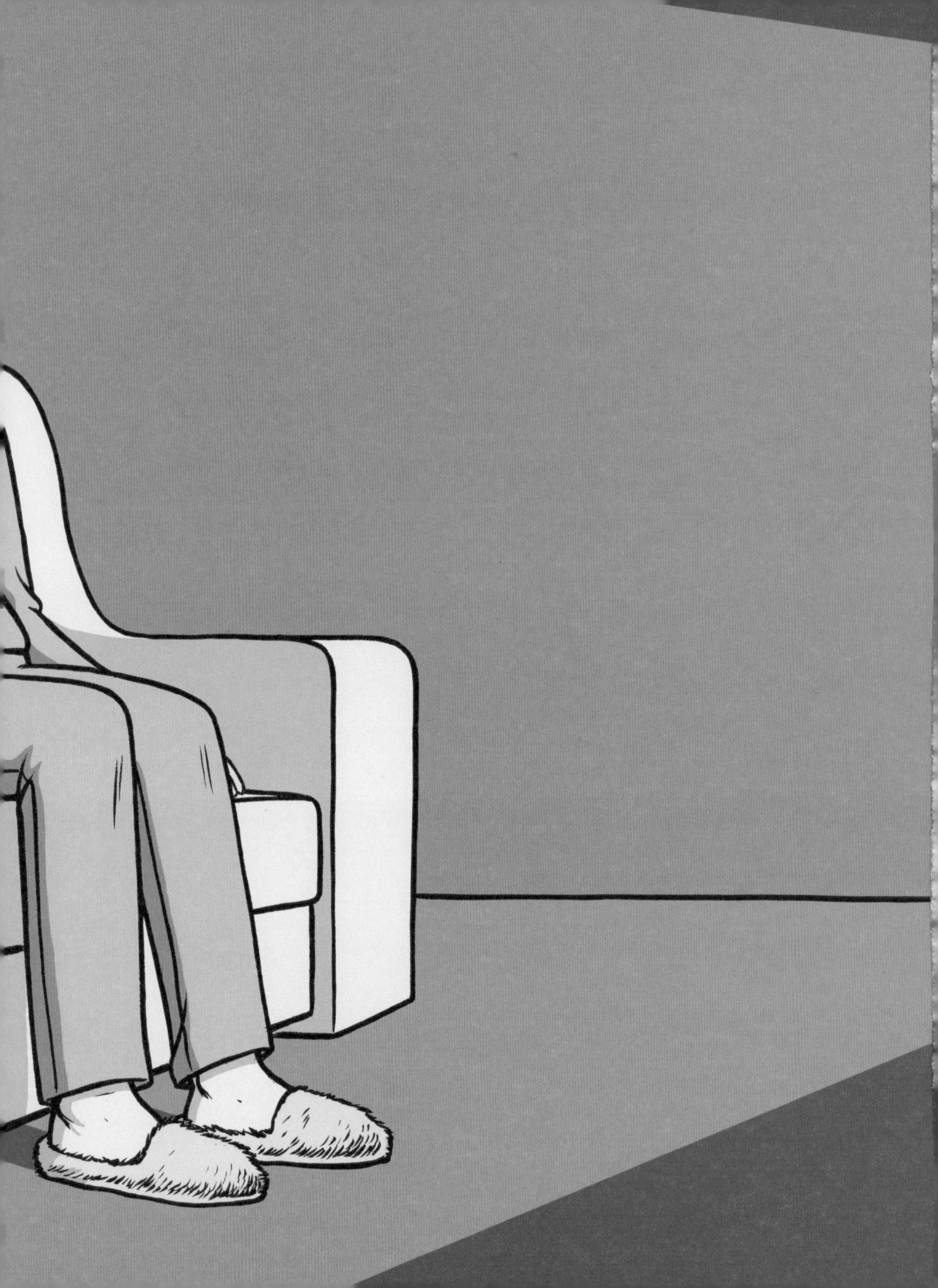

Life with MR. Dangerous

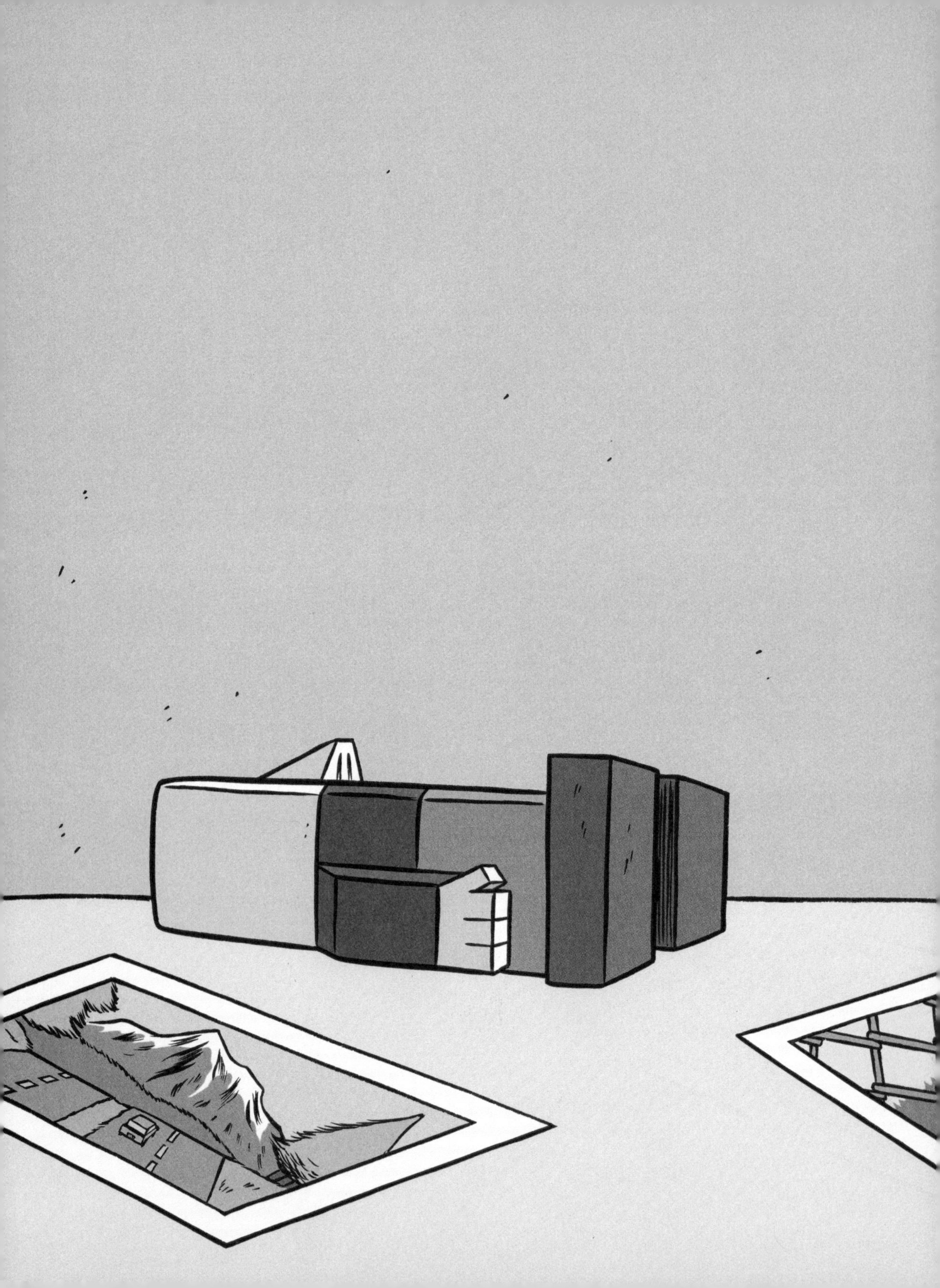

Life with MR. Dangerous

A CARTOON
BY
PAUL HORNSCHEMEIER

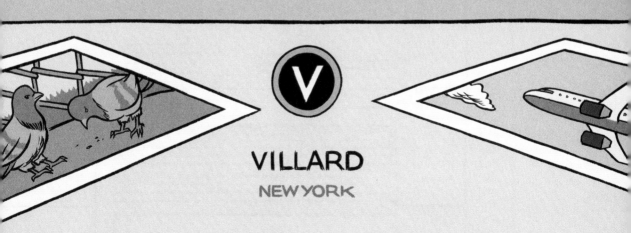

VILLARD

NEW YORK

PUBLISHED IN THE UNITED STATES BY VILLARD BOOKS,
AN IMPRINT OF THE RANDOM HOUSE PUBLISHING GROUP,
A DIVISION OF RANDOM HOUSE, INC., NEW YORK.

VILLARD AND "V" CIRCLED DESIGN ARE REGISTERED
TRADEMARKS OF RANDOM HOUSE, INC.

SOME OF THE MATERIAL IN THIS BOOK ORIGINALLY APPEARED
SERIALIZED IN "MOME," AN ANTHOLOGY PUBLISHED BY
FANTAGRAPHICS BOOKS, INC.

ISBN 978-0-345-49441-2

PRINTED IN THE UNITED STATES OF AMERICA
ON ACID FREE PAPER.

WWW.VILLARD.COM

9 8 7 6 5 4 3 2 1

FIRST EDITION

BOOK DESIGN BY THE AUTHOR.

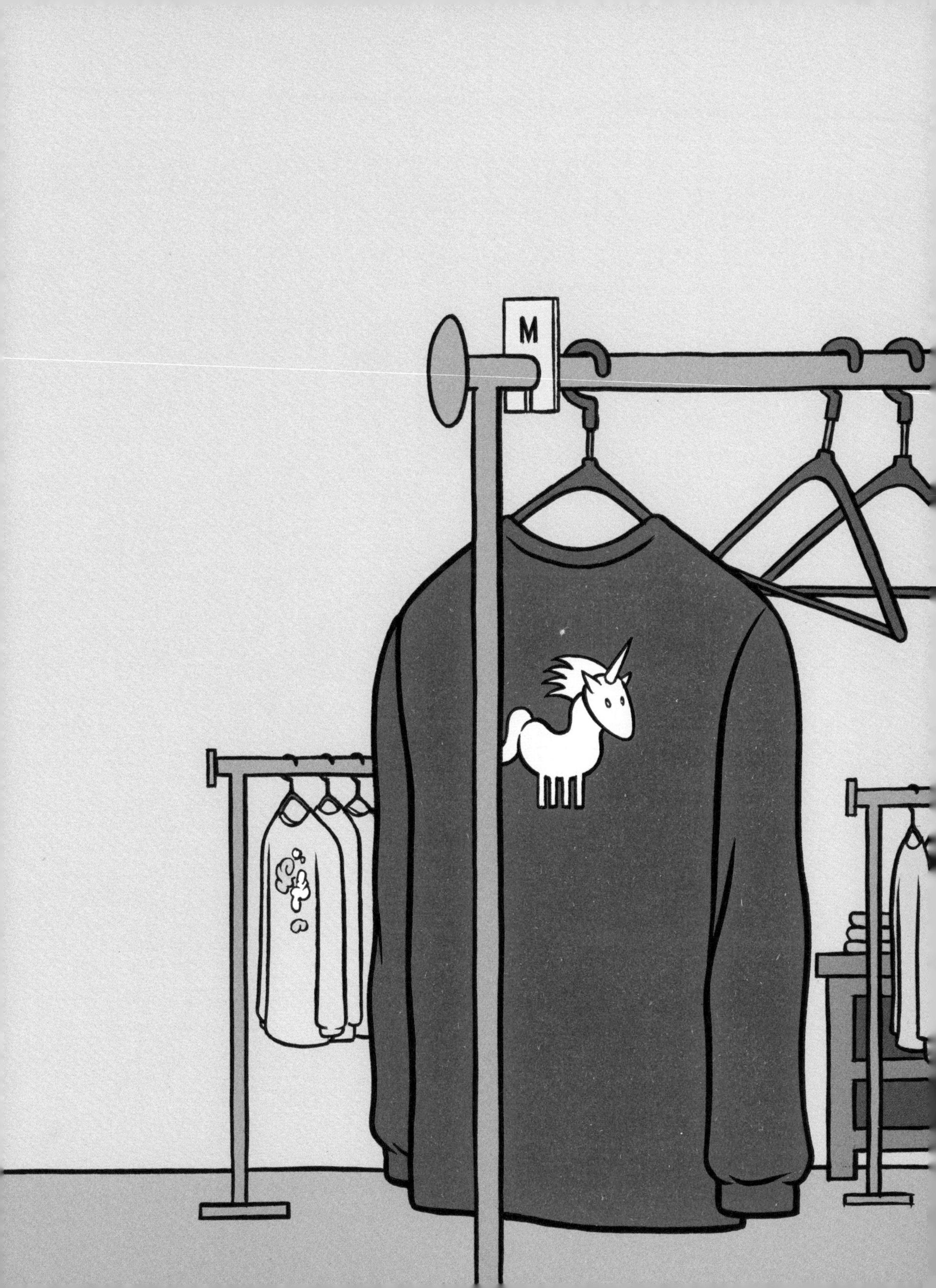
M

Contents

For Emily

WITH WHOM IT'S ALWAYS BETTER

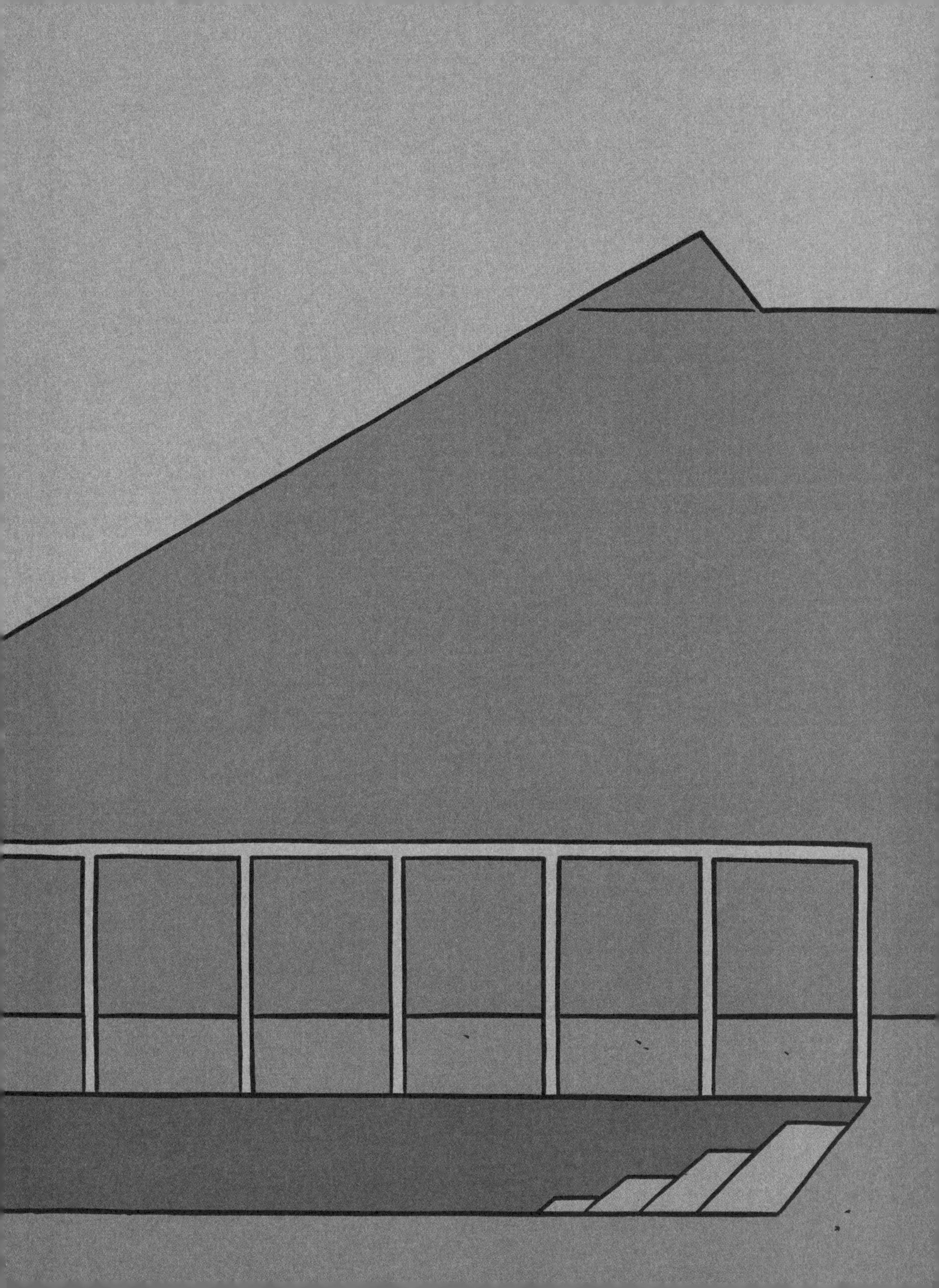

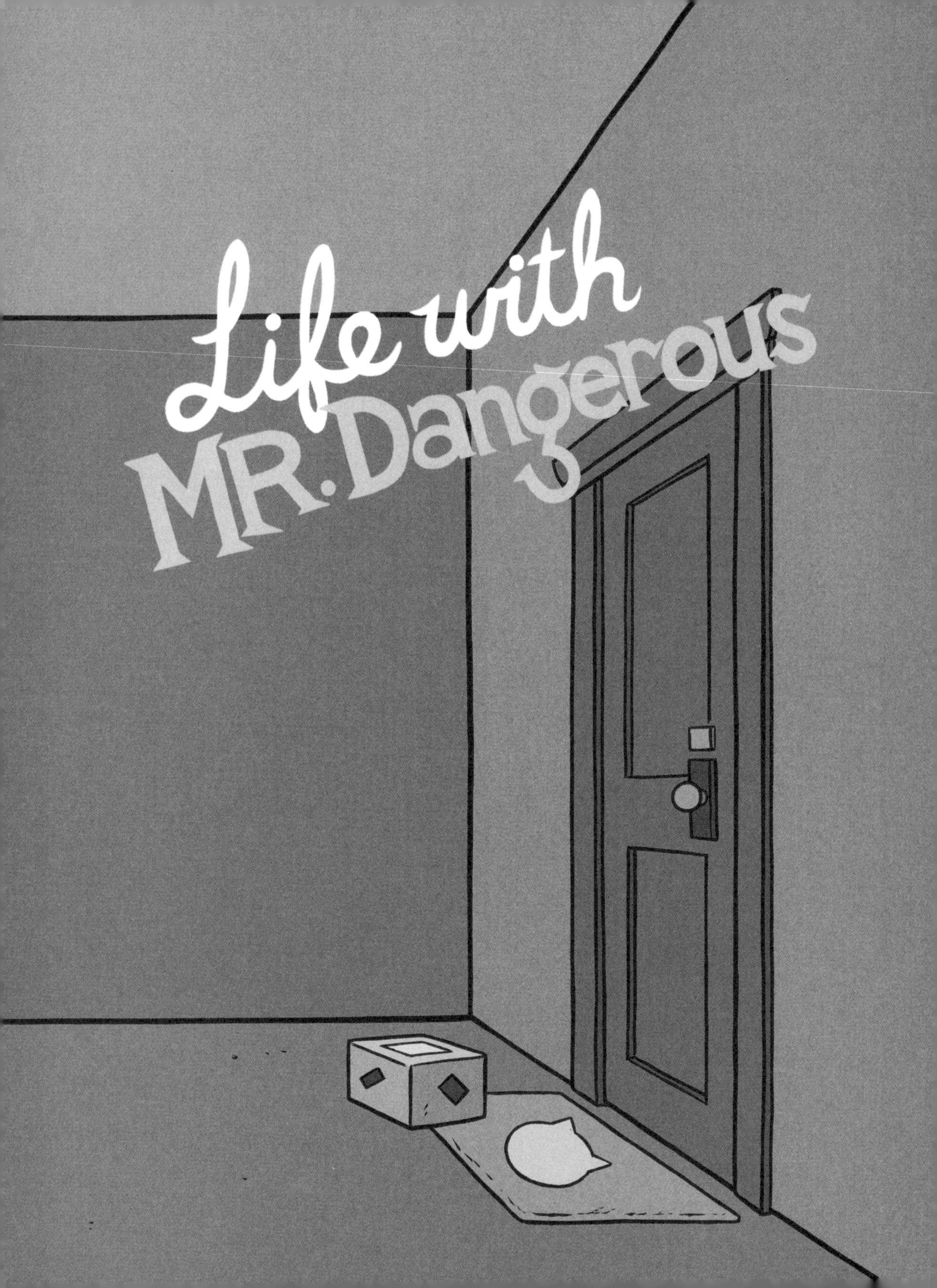
Life with
MR. Dangerous

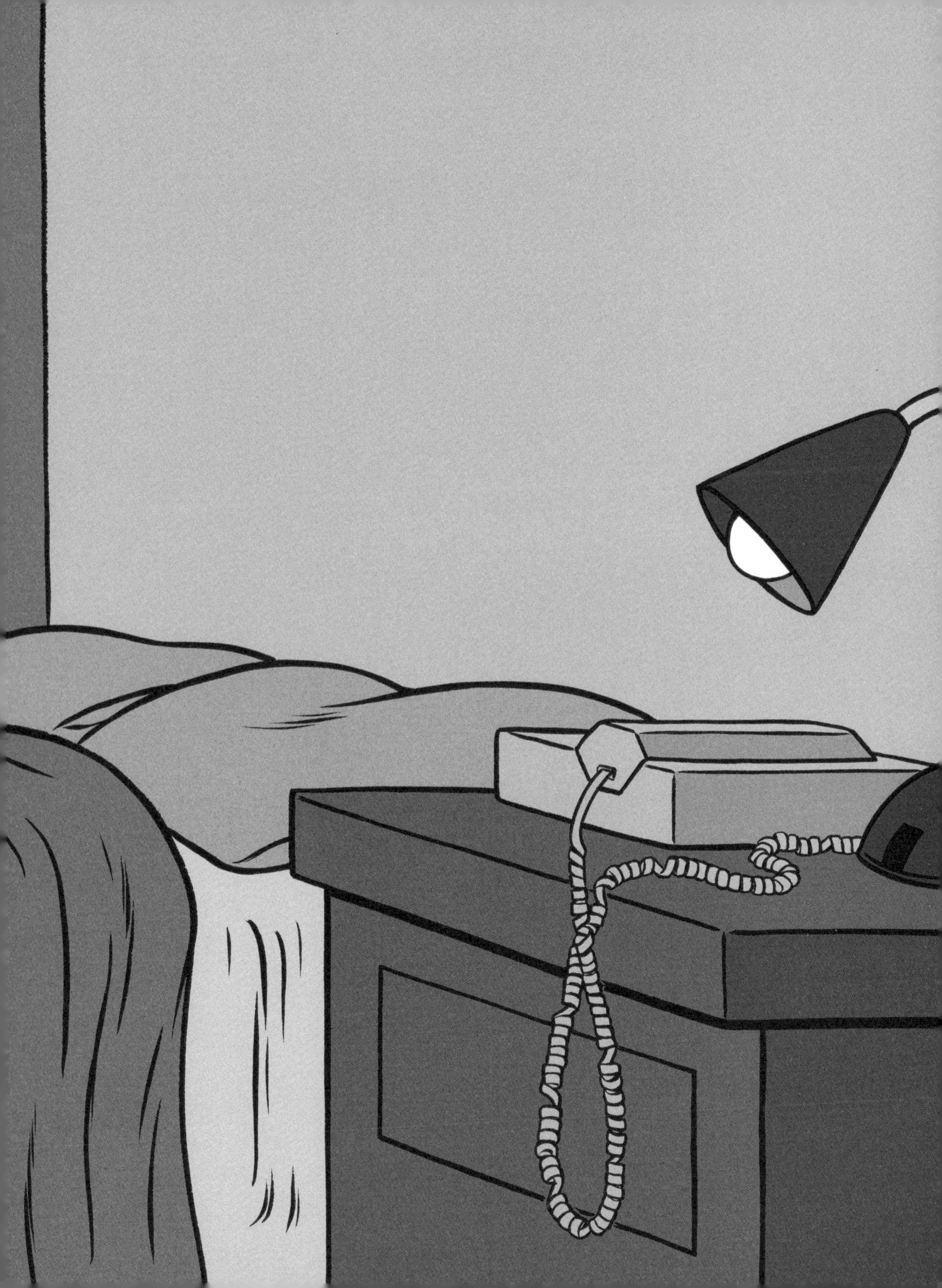

1
Long Distance
Phone Calls

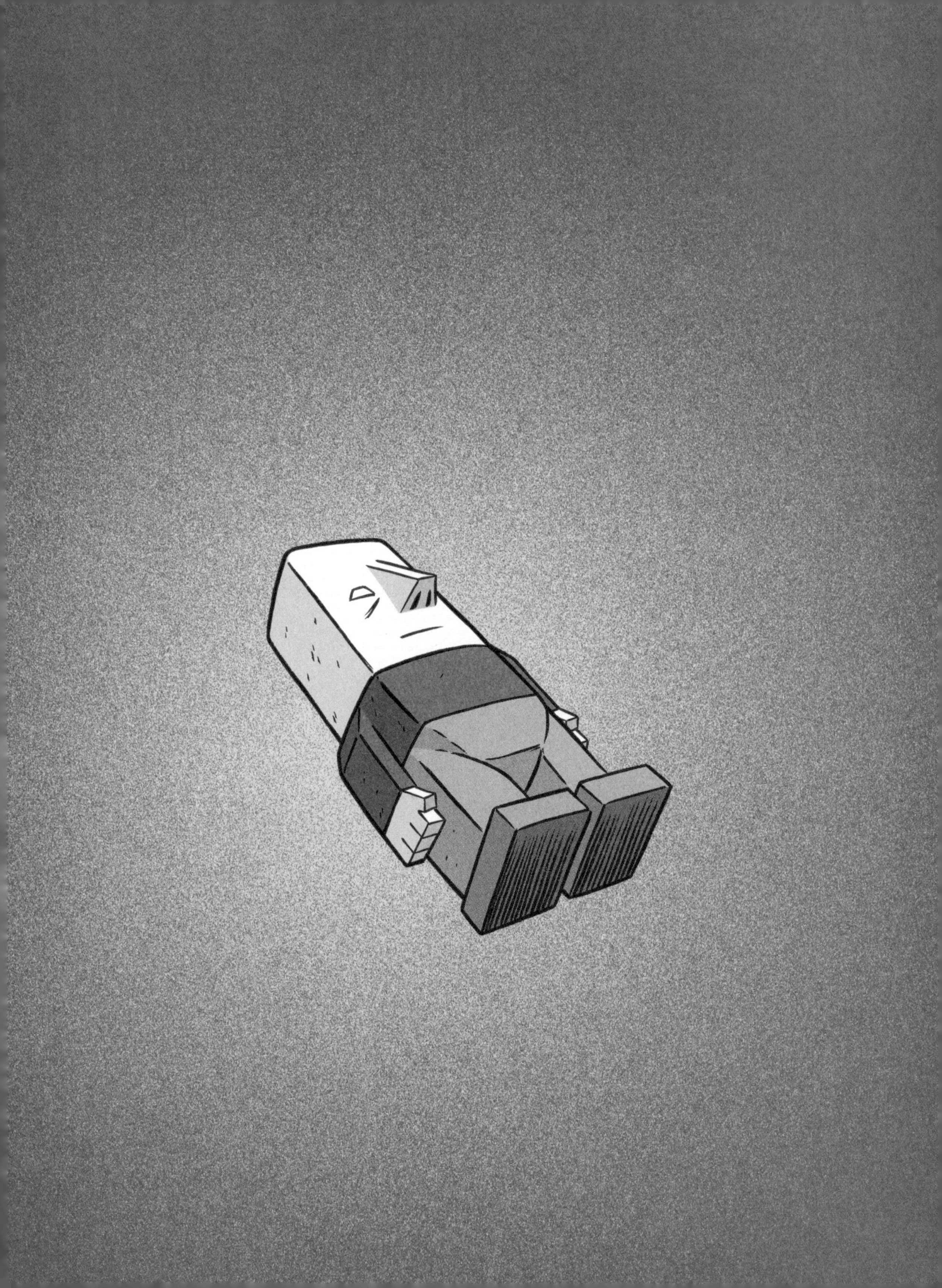

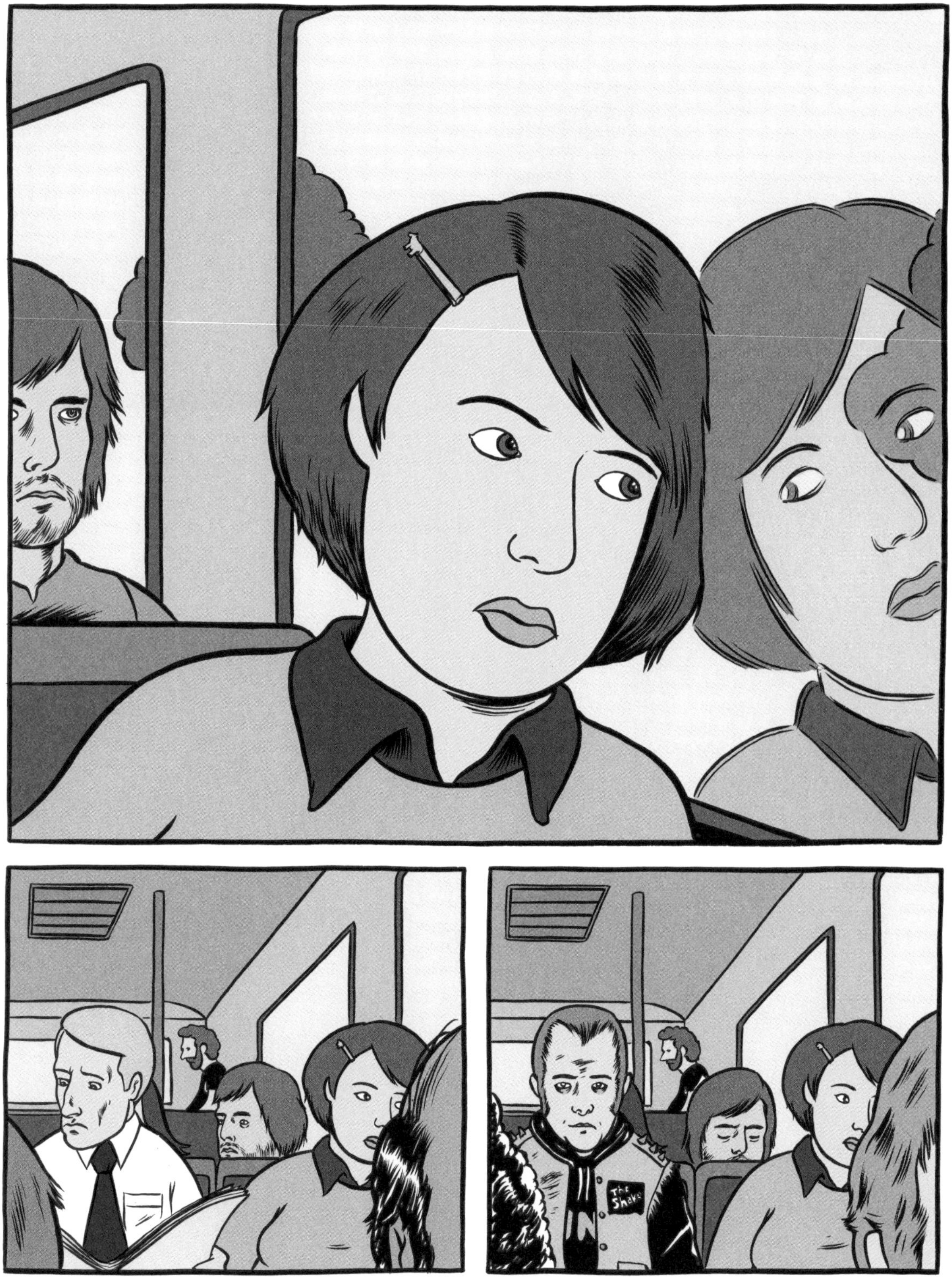
The Shake

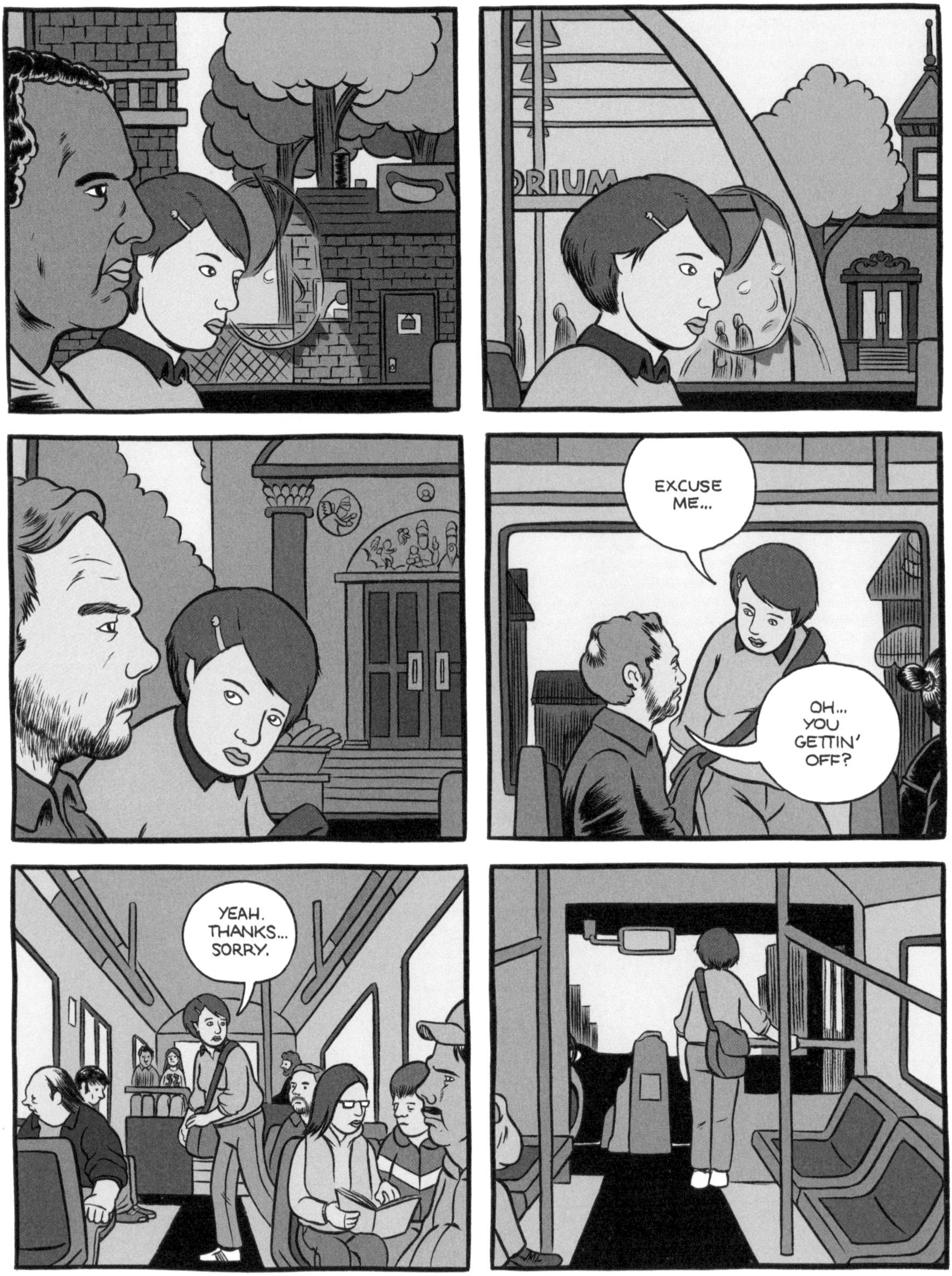
EXCUSE ME...
OH... YOU GETTIN' OFF?
YEAH. THANKS... SORRY.

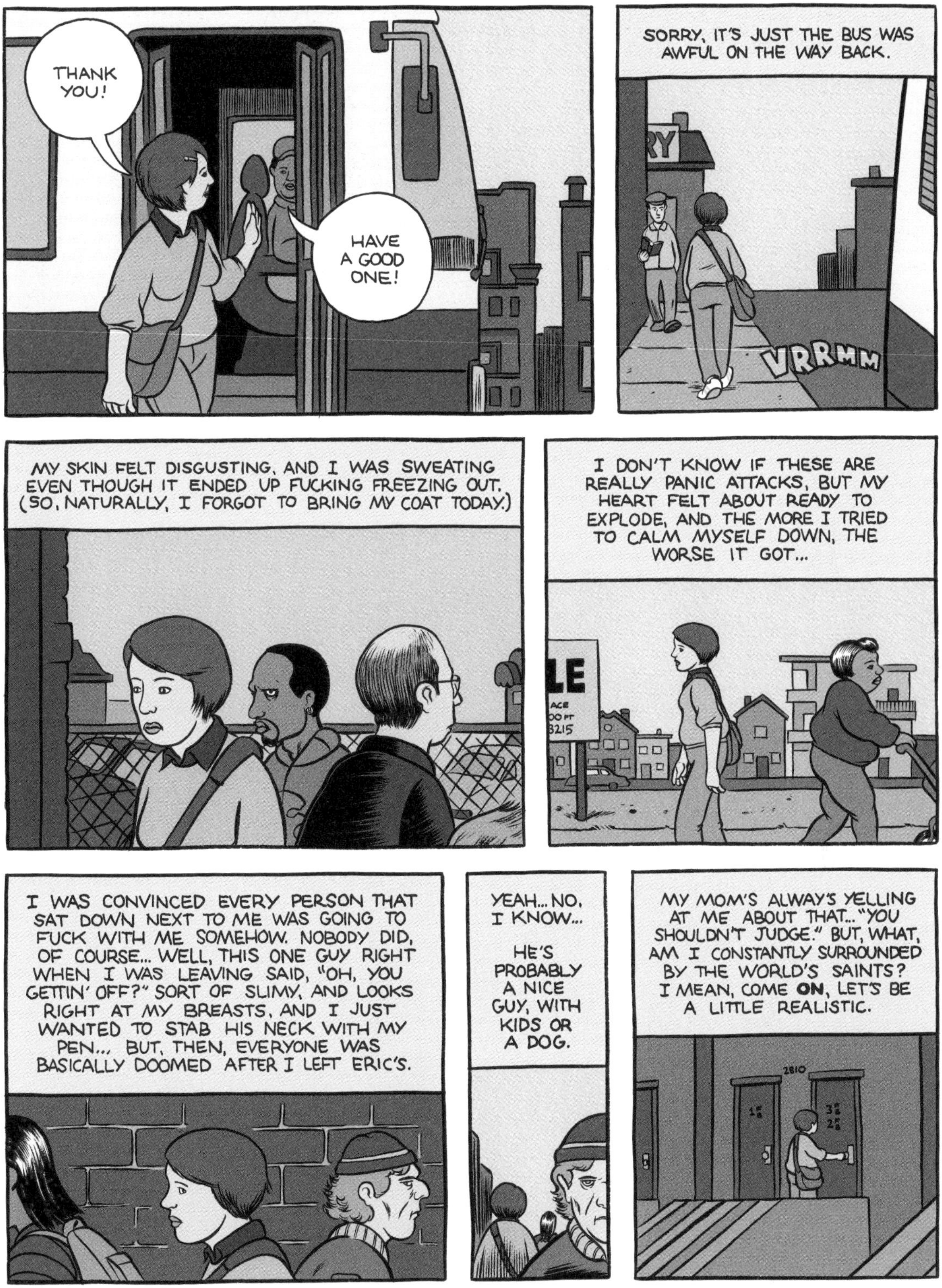
THANK YOU!
HAVE A GOOD ONE!
SORRY, IT'S JUST THE BUS WAS AWFUL ON THE WAY BACK.
VRRMM
MY SKIN FELT DISGUSTING, AND I WAS SWEATING EVEN THOUGH IT ENDED UP FUCKING FREEZING OUT. (SO, NATURALLY, I FORGOT TO BRING MY COAT TODAY.)
I DON'T KNOW IF THESE ARE REALLY PANIC ATTACKS, BUT MY HEART FELT ABOUT READY TO EXPLODE, AND THE MORE I TRIED TO CALM MYSELF DOWN, THE WORSE IT GOT...
I WAS CONVINCED EVERY PERSON THAT SAT DOWN NEXT TO ME WAS GOING TO FUCK WITH ME SOMEHOW. NOBODY DID, OF COURSE... WELL, THIS ONE GUY RIGHT WHEN I WAS LEAVING SAID, "OH, YOU GETTIN' OFF?" SORT OF SLIMY, AND LOOKS RIGHT AT MY BREASTS, AND I JUST WANTED TO STAB HIS NECK WITH MY PEN... BUT, THEN, EVERYONE WAS BASICALLY DOOMED AFTER I LEFT ERIC'S.
YEAH... NO, I KNOW...
HE'S PROBABLY A NICE GUY, WITH KIDS OR A DOG.
MY MOM'S ALWAYS YELLING AT ME ABOUT THAT... "YOU SHOULDN'T JUDGE." BUT, WHAT, AM I CONSTANTLY SURROUNDED BY THE WORLD'S SAINTS? I MEAN, COME ON, LET'S BE A LITTLE REALISTIC.
2810

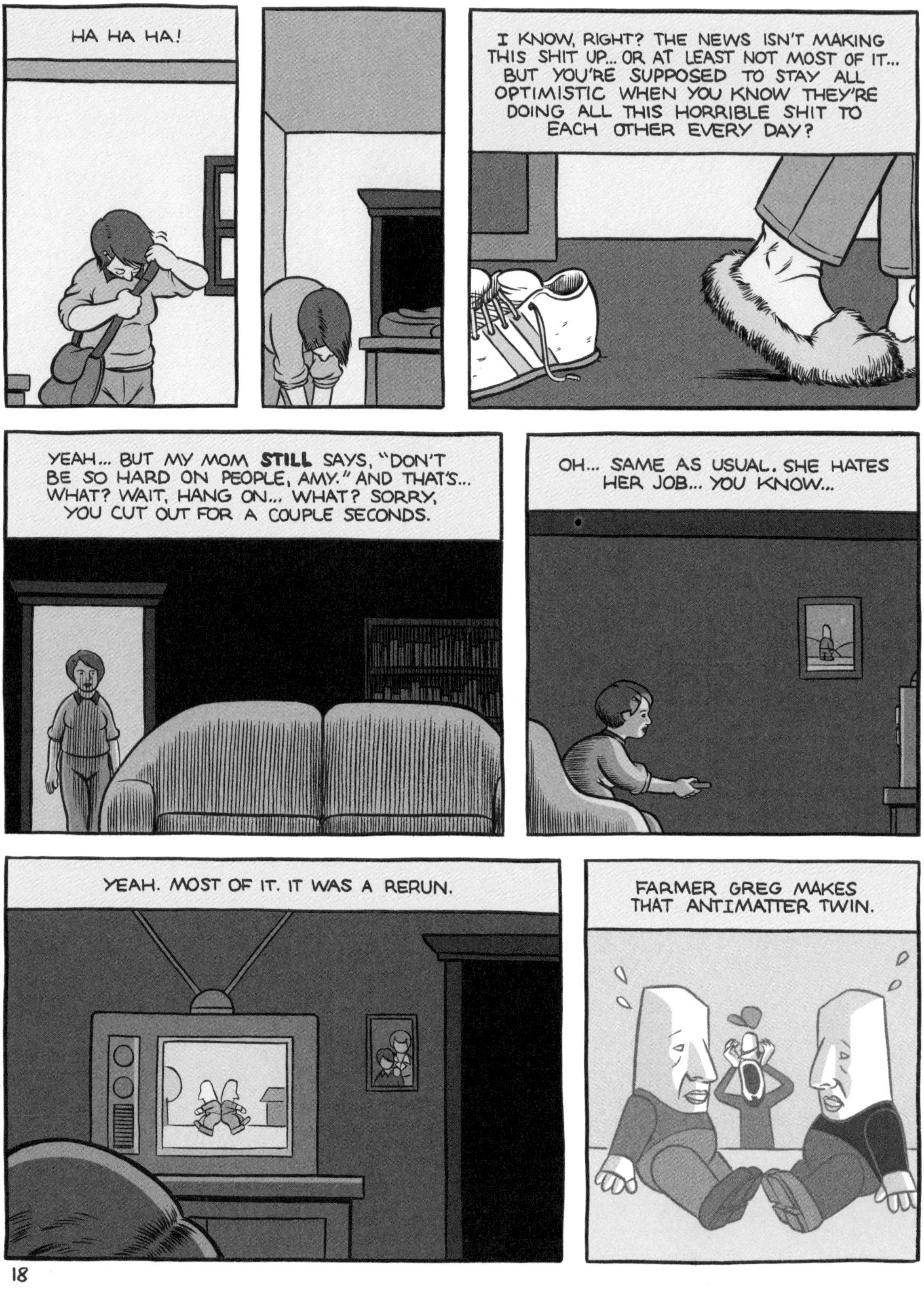
HA HA HA!
I KNOW, RIGHT? THE NEWS ISN'T MAKING THIS SHIT UP... OR AT LEAST NOT MOST OF IT... BUT YOU'RE SUPPOSED TO STAY ALL OPTIMISTIC WHEN YOU KNOW THEY'RE DOING ALL THIS HORRIBLE SHIT TO EACH OTHER EVERY DAY?
YEAH... BUT MY MOM **STILL** SAYS, "DON'T BE SO HARD ON PEOPLE, AMY." AND THAT'S... WHAT? WAIT, HANG ON... WHAT? SORRY, YOU CUT OUT FOR A COUPLE SECONDS.
OH... SAME AS USUAL. SHE HATES HER JOB... YOU KNOW...
YEAH. MOST OF IT. IT WAS A RERUN.
FARMER GREG MAKES THAT ANTIMATTER TWIN.

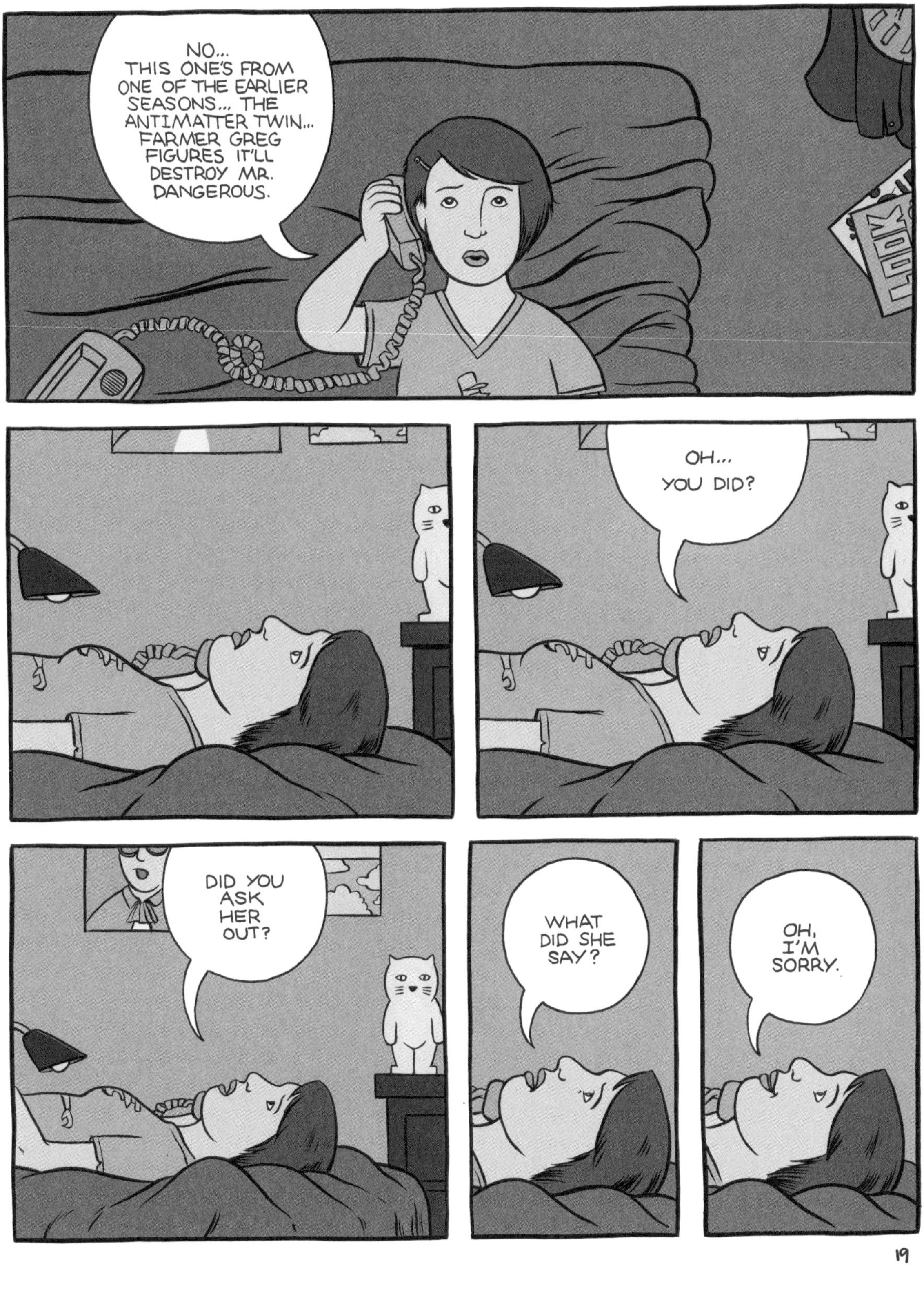
NO... THIS ONE'S FROM ONE OF THE EARLIER SEASONS... THE ANTIMATTER TWIN... FARMER GREG FIGURES IT'LL DESTROY MR. DANGEROUS.
LOOK
OH... YOU DID?
DID YOU ASK HER OUT?
WHAT DID SHE SAY?
OH, I'M SORRY.

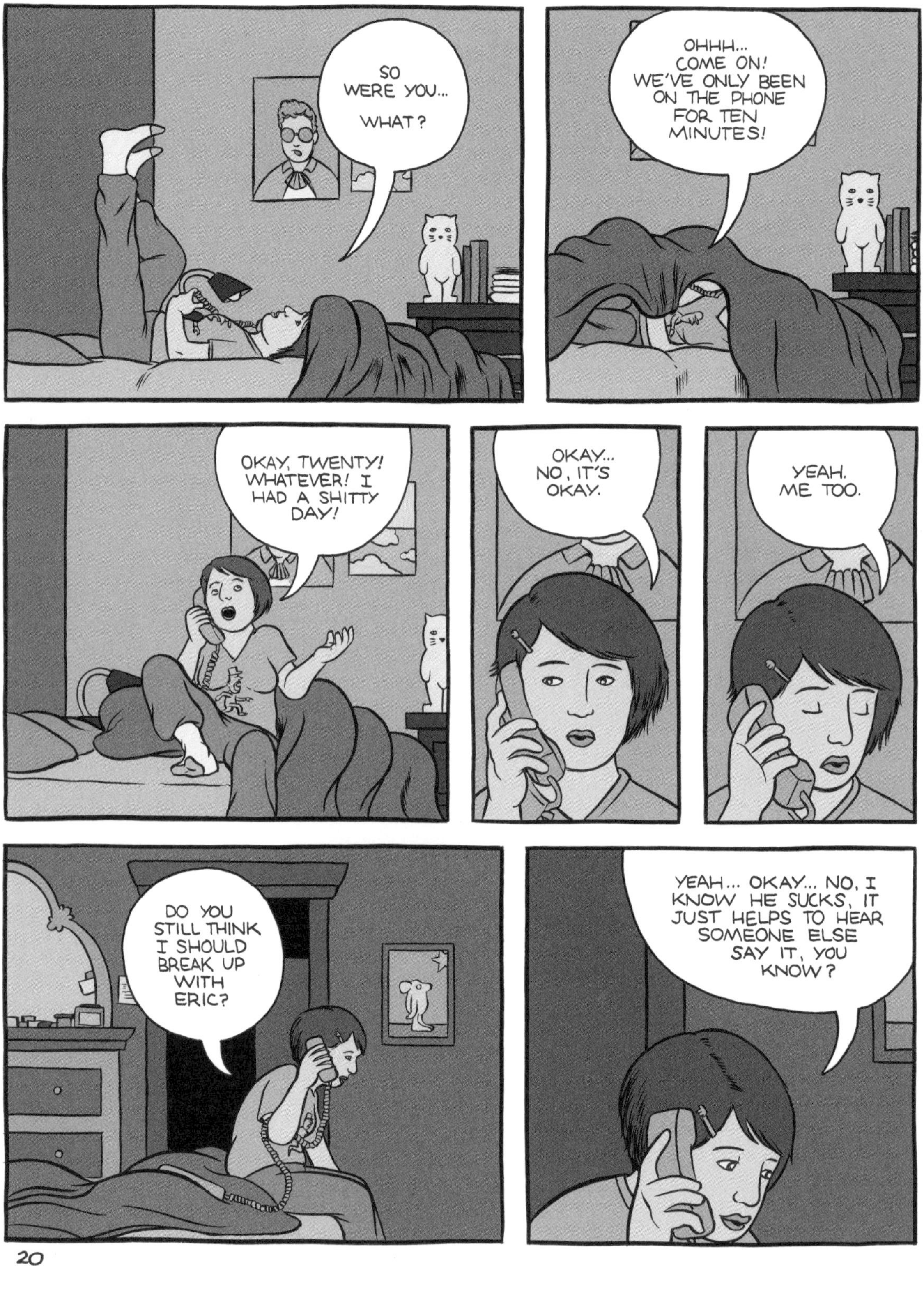
SO WERE YOU... WHAT?
OHHH... COME ON! WE'VE ONLY BEEN ON THE PHONE FOR TEN MINUTES!
OKAY, TWENTY! WHATEVER! I HAD A SHITTY DAY!
OKAY... NO, IT'S OKAY.
YEAH. ME TOO.
DO YOU STILL THINK I SHOULD BREAK UP WITH ERIC?
YEAH... OKAY... NO, I KNOW HE SUCKS, IT JUST HELPS TO HEAR SOMEONE ELSE SAY IT, YOU KNOW?

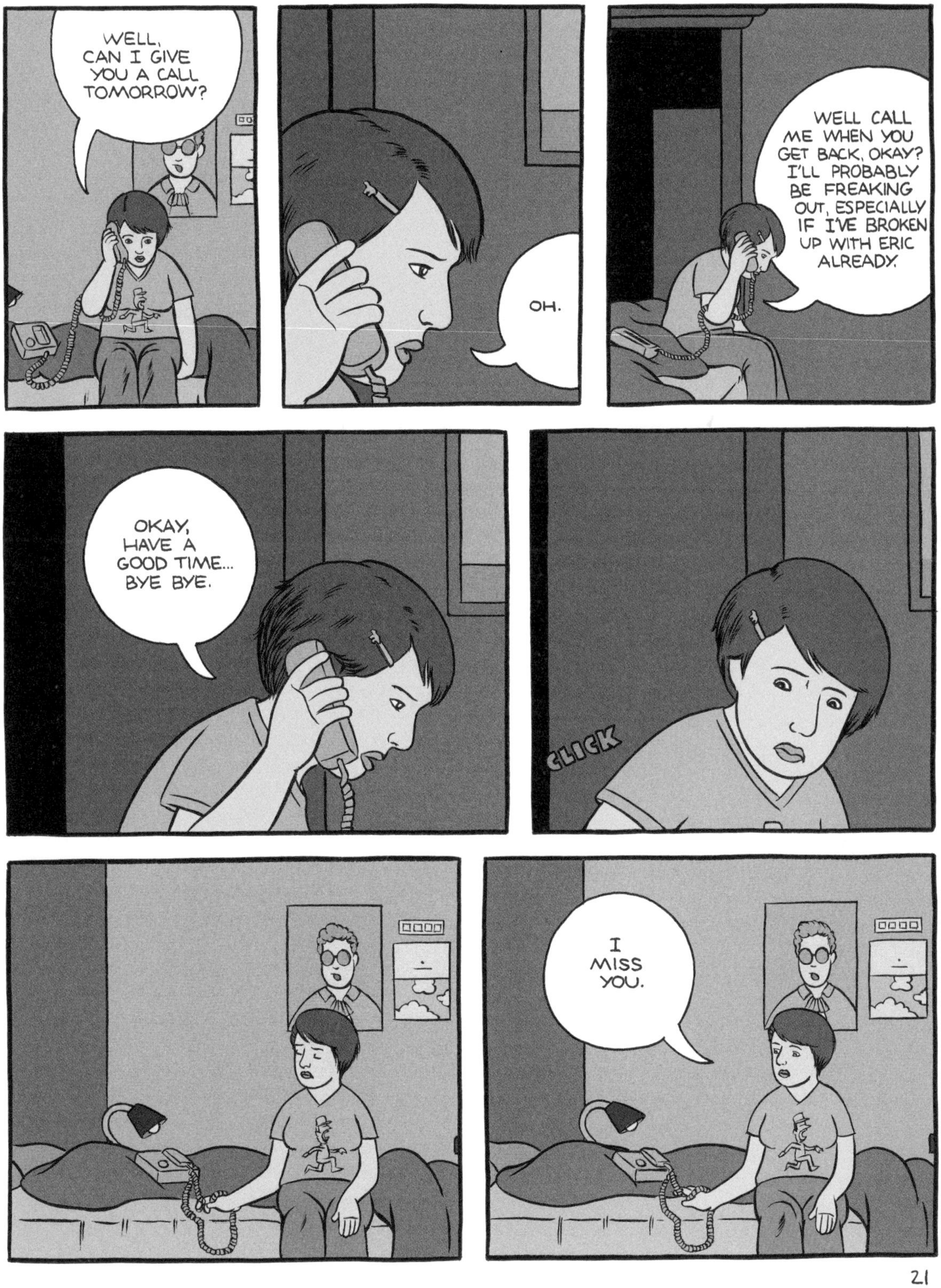
WELL, CAN I GIVE YOU A CALL TOMORROW?
OH.
WELL CALL ME WHEN YOU GET BACK, OKAY? I'LL PROBABLY BE FREAKING OUT, ESPECIALLY IF I'VE BROKEN UP WITH ERIC ALREADY.
OKAY, HAVE A GOOD TIME... BYE BYE.
CLICK
I MISS YOU.

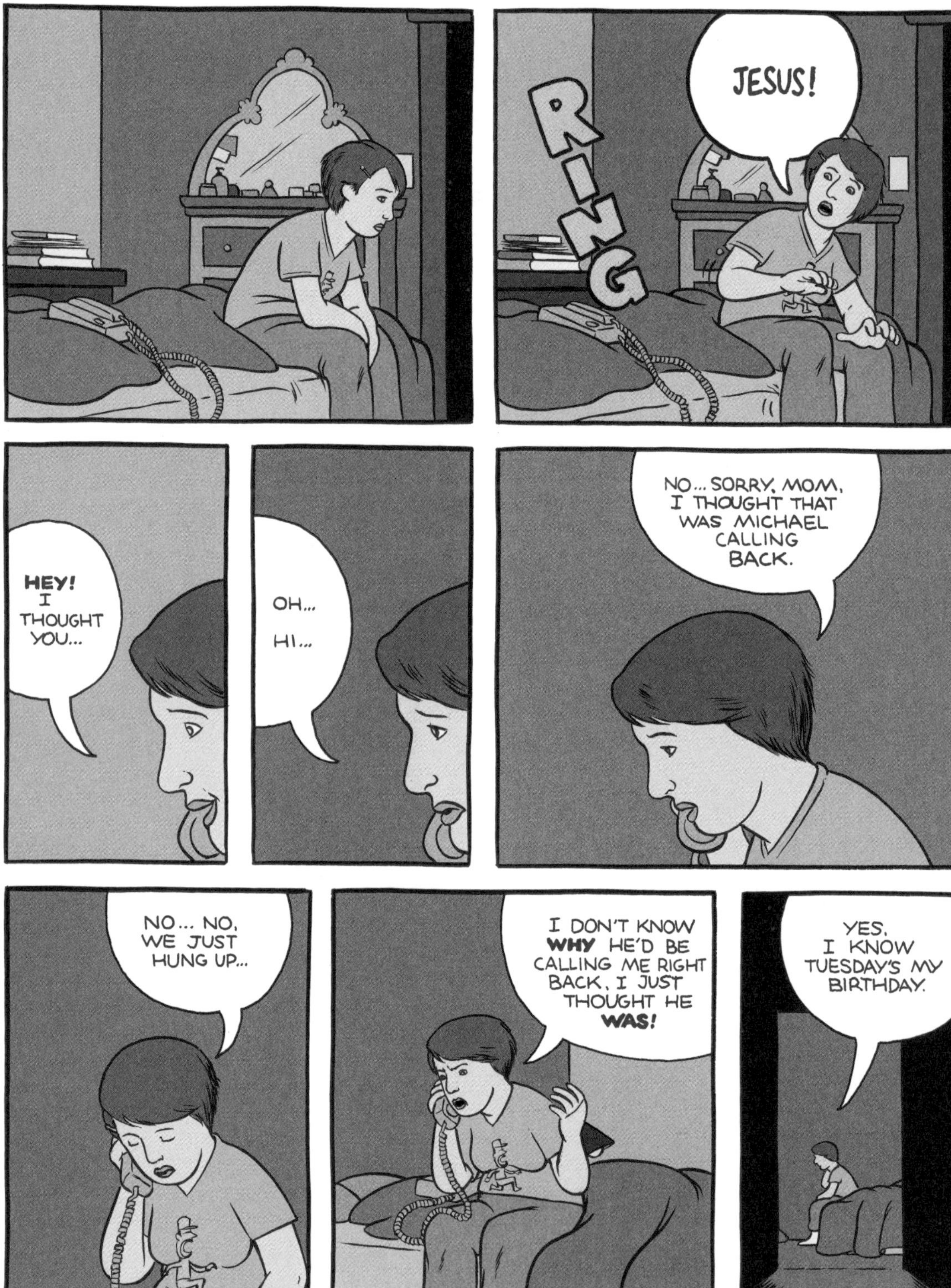

RING
JESUS!
HEY! I THOUGHT YOU...
OH... HI...
NO... SORRY, MOM, I THOUGHT THAT WAS MICHAEL CALLING BACK.
NO... NO, WE JUST HUNG UP...
I DON'T KNOW WHY HE'D BE CALLING ME RIGHT BACK. I JUST THOUGHT HE WAS!
YES, I KNOW TUESDAY'S MY BIRTHDAY.

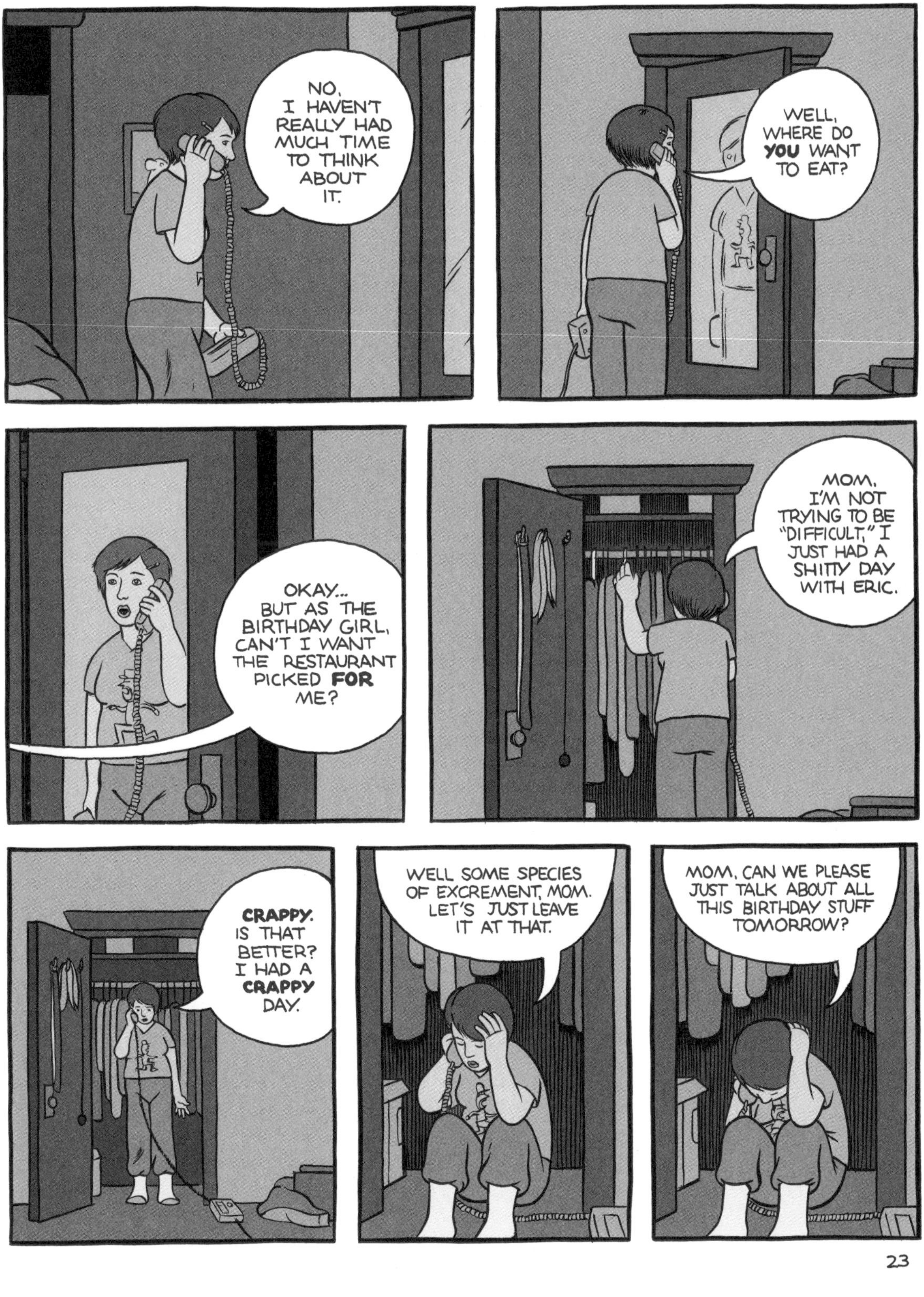
NO, I HAVEN'T REALLY HAD MUCH TIME TO THINK ABOUT IT.
WELL, WHERE DO **YOU** WANT TO EAT?
OKAY... BUT AS THE BIRTHDAY GIRL, CAN'T I WANT THE RESTAURANT PICKED **FOR** ME?
MOM, I'M NOT TRYING TO BE "DIFFICULT," I JUST HAD A SHITTY DAY WITH ERIC.
CRAPPY. IS THAT BETTER? I HAD A **CRAPPY** DAY.
WELL SOME SPECIES OF EXCREMENT, MOM. LET'S JUST LEAVE IT AT THAT.
MOM, CAN WE PLEASE JUST TALK ABOUT ALL THIS BIRTHDAY STUFF TOMORROW?

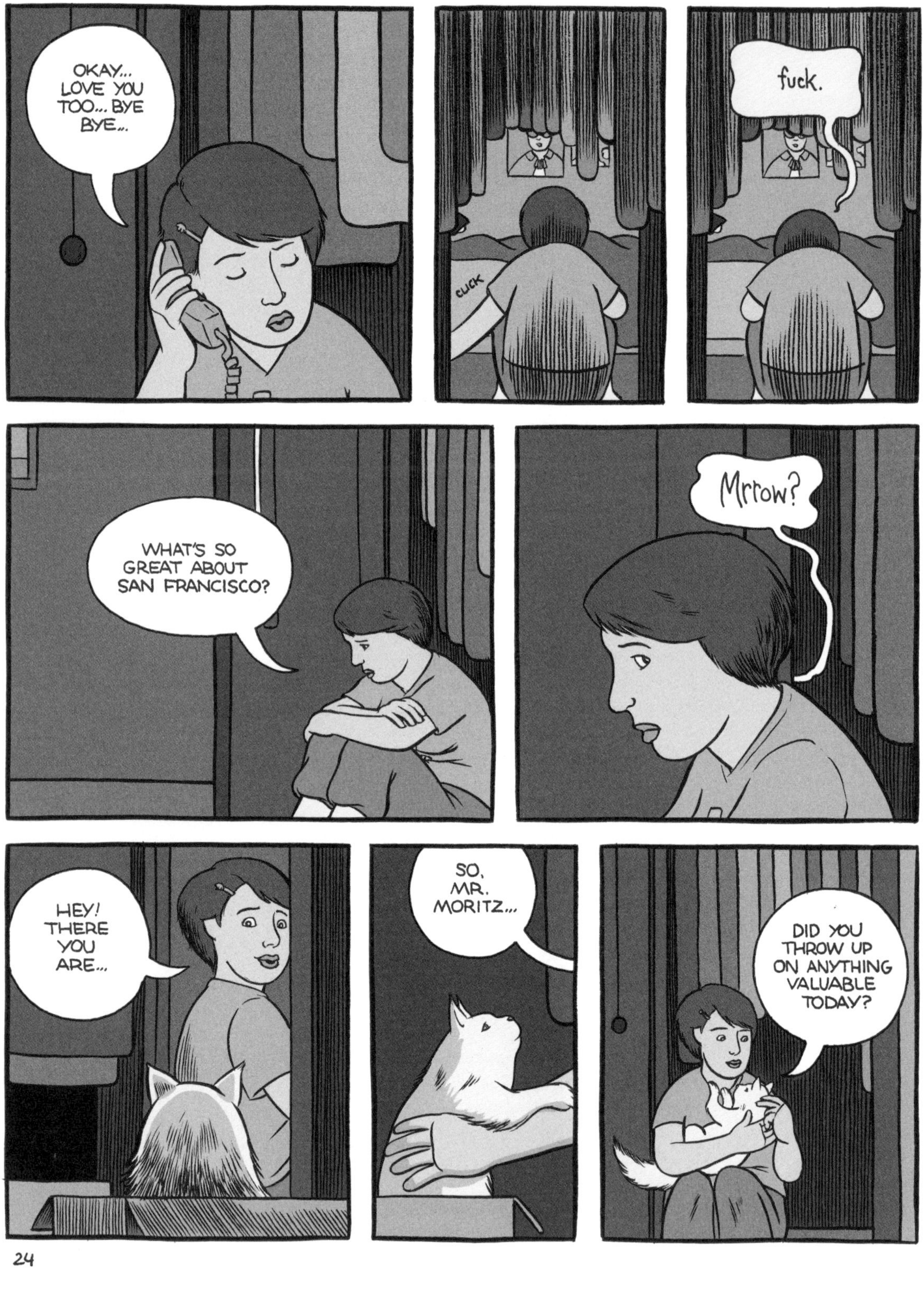
OKAY... LOVE YOU TOO... BYE BYE...
CLICK
fuck.
WHAT'S SO GREAT ABOUT SAN FRANCISCO?
Mrrow?
HEY! THERE YOU ARE...
SO, MR. MORITZ...
DID YOU THROW UP ON ANYTHING VALUABLE TODAY?

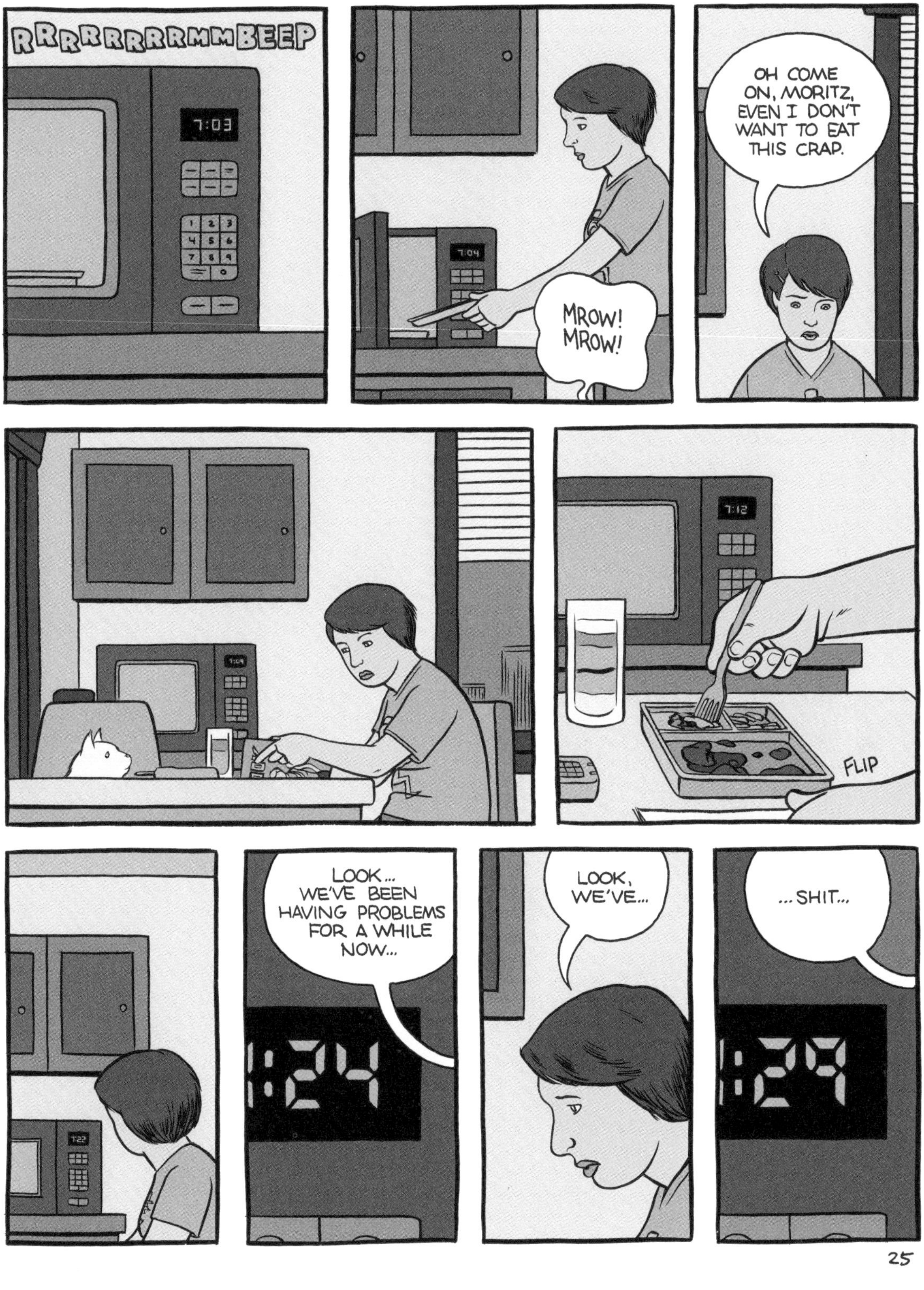
RRRRRRRRRMMBEEP
7:03
7:04
MROW! MROW!
OH COME ON, MORITZ, EVEN I DON'T WANT TO EAT THIS CRAP.
7:12
FLIP
7:22
LOOK... WE'VE BEEN HAVING PROBLEMS FOR A WHILE NOW...
LOOK, WE'VE...
...SHIT...

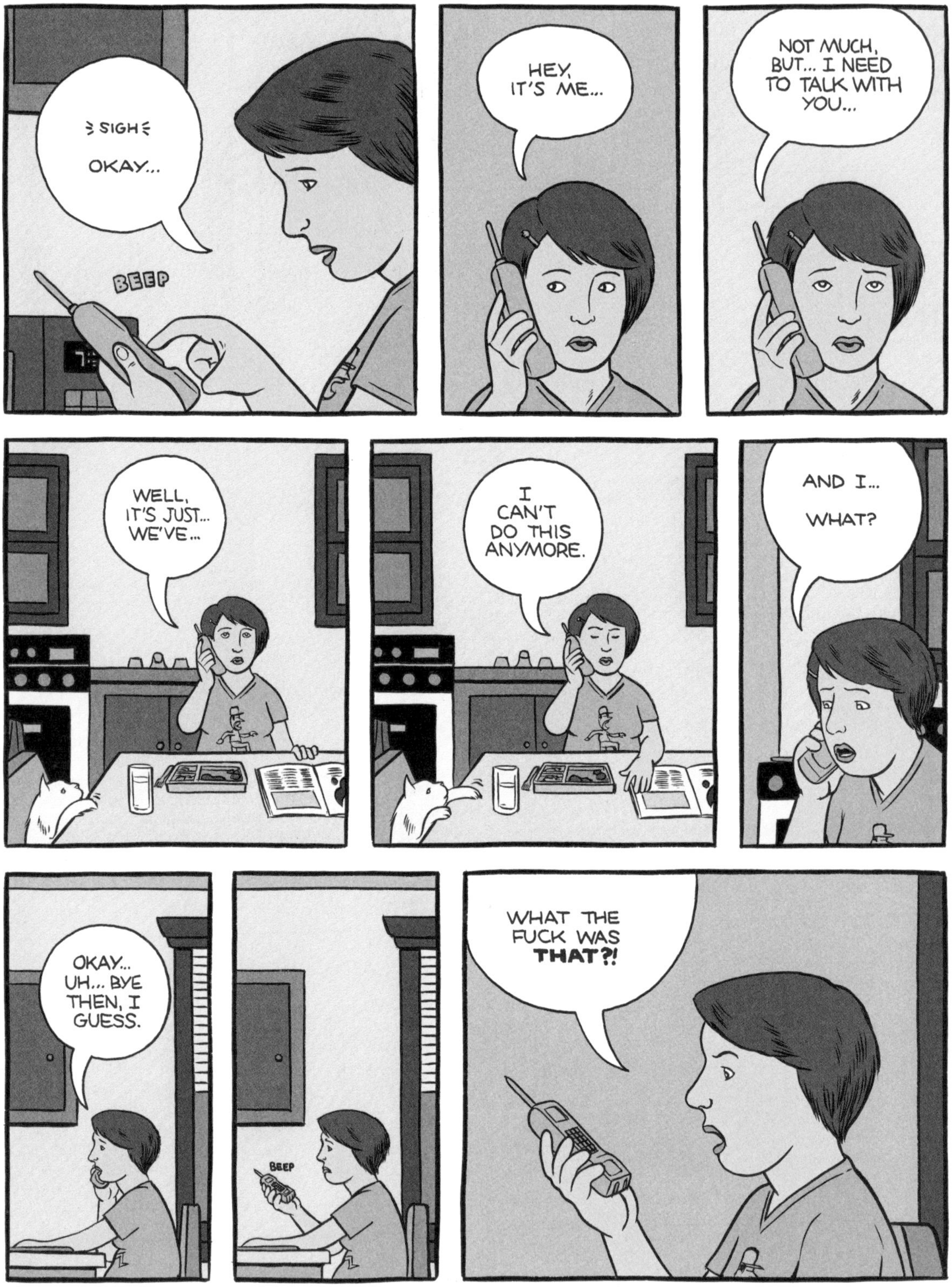

≷ SIGH ≶
OKAY...
BEEP
HEY, IT'S ME...
NOT MUCH, BUT... I NEED TO TALK WITH YOU...
WELL, IT'S JUST... WE'VE...
I CAN'T DO THIS ANYMORE.
AND I...
WHAT?
OKAY... UH... BYE THEN, I GUESS.
BEEP
WHAT THE FUCK WAS **THAT?!**

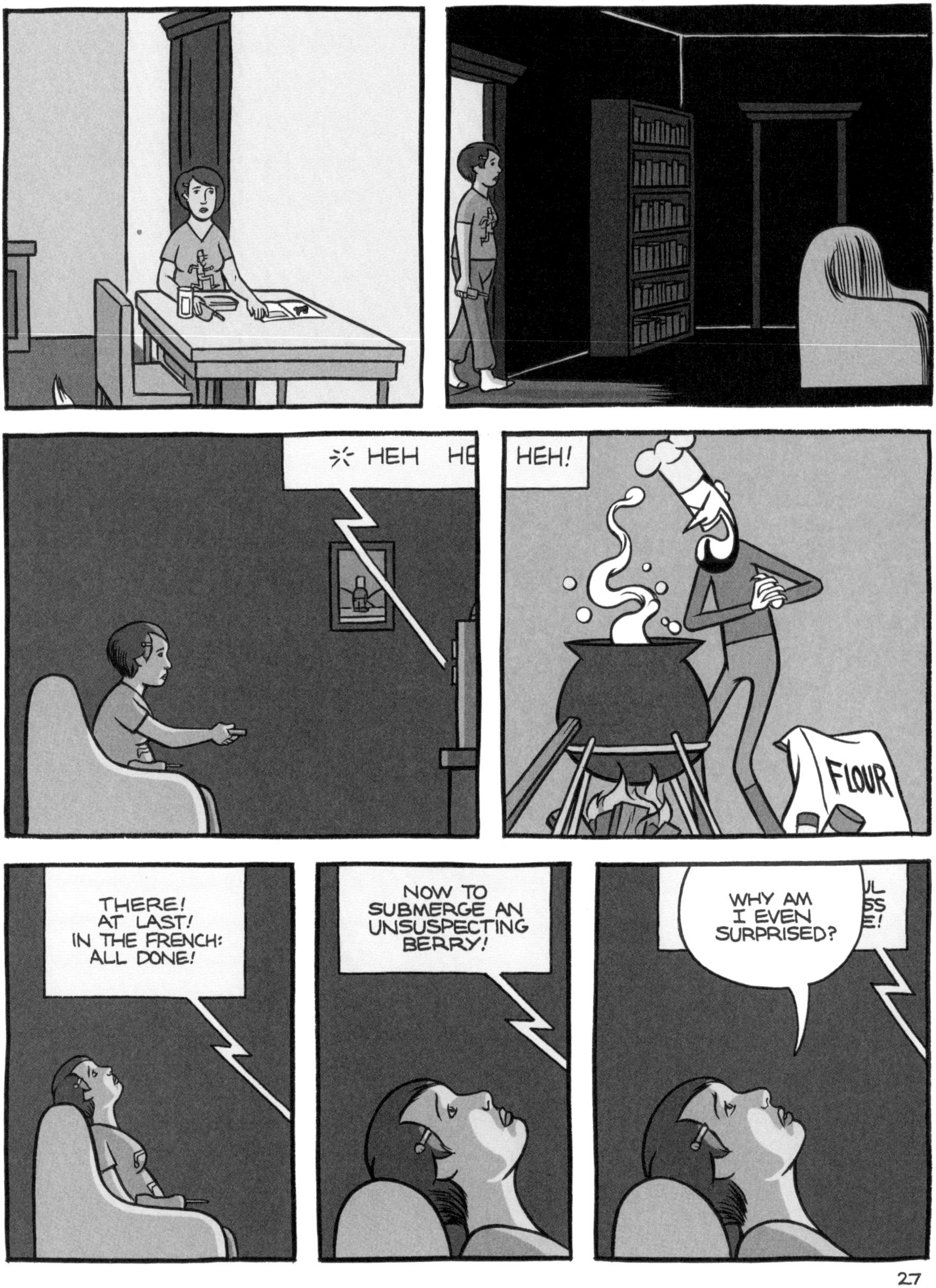

HEH HE
HEH!
THERE! AT LAST! IN THE FRENCH: ALL DONE!
NOW TO SUBMERGE AN UNSUSPECTING BERRY!
WHY AM I EVEN SURPRISED?
FLOUR

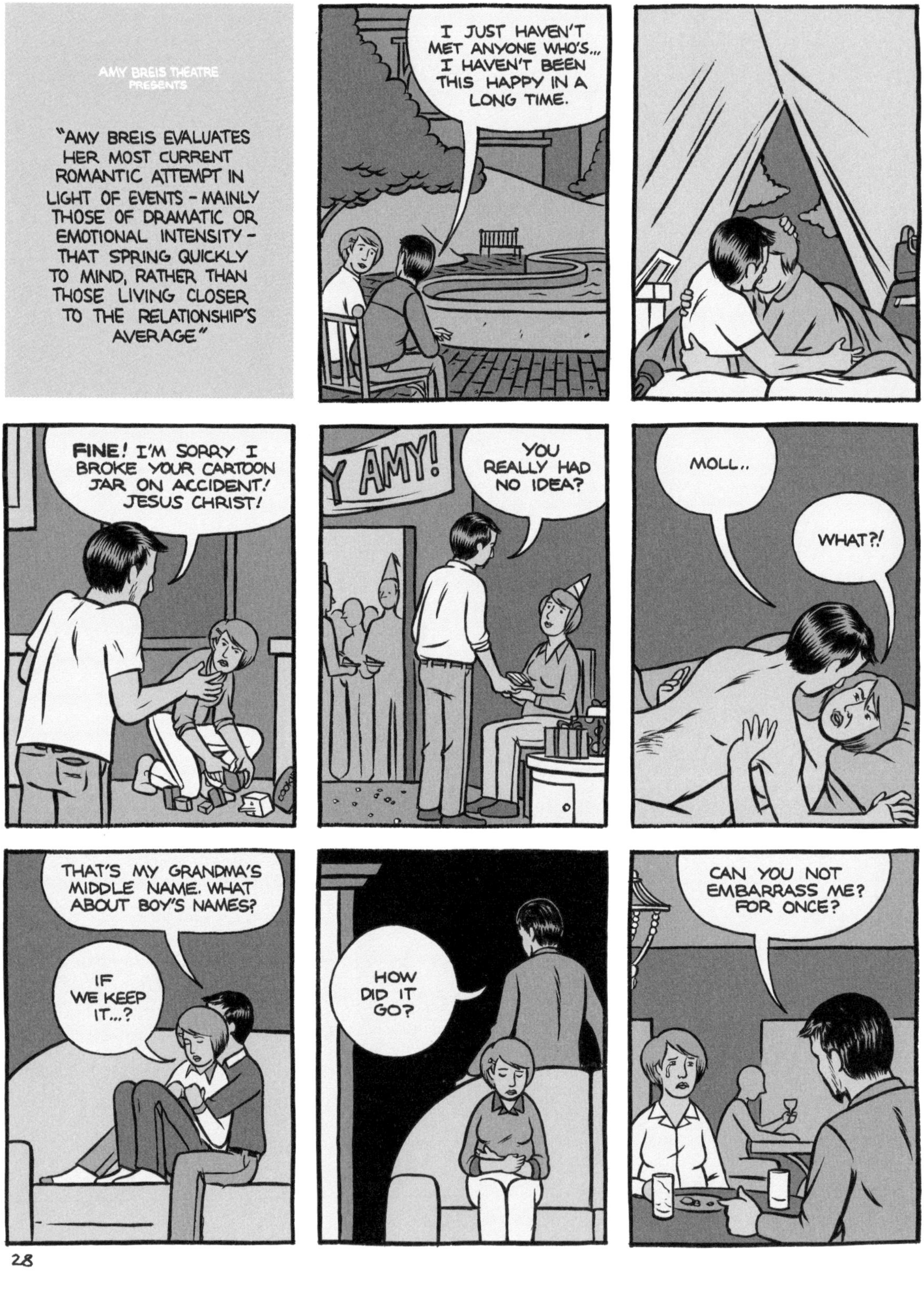
AMY BREIS THEATRE PRESENTS
"AMY BREIS EVALUATES HER MOST CURRENT ROMANTIC ATTEMPT IN LIGHT OF EVENTS - MAINLY THOSE OF DRAMATIC OR EMOTIONAL INTENSITY - THAT SPRING QUICKLY TO MIND, RATHER THAN THOSE LIVING CLOSER TO THE RELATIONSHIP'S AVERAGE"
I JUST HAVEN'T MET ANYONE WHO'S... I HAVEN'T BEEN THIS HAPPY IN A LONG TIME.
FINE! I'M SORRY I BROKE YOUR CARTOON JAR ON ACCIDENT! JESUS CHRIST!
Y AMY!
YOU REALLY HAD NO IDEA?
MOLL..
WHAT?!
THAT'S MY GRANDMA'S MIDDLE NAME. WHAT ABOUT BOY'S NAMES?
IF WE KEEP IT...?
HOW DID IT GO?
CAN YOU NOT EMBARRASS ME? FOR ONCE?

O GLOOPISH BLISS!

RING RING

HELLO?

OH...
HEY, MOM.

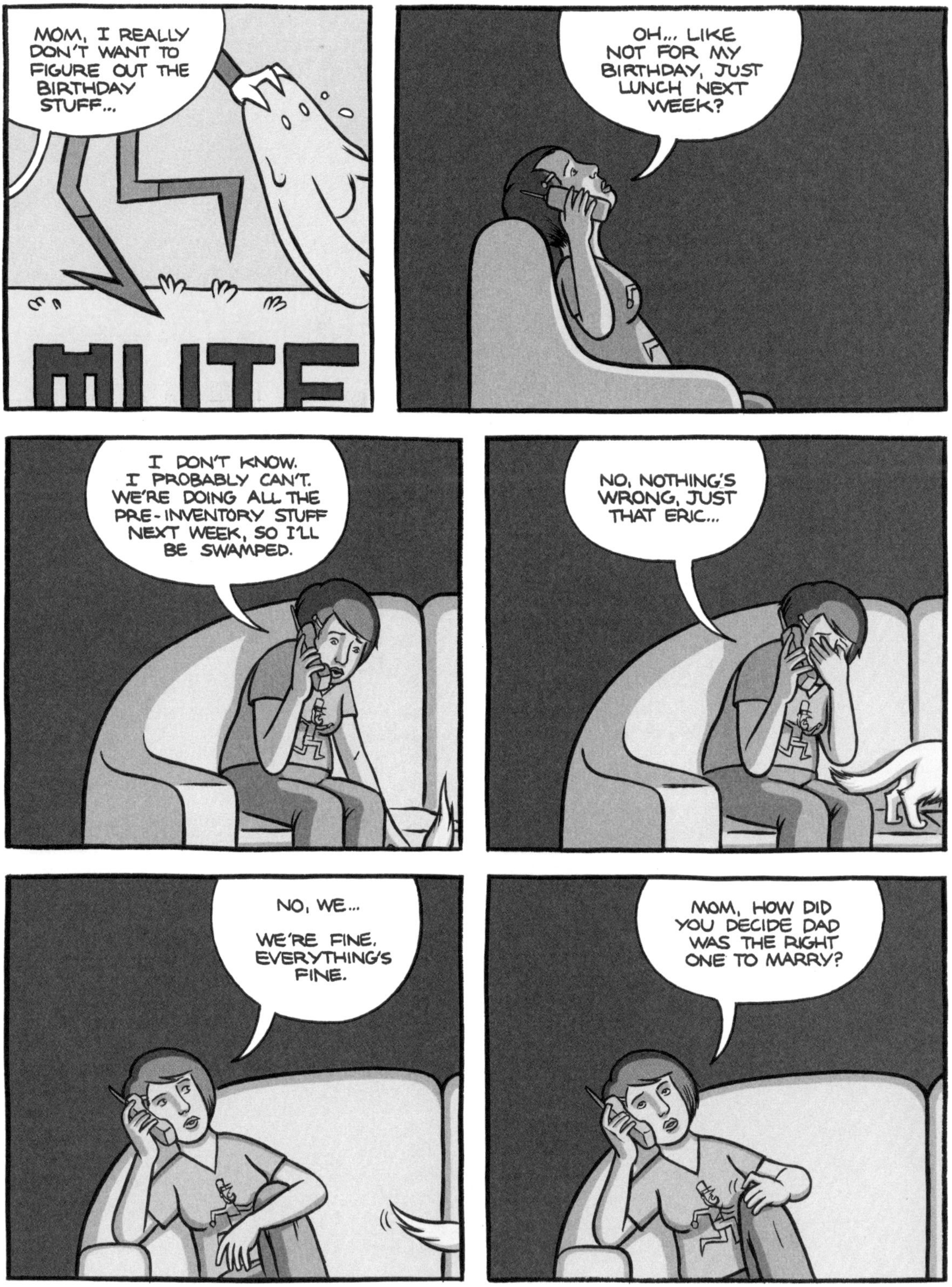
MOM, I REALLY DON'T WANT TO FIGURE OUT THE BIRTHDAY STUFF...
MUTE
OH... LIKE NOT FOR MY BIRTHDAY, JUST LUNCH NEXT WEEK?
I DON'T KNOW. I PROBABLY CAN'T. WE'RE DOING ALL THE PRE-INVENTORY STUFF NEXT WEEK, SO I'LL BE SWAMPED.
NO, NOTHING'S WRONG, JUST THAT ERIC...
NO, WE...
WE'RE FINE. EVERYTHING'S FINE.
MOM, HOW DID YOU DECIDE DAD WAS THE RIGHT ONE TO MARRY?

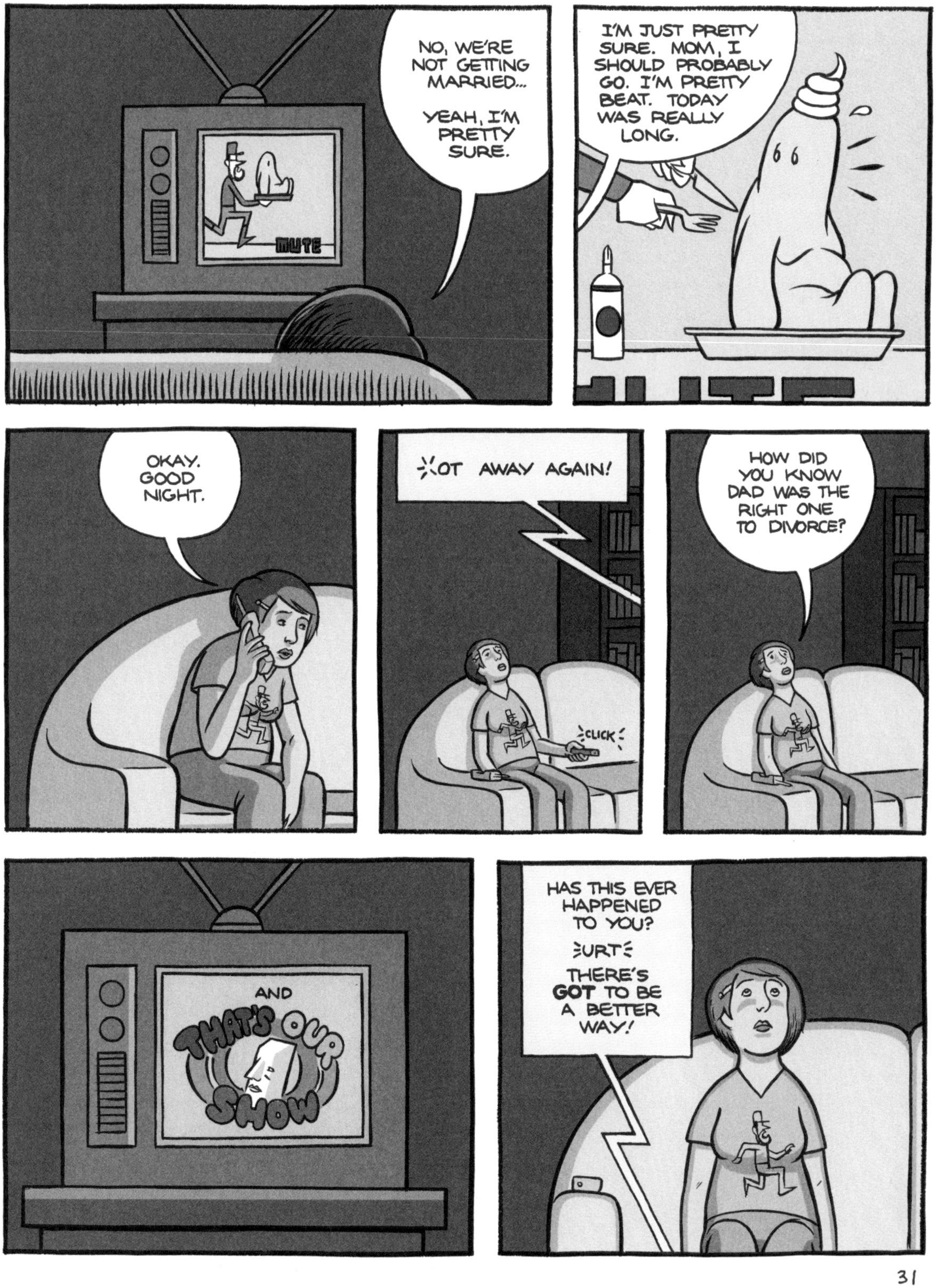
NO, WE'RE NOT GETTING MARRIED...
YEAH, I'M PRETTY SURE.
MUTE
I'M JUST PRETTY SURE. MOM, I SHOULD PROBABLY GO. I'M PRETTY BEAT. TODAY WAS REALLY LONG.
OKAY. GOOD NIGHT.
OT AWAY AGAIN!
CLICK
HOW DID YOU KNOW DAD WAS THE RIGHT ONE TO DIVORCE?
AND THAT'S OUR SHOW
HAS THIS EVER HAPPENED TO YOU?
URT
THERE'S GOT TO BE A BETTER WAY!

2
At Last,
the Weekend

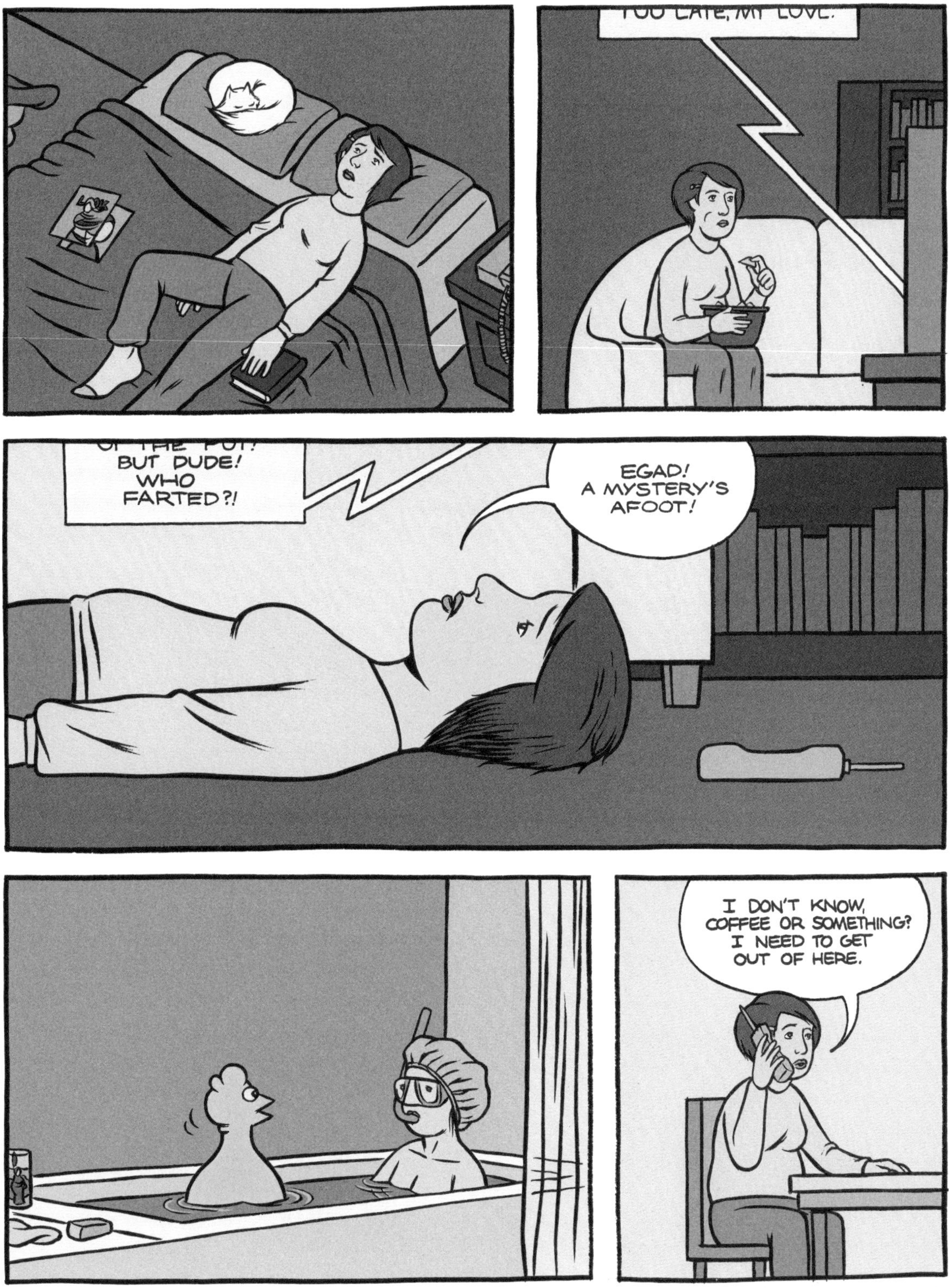
TOO LATE, MY LOVE.
BUT DUDE! WHO FARTED?!
EGAD! A MYSTERY'S AFOOT!
I DON'T KNOW, COFFEE OR SOMETHING? I NEED TO GET OUT OF HERE.

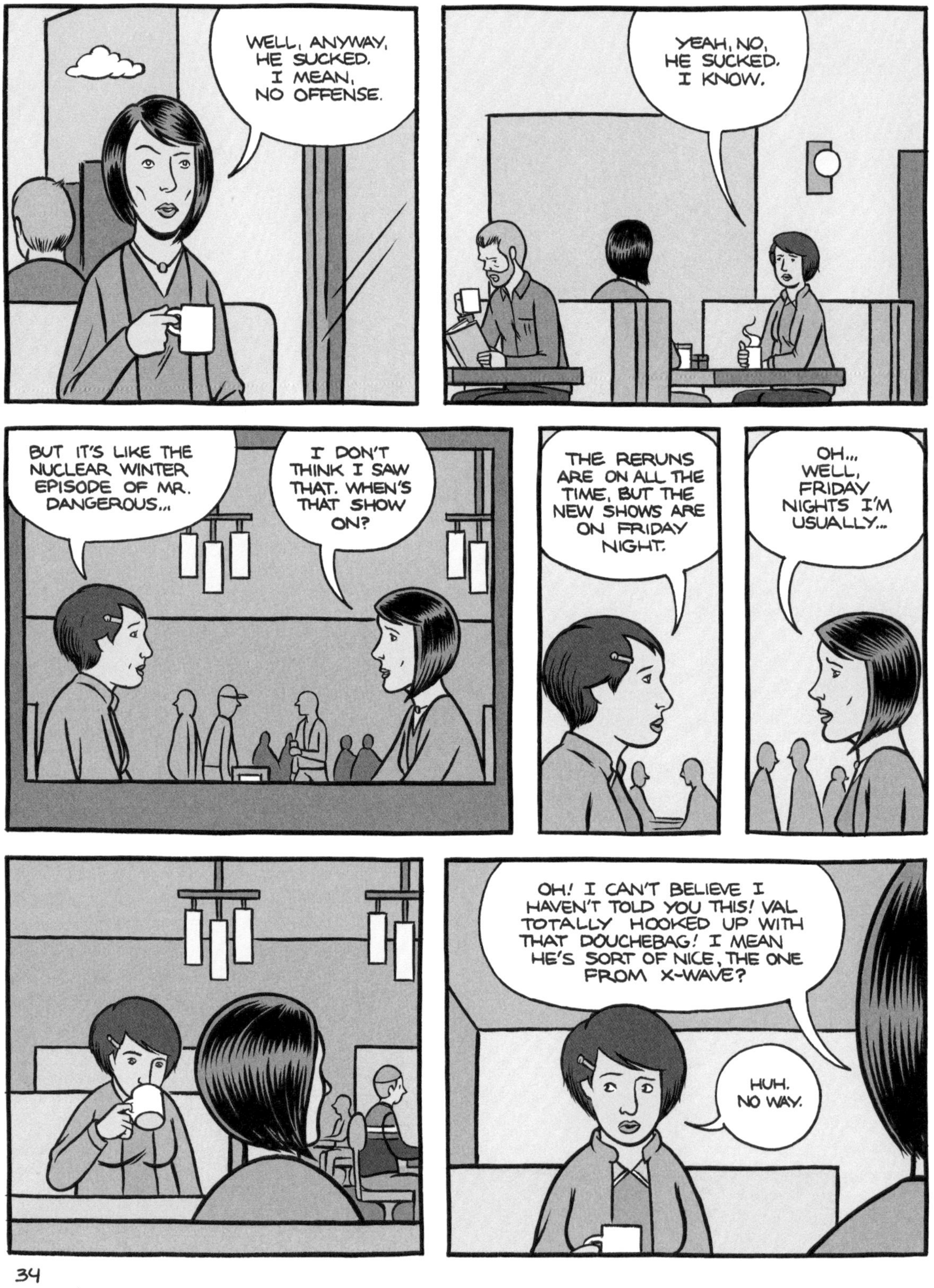
WELL, ANYWAY, HE SUCKED. I MEAN, NO OFFENSE.
YEAH, NO, HE SUCKED. I KNOW.
BUT IT'S LIKE THE NUCLEAR WINTER EPISODE OF MR. DANGEROUS...
I DON'T THINK I SAW THAT. WHEN'S THAT SHOW ON?
THE RERUNS ARE ON ALL THE TIME, BUT THE NEW SHOWS ARE ON FRIDAY NIGHT.
OH... WELL, FRIDAY NIGHTS I'M USUALLY...
OH! I CAN'T BELIEVE I HAVEN'T TOLD YOU THIS! VAL TOTALLY HOOKED UP WITH THAT DOUCHEBAG! I MEAN HE'S SORT OF NICE, THE ONE FROM X-WAVE?
HUH. NO WAY.

3
The Day Before
You're Older

CAN I HELP YOU WITH ANYTHING? WE HAVE FITTING ROOMS IF YOU'D LIKE TO..

NO, THIS IS A LITTLE TOO...

I DON'T REALLY SEE ANYTHING I LIKE.

EVERYTHING OKAY, AMY?

YEAH, SURE.

WELL, LET'S GET THOSE FOLDED UP. THERE'S MORE TO PUT OUT. IT'S A MESS IN THE BACK.

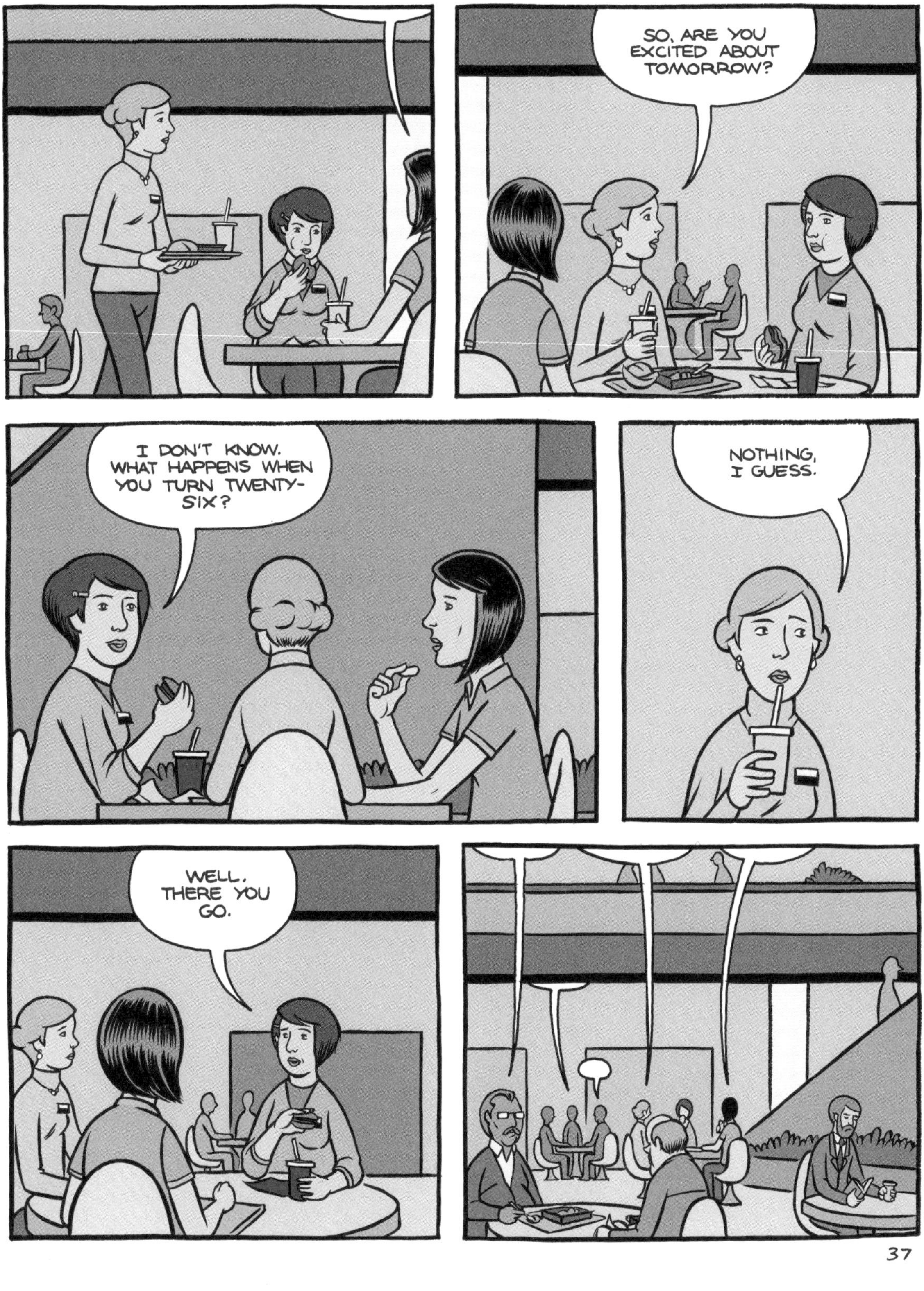
SO, ARE YOU EXCITED ABOUT TOMORROW?
I DON'T KNOW. WHAT HAPPENS WHEN YOU TURN TWENTY-SIX?
NOTHING, I GUESS.
WELL. THERE YOU GO.

4
Happy Birthday, Amy

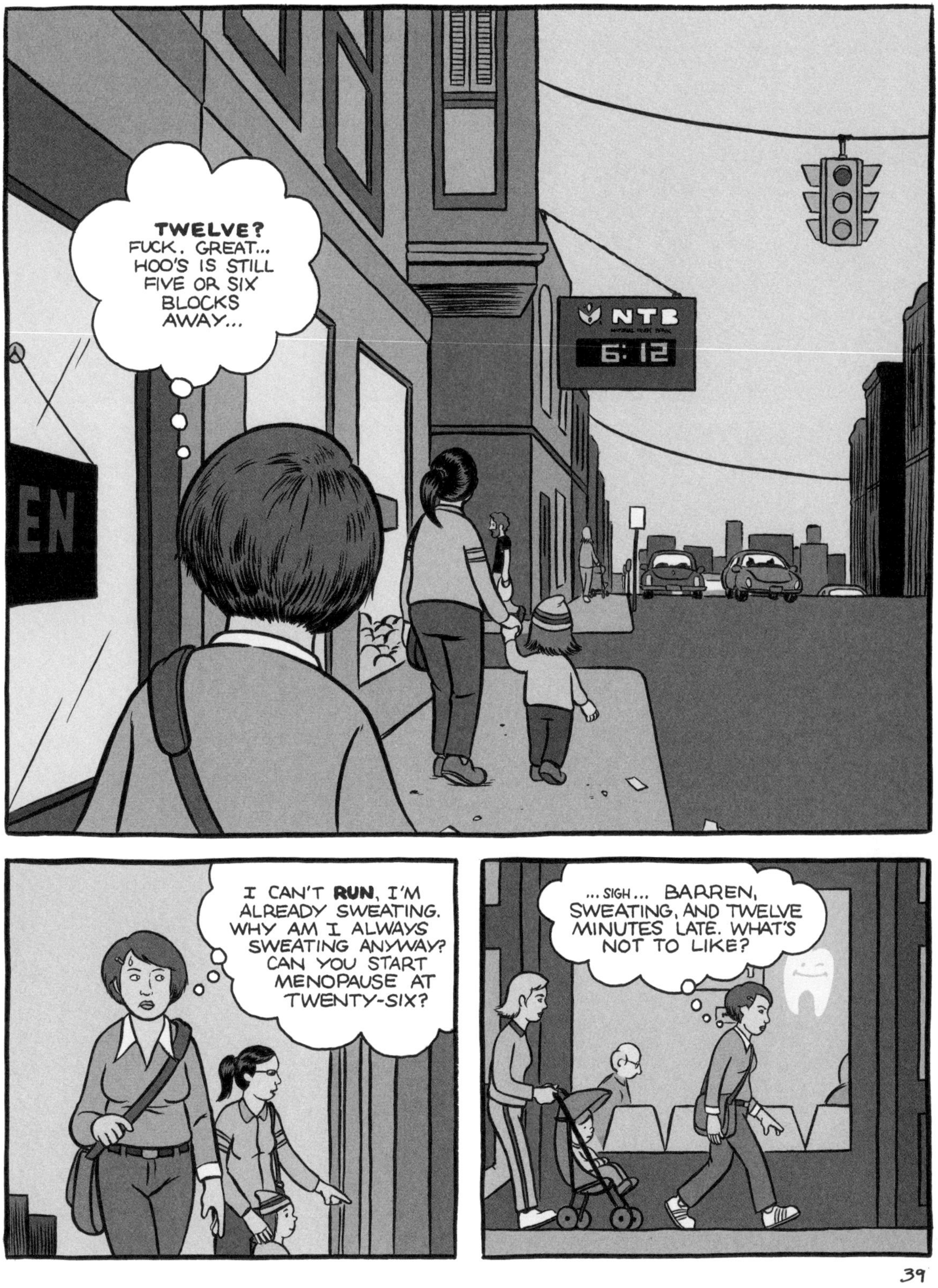
TWELVE? FUCK. GREAT... HOO'S IS STILL FIVE OR SIX BLOCKS AWAY...
NTB
6:12
EN
I CAN'T RUN, I'M ALREADY SWEATING. WHY AM I ALWAYS SWEATING ANYWAY? CAN YOU START MENOPAUSE AT TWENTY-SIX?
...SIGH... BARREN, SWEATING, AND TWELVE MINUTES LATE. WHAT'S NOT TO LIKE?

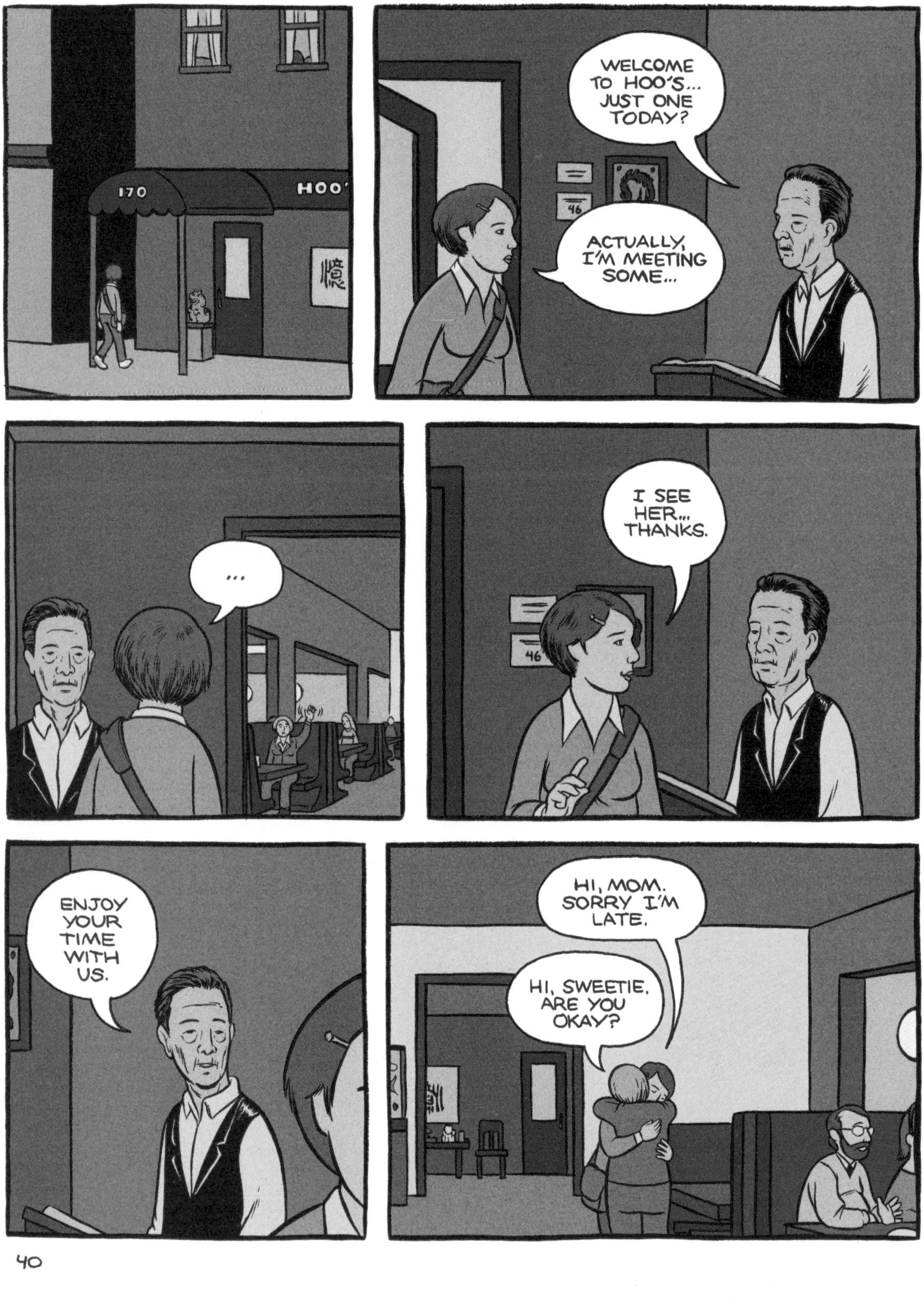
170
HOO'
WELCOME TO HOO'S... JUST ONE TODAY?
ACTUALLY, I'M MEETING SOME...
46
...
I SEE HER... THANKS.
46
ENJOY YOUR TIME WITH US.
HI, MOM. SORRY I'M LATE.
HI, SWEETIE. ARE YOU OKAY?

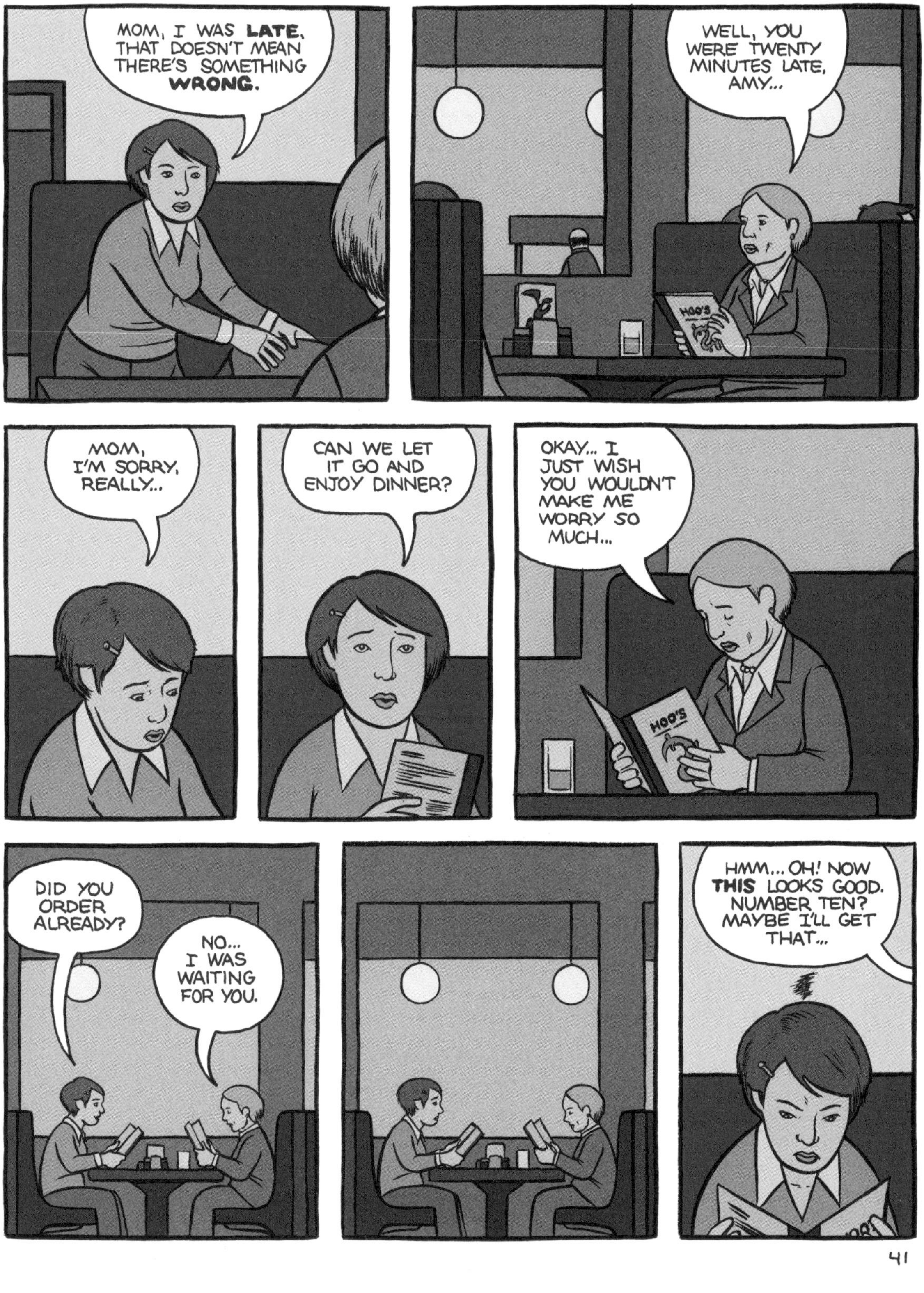
MOM, I WAS **LATE**. THAT DOESN'T MEAN THERE'S SOMETHING **WRONG**.
WELL, YOU WERE TWENTY MINUTES LATE, AMY...
MOM, I'M SORRY, REALLY...
CAN WE LET IT GO AND ENJOY DINNER?
OKAY... I JUST WISH YOU WOULDN'T MAKE ME WORRY SO MUCH...
HOO'S
DID YOU ORDER ALREADY?
NO... I WAS WAITING FOR YOU.
HMM... OH! NOW **THIS** LOOKS GOOD. NUMBER TEN? MAYBE I'LL GET THAT...

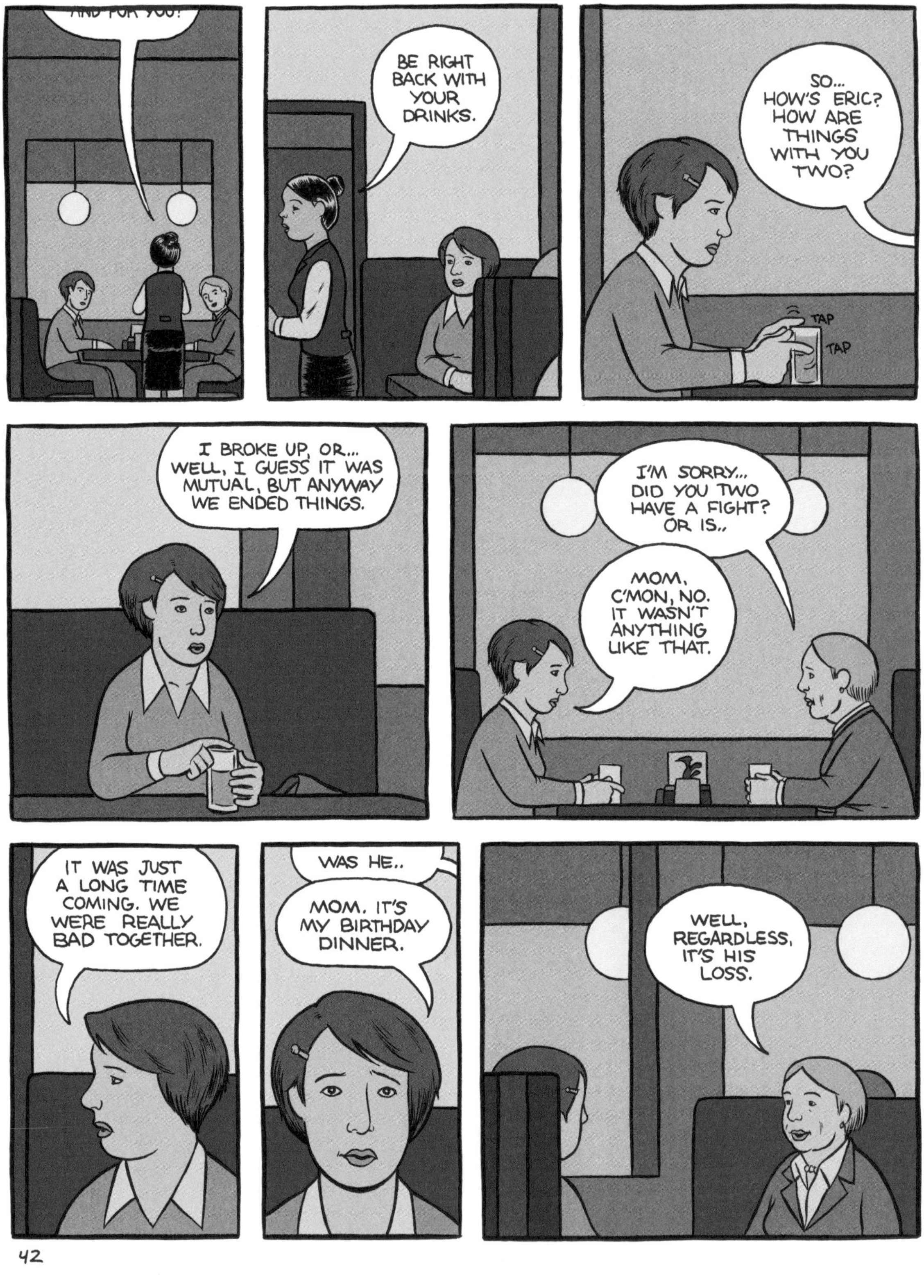
AND FOR YOU?
BE RIGHT BACK WITH YOUR DRINKS.
SO... HOW'S ERIC? HOW ARE THINGS WITH YOU TWO?
TAP
TAP
I BROKE UP, OR... WELL, I GUESS IT WAS MUTUAL, BUT ANYWAY WE ENDED THINGS.
I'M SORRY... DID YOU TWO HAVE A FIGHT? OR IS..
MOM, C'MON, NO. IT WASN'T ANYTHING LIKE THAT.
IT WAS JUST A LONG TIME COMING. WE WERE REALLY BAD TOGETHER.
WAS HE..
MOM. IT'S MY BIRTHDAY DINNER.
WELL, REGARDLESS, IT'S HIS LOSS.

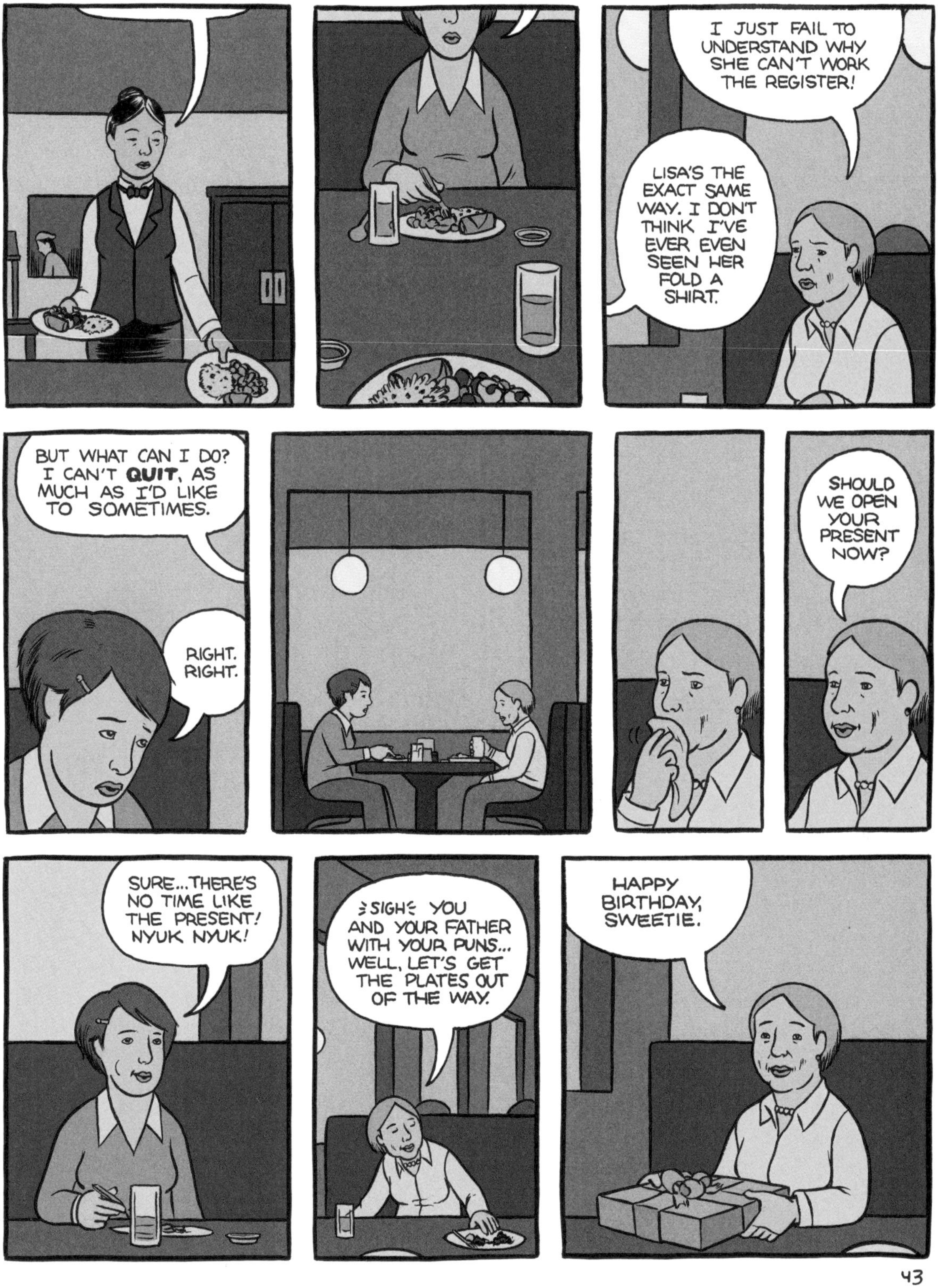
I JUST FAIL TO UNDERSTAND WHY SHE CAN'T WORK THE REGISTER!
LISA'S THE EXACT SAME WAY. I DON'T THINK I'VE EVER EVEN SEEN HER FOLD A SHIRT.
BUT WHAT CAN I DO? I CAN'T **QUIT**, AS MUCH AS I'D LIKE TO SOMETIMES.
RIGHT. RIGHT.
SHOULD WE OPEN YOUR PRESENT NOW?
SURE...THERE'S NO TIME LIKE THE PRESENT! NYUK NYUK!
≷SIGH≶ YOU AND YOUR FATHER WITH YOUR PUNS... WELL, LET'S GET THE PLATES OUT OF THE WAY.
HAPPY BIRTHDAY, SWEETIE.

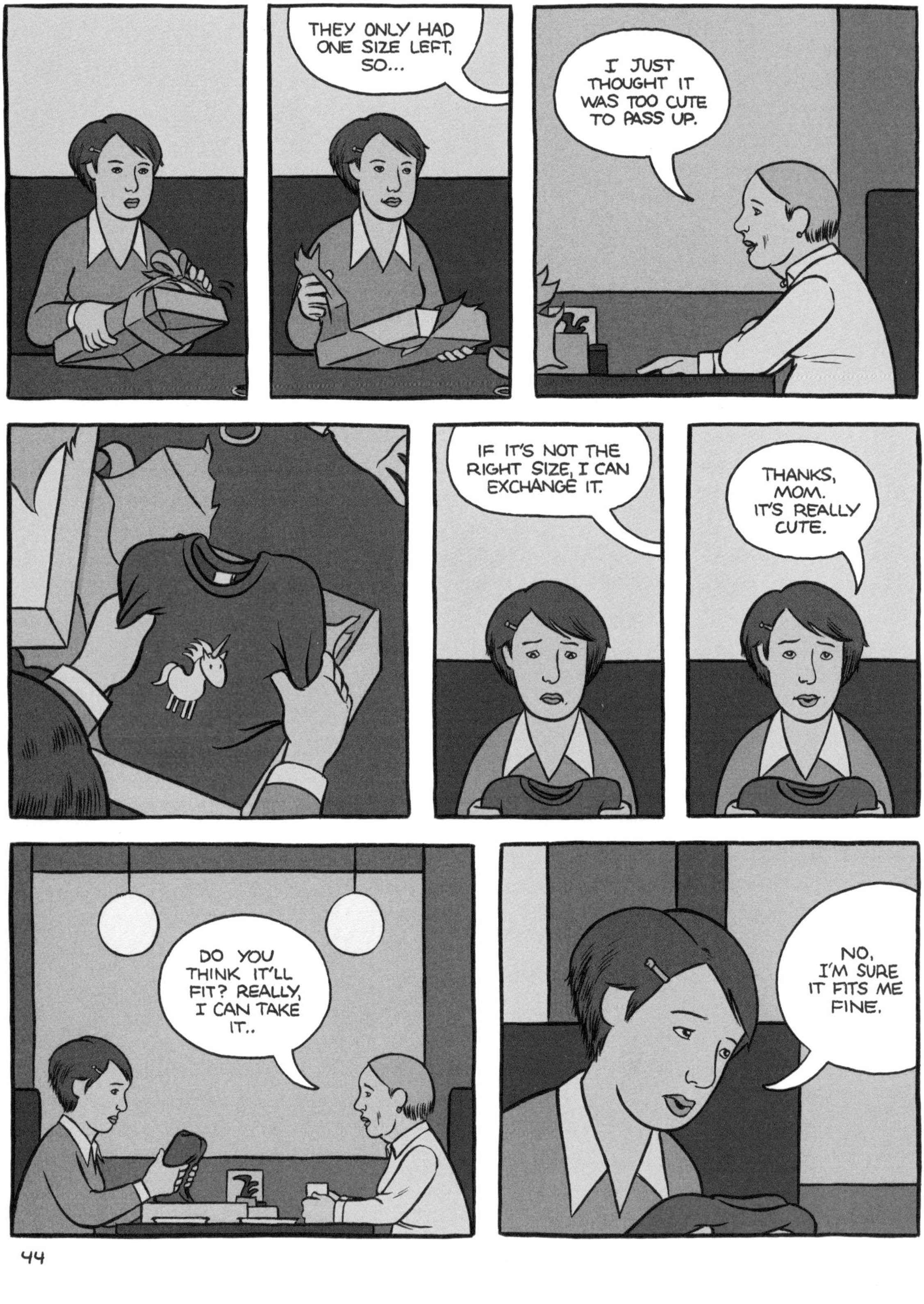
THEY ONLY HAD ONE SIZE LEFT, SO...
I JUST THOUGHT IT WAS TOO CUTE TO PASS UP.
IF IT'S NOT THE RIGHT SIZE, I CAN EXCHANGE IT.
THANKS, MOM. IT'S REALLY CUTE.
DO YOU THINK IT'LL FIT? REALLY, I CAN TAKE IT..
NO, I'M SURE IT FITS ME FINE.

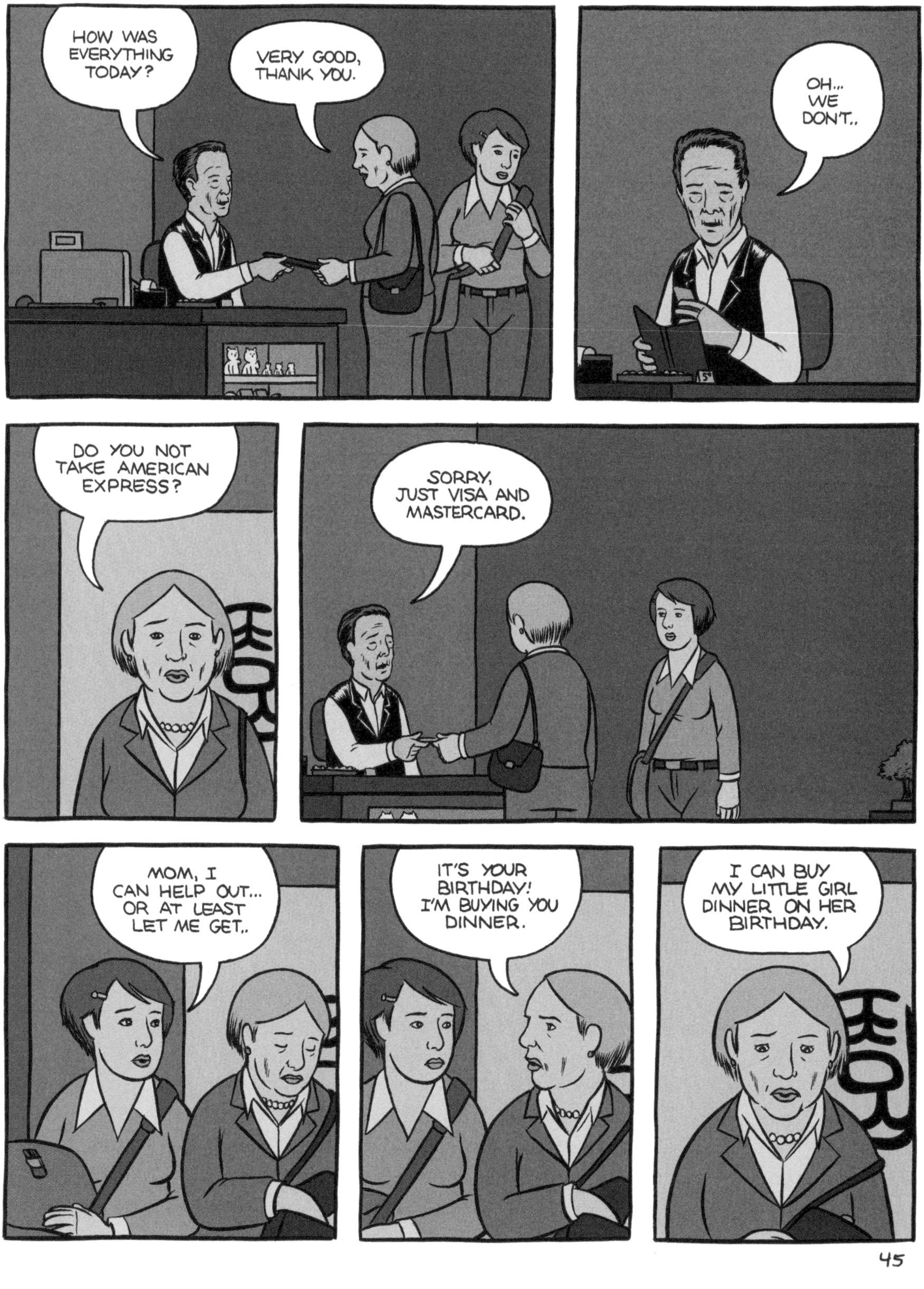
HOW WAS EVERYTHING TODAY?
VERY GOOD, THANK YOU.
OH... WE DON'T..
DO YOU NOT TAKE AMERICAN EXPRESS?
SORRY, JUST VISA AND MASTERCARD.
MOM, I CAN HELP OUT... OR AT LEAST LET ME GET..
IT'S YOUR BIRTHDAY! I'M BUYING YOU DINNER.
I CAN BUY MY LITTLE GIRL DINNER ON HER BIRTHDAY.

YOU'RE HEADED THAT WAY?

YEAH, I'M PARKED OVER ON MORRIS.

HAPPY BIRTHDAY, SWEETIE. I LOVE YOU.

THANKS, MOM. LOVE YOU TOO.

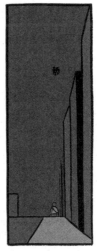

READY TO GO, HUBERT?

AND HOW OLD ARE YOU TODAY, LITTLE GIRL?

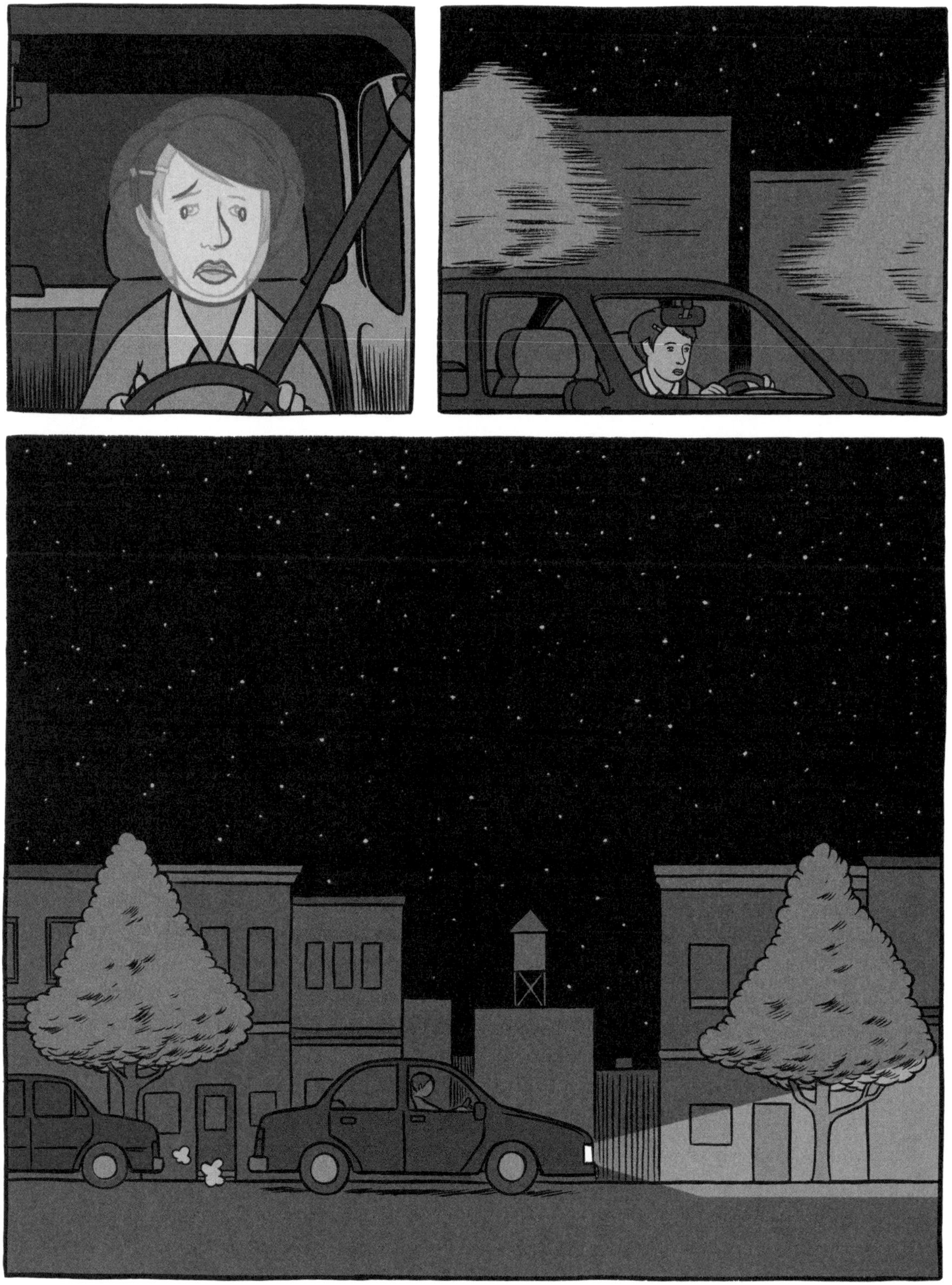

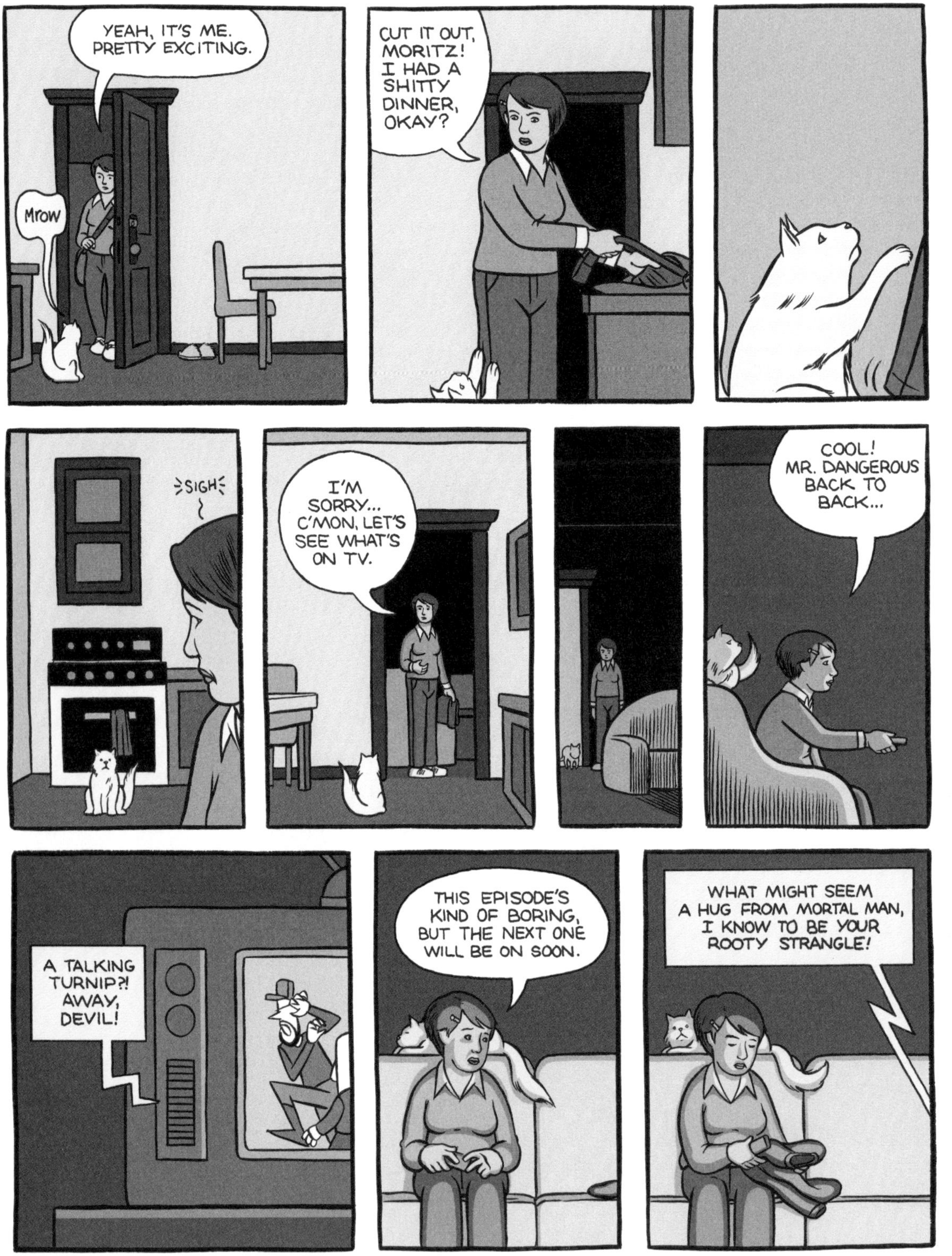
YEAH, IT'S ME. PRETTY EXCITING.
Mrow
CUT IT OUT, MORITZ! I HAD A SHITTY DINNER, OKAY?
SIGH
I'M SORRY... C'MON, LET'S SEE WHAT'S ON TV.
COOL! MR. DANGEROUS BACK TO BACK...
A TALKING TURNIP?! AWAY, DEVIL!
THIS EPISODE'S KIND OF BORING, BUT THE NEXT ONE WILL BE ON SOON.
WHAT MIGHT SEEM A HUG FROM MORTAL MAN, I KNOW TO BE YOUR ROOTY STRANGLE!

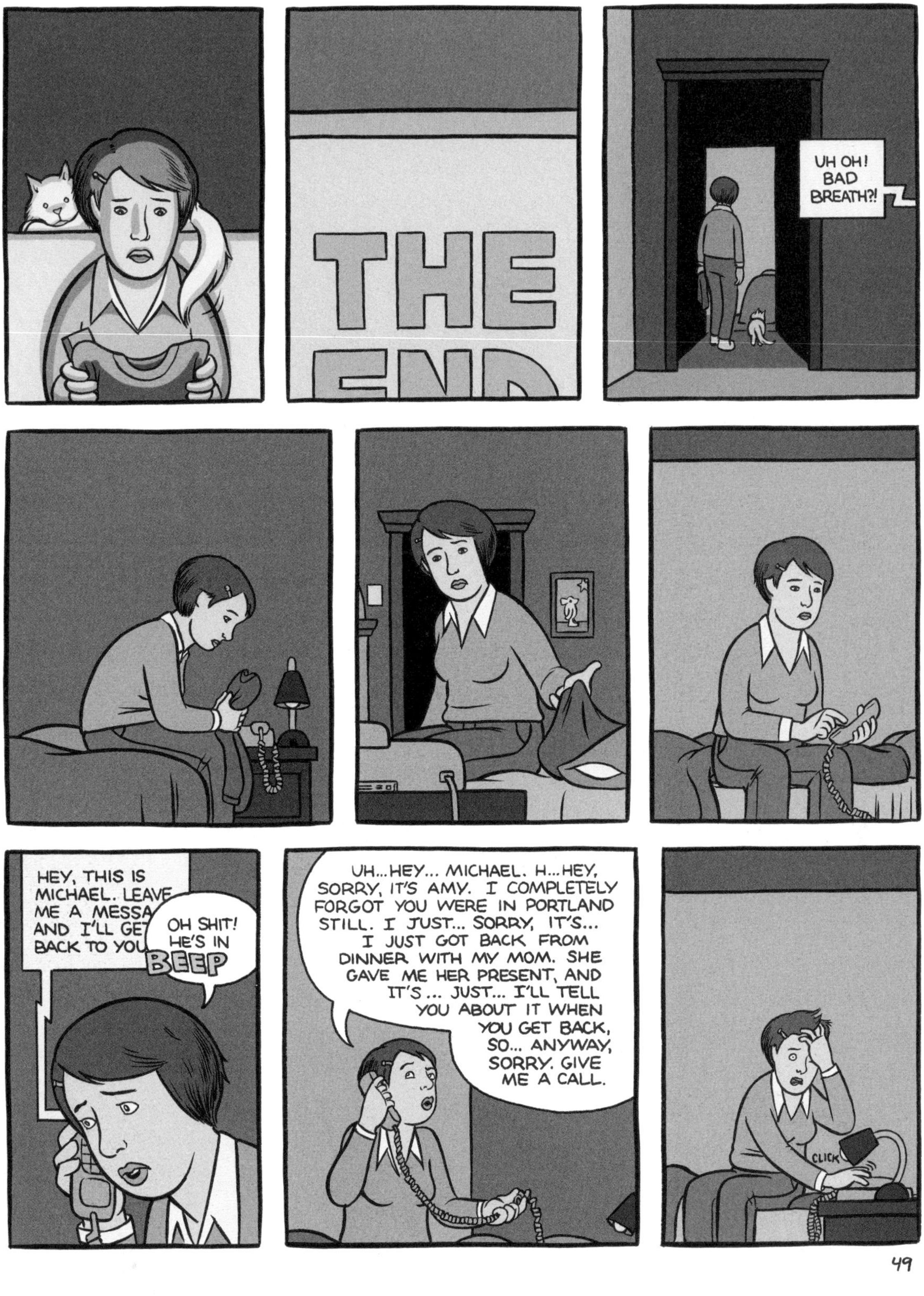
THE END
UH OH! BAD BREATH?!
HEY, THIS IS MICHAEL. LEAVE ME A MESSA AND I'LL GET BACK TO YOU
OH SHIT! HE'S IN
BEEP
UH... HEY... MICHAEL. H...HEY, SORRY, IT'S AMY. I COMPLETELY FORGOT YOU WERE IN PORTLAND STILL. I JUST... SORRY, IT'S... I JUST GOT BACK FROM DINNER WITH MY MOM. SHE GAVE ME HER PRESENT, AND IT'S ... JUST... I'LL TELL YOU ABOUT IT WHEN YOU GET BACK, SO... ANYWAY, SORRY. GIVE ME A CALL.
CLICK

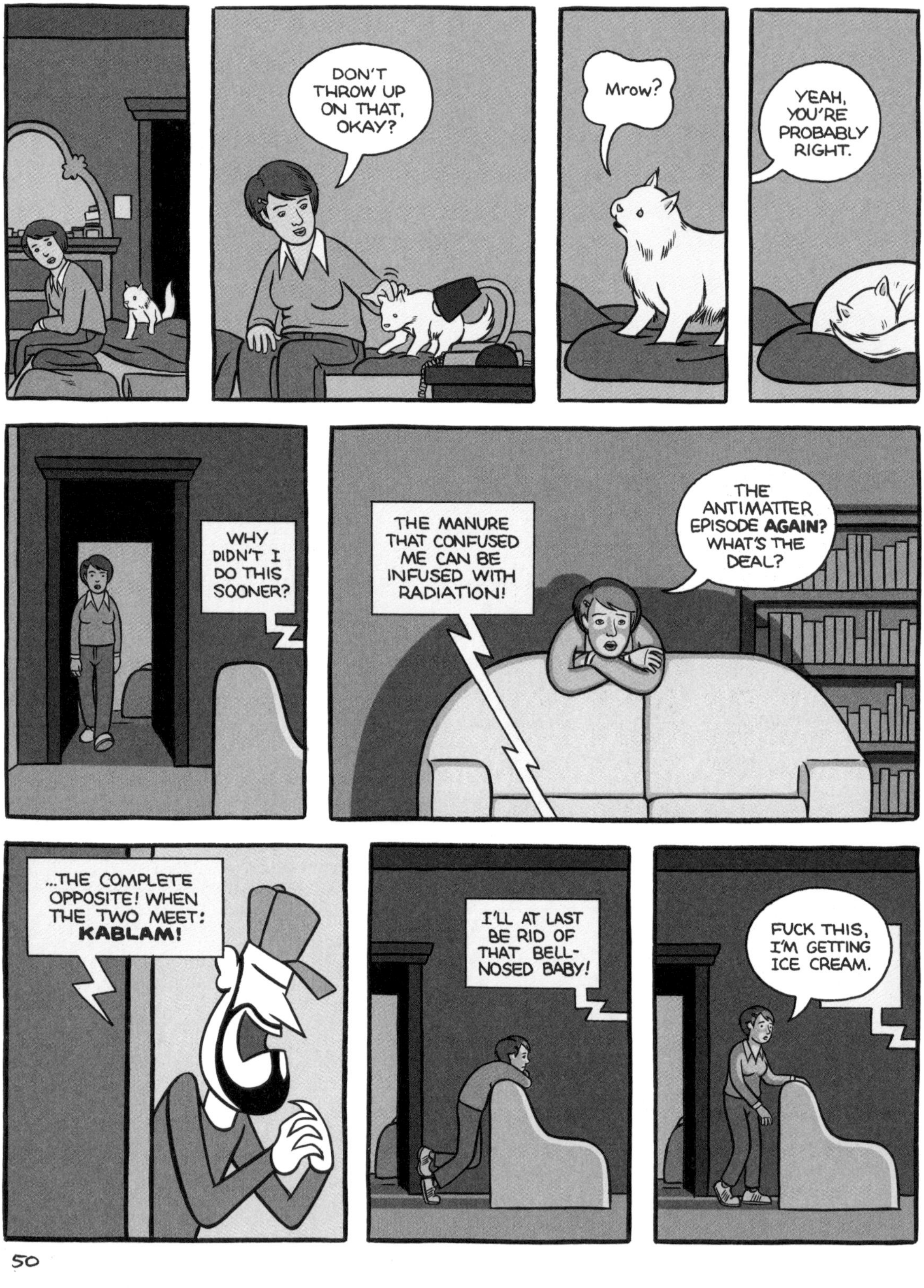

DON'T THROW UP ON THAT, OKAY?
Mrow?
YEAH, YOU'RE PROBABLY RIGHT.
WHY DIDN'T I DO THIS SOONER?
THE MANURE THAT CONFUSED ME CAN BE INFUSED WITH RADIATION!
THE ANTIMATTER EPISODE **AGAIN?** WHAT'S THE DEAL?
...THE COMPLETE OPPOSITE! WHEN THE TWO MEET: **KABLAM!**
I'LL AT LAST BE RID OF THAT BELL-NOSED BABY!
FUCK THIS, I'M GETTING ICE CREAM.

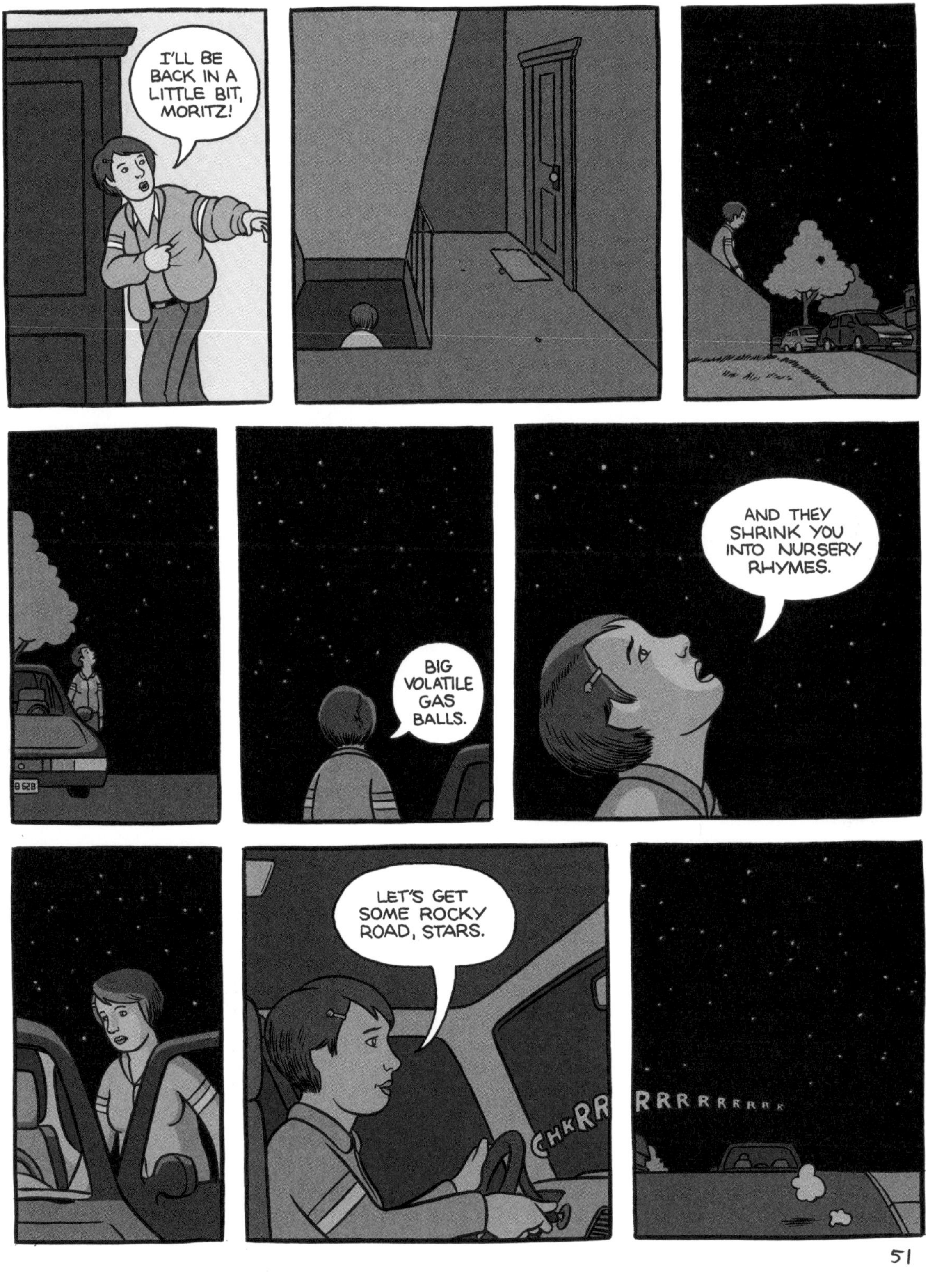
I'LL BE BACK IN A LITTLE BIT, MORITZ!
B 62B
BIG VOLATILE GAS BALLS.
AND THEY SHRINK YOU INTO NURSERY RHYMES.
LET'S GET SOME ROCKY ROAD, STARS.
CHKRRRRRRRRRRR

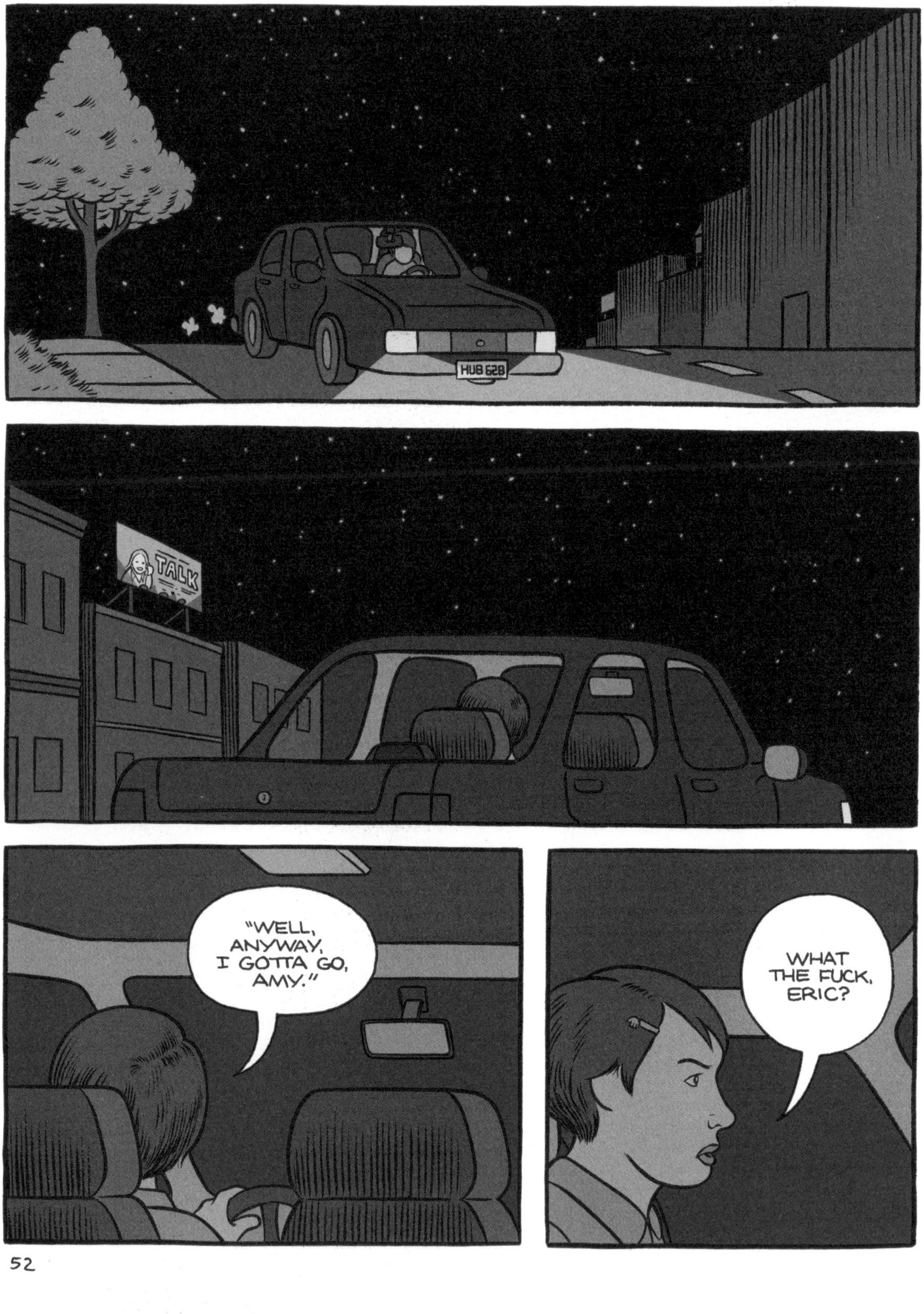
HUB 628
TALK
"WELL, ANYWAY, I GOTTA GO, AMY."
WHAT THE FUCK, ERIC?

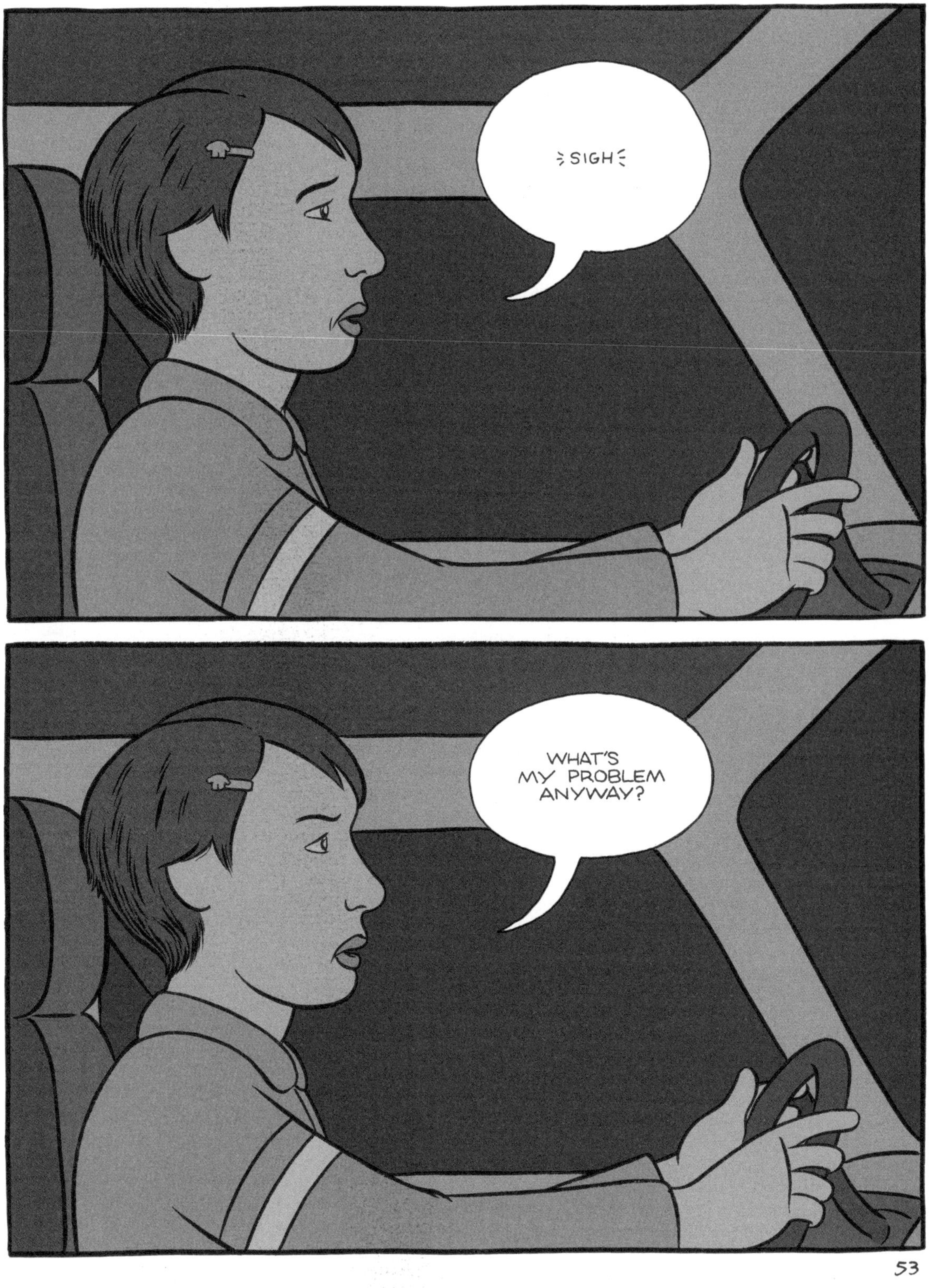
SIGH
WHAT'S MY PROBLEM ANYWAY?

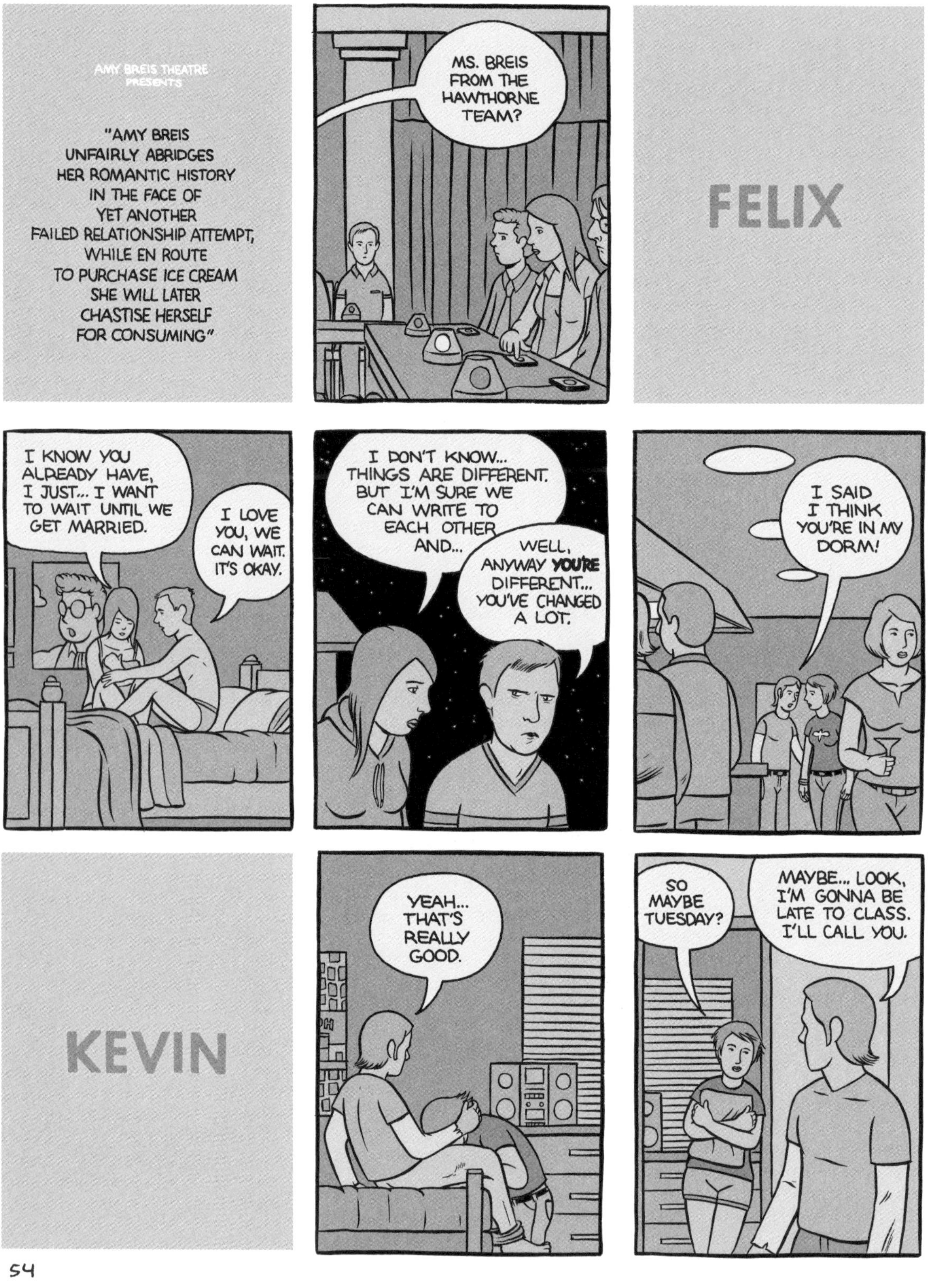
AMY BREIS THEATRE PRESENTS
"AMY BREIS UNFAIRLY ABRIDGES HER ROMANTIC HISTORY IN THE FACE OF YET ANOTHER FAILED RELATIONSHIP ATTEMPT, WHILE EN ROUTE TO PURCHASE ICE CREAM SHE WILL LATER CHASTISE HERSELF FOR CONSUMING"
MS. BREIS FROM THE HAWTHORNE TEAM?
FELIX
I KNOW YOU ALREADY HAVE, I JUST... I WANT TO WAIT UNTIL WE GET MARRIED.
I LOVE YOU, WE CAN WAIT. IT'S OKAY.
I DON'T KNOW... THINGS ARE DIFFERENT. BUT I'M SURE WE CAN WRITE TO EACH OTHER AND...
WELL, ANYWAY YOU'RE DIFFERENT... YOU'VE CHANGED A LOT.
I SAID I THINK YOU'RE IN MY DORM!
KEVIN
YEAH... THAT'S REALLY GOOD.
SO MAYBE TUESDAY?
MAYBE... LOOK, I'M GONNA BE LATE TO CLASS. I'LL CALL YOU.

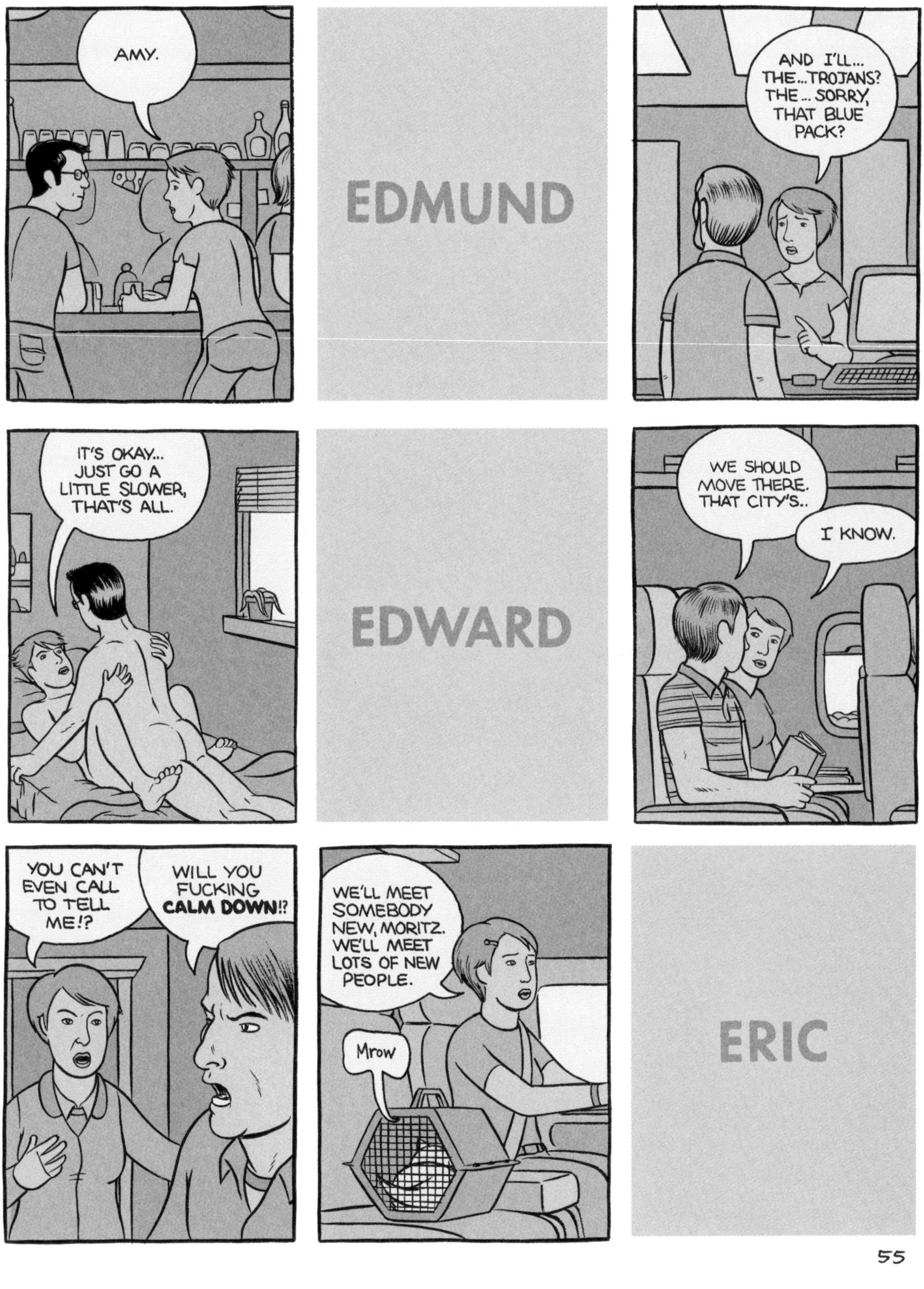
AMY.
EDMUND
AND I'LL... THE...TROJANS? THE... SORRY, THAT BLUE PACK?
IT'S OKAY... JUST GO A LITTLE SLOWER, THAT'S ALL.
EDWARD
WE SHOULD MOVE THERE. THAT CITY'S..
I KNOW.
YOU CAN'T EVEN CALL TO TELL ME!?
WILL YOU FUCKING **CALM DOWN**!?
WE'LL MEET SOMEBODY NEW, MORITZ. WE'LL MEET LOTS OF NEW PEOPLE.
Mrow
ERIC

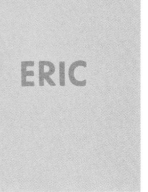

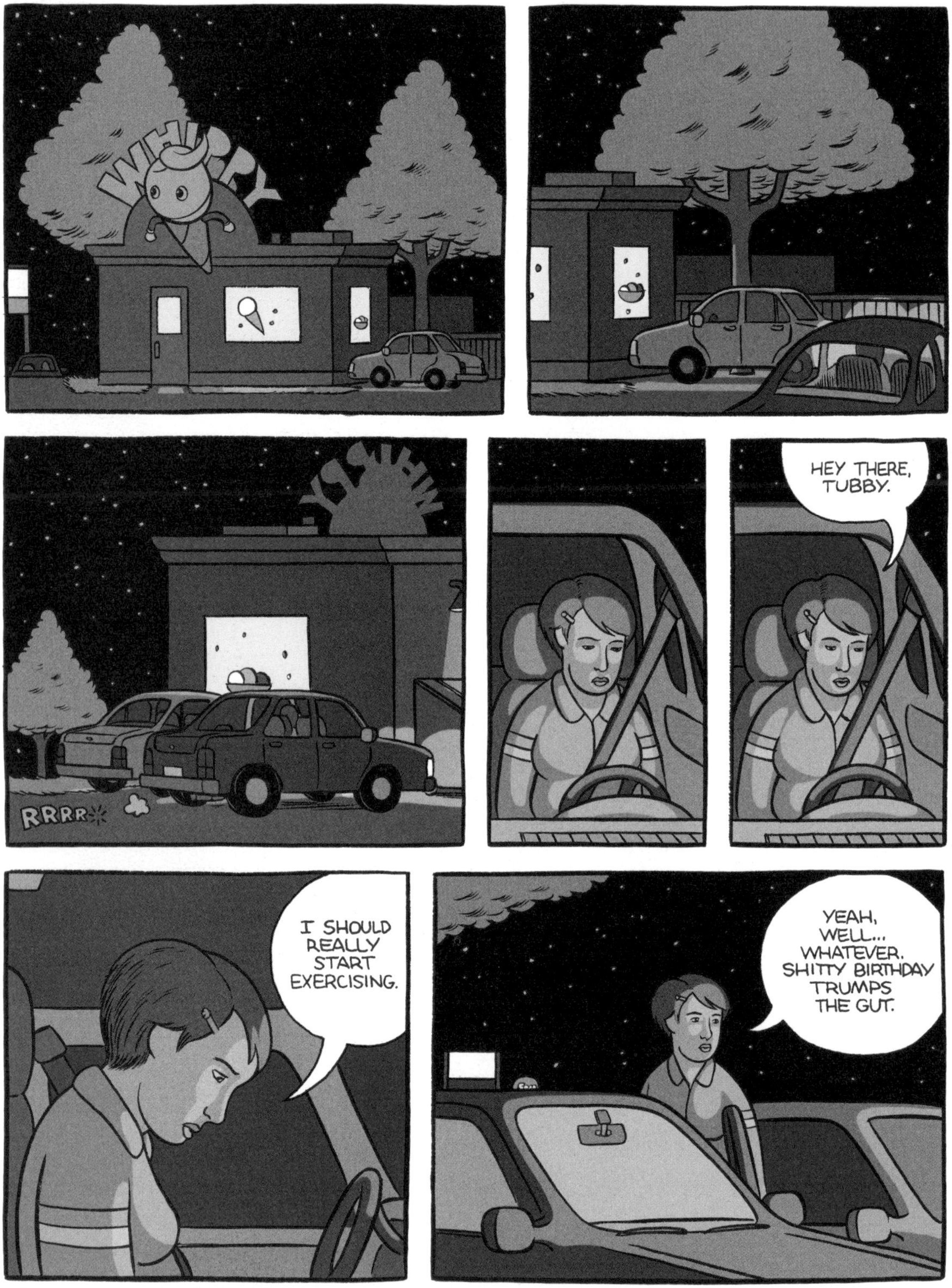
RRRR
HEY THERE, TUBBY.
I SHOULD REALLY START EXERCISING.
YEAH, WELL... WHATEVER. SHITTY BIRTHDAY TRUMPS THE GUT.

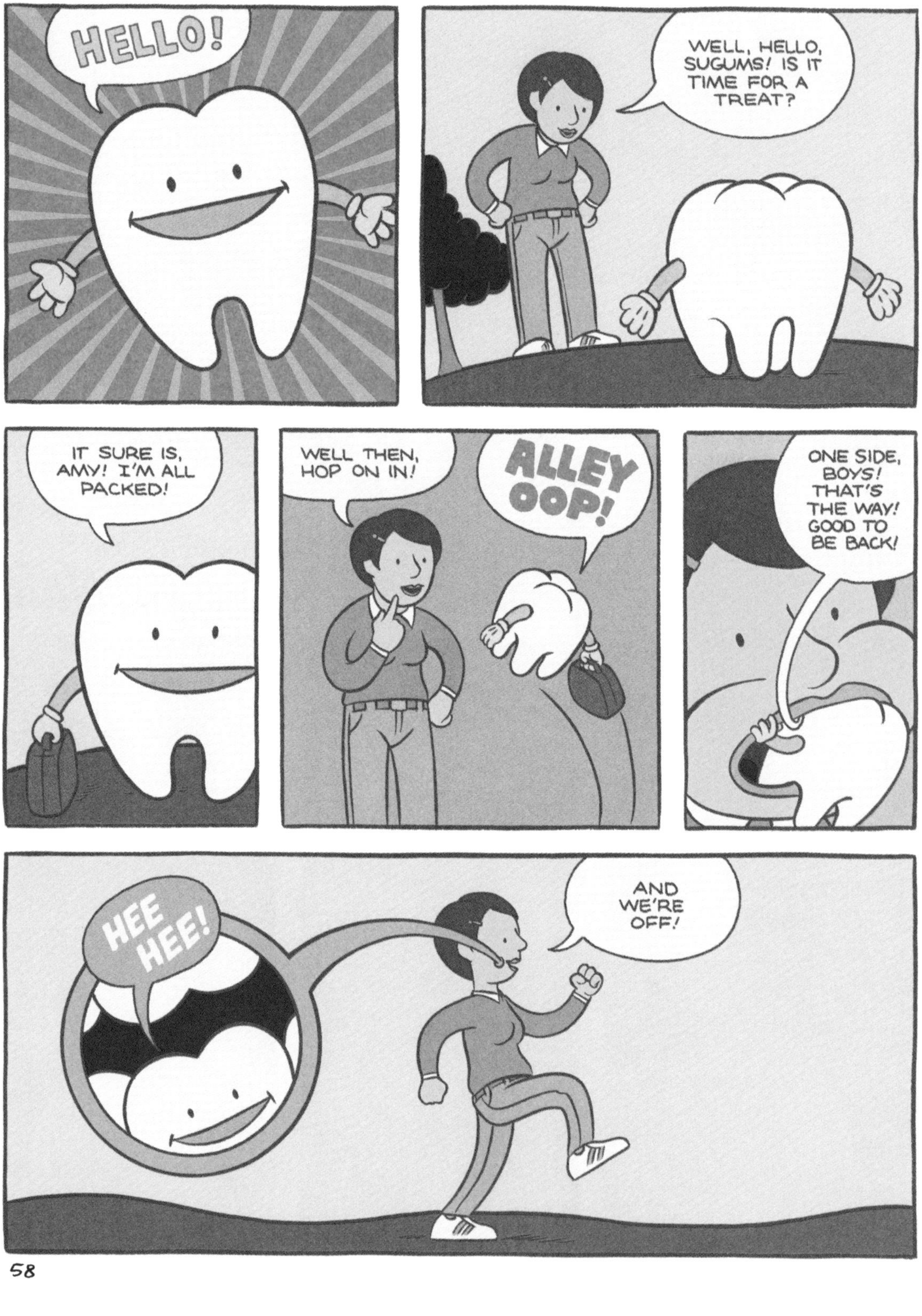
HELLO!
WELL, HELLO, SUGUMS! IS IT TIME FOR A TREAT?
IT SURE IS, AMY! I'M ALL PACKED!
WELL THEN, HOP ON IN!
ALLEY OOP!
ONE SIDE, BOYS! THAT'S THE WAY! GOOD TO BE BACK!
HEE HEE!
AND WE'RE OFF!

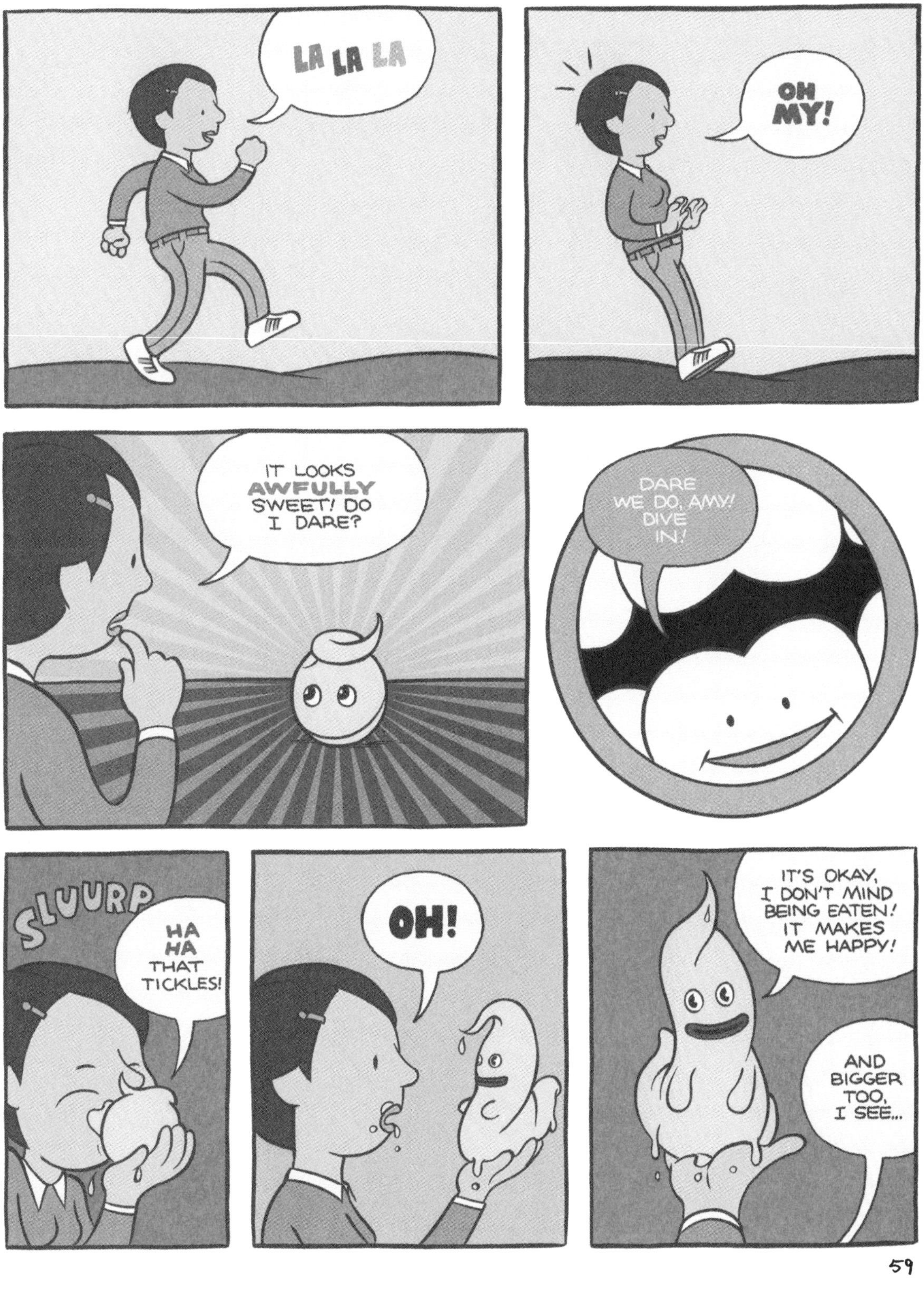
LA LA LA
OH MY!
IT LOOKS AWFULLY SWEET! DO I DARE?
DARE WE DO, AMY! DIVE IN!
SLUURP
HA HA THAT TICKLES!
OH!
IT'S OKAY, I DON'T MIND BEING EATEN! IT MAKES ME HAPPY!
AND BIGGER TOO, I SEE...

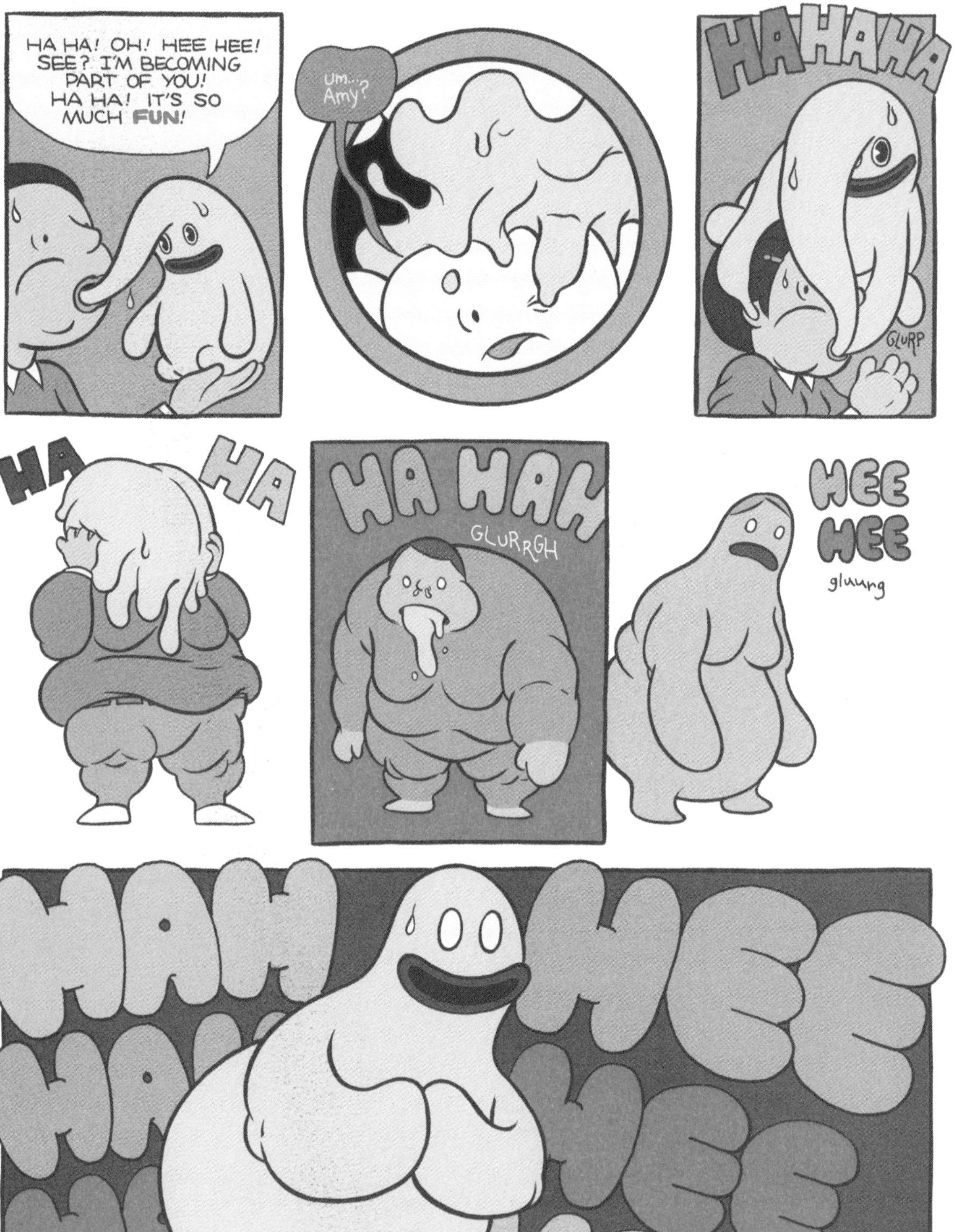
HA HA! OH! HEE HEE! SEE? I'M BECOMING PART OF YOU! HA HA! IT'S SO MUCH FUN!
Um...? Amy?
HAHAHA
GLURP
HA HA
HA HAH
GLURRGH
HEE HEE
gluurg
HAH HEE

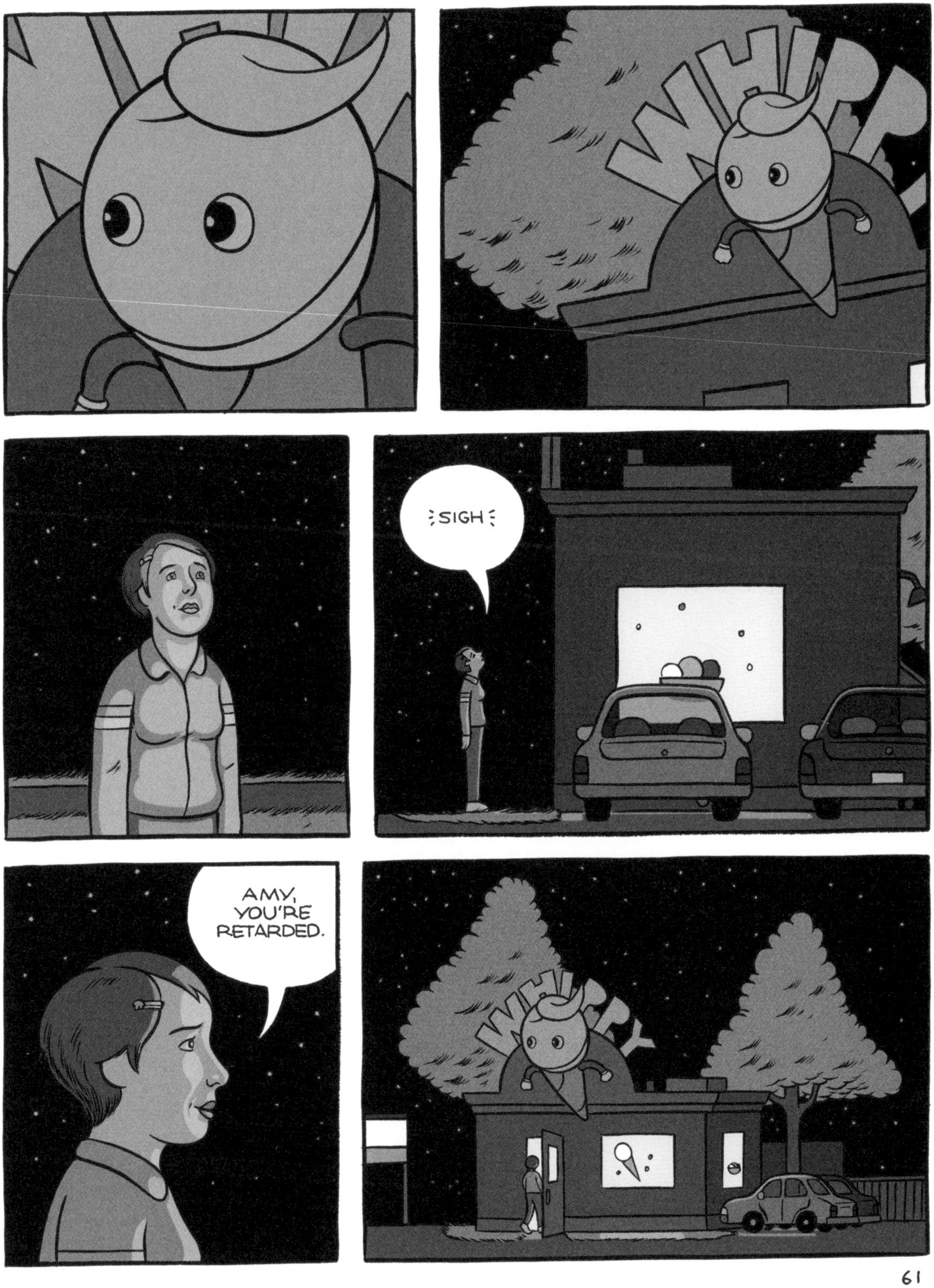
WHIPPY
SIGH
AMY, YOU'RE RETARDED.
WHIPPY

5
Dessert Before Bed

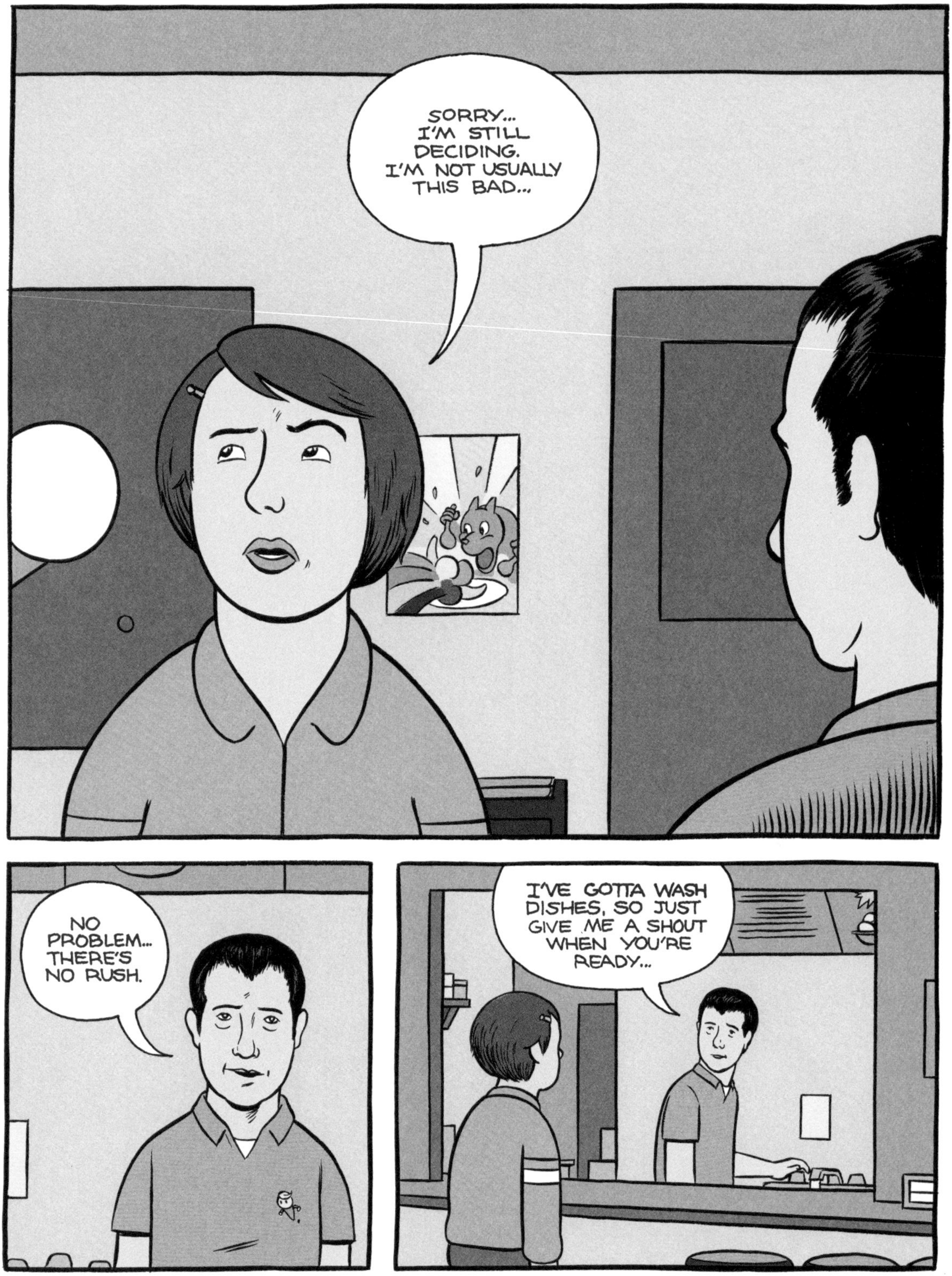
SORRY... I'M STILL DECIDING. I'M NOT USUALLY THIS BAD...
NO PROBLEM... THERE'S NO RUSH.
I'VE GOTTA WASH DISHES, SO JUST GIVE ME A SHOUT WHEN YOU'RE READY...

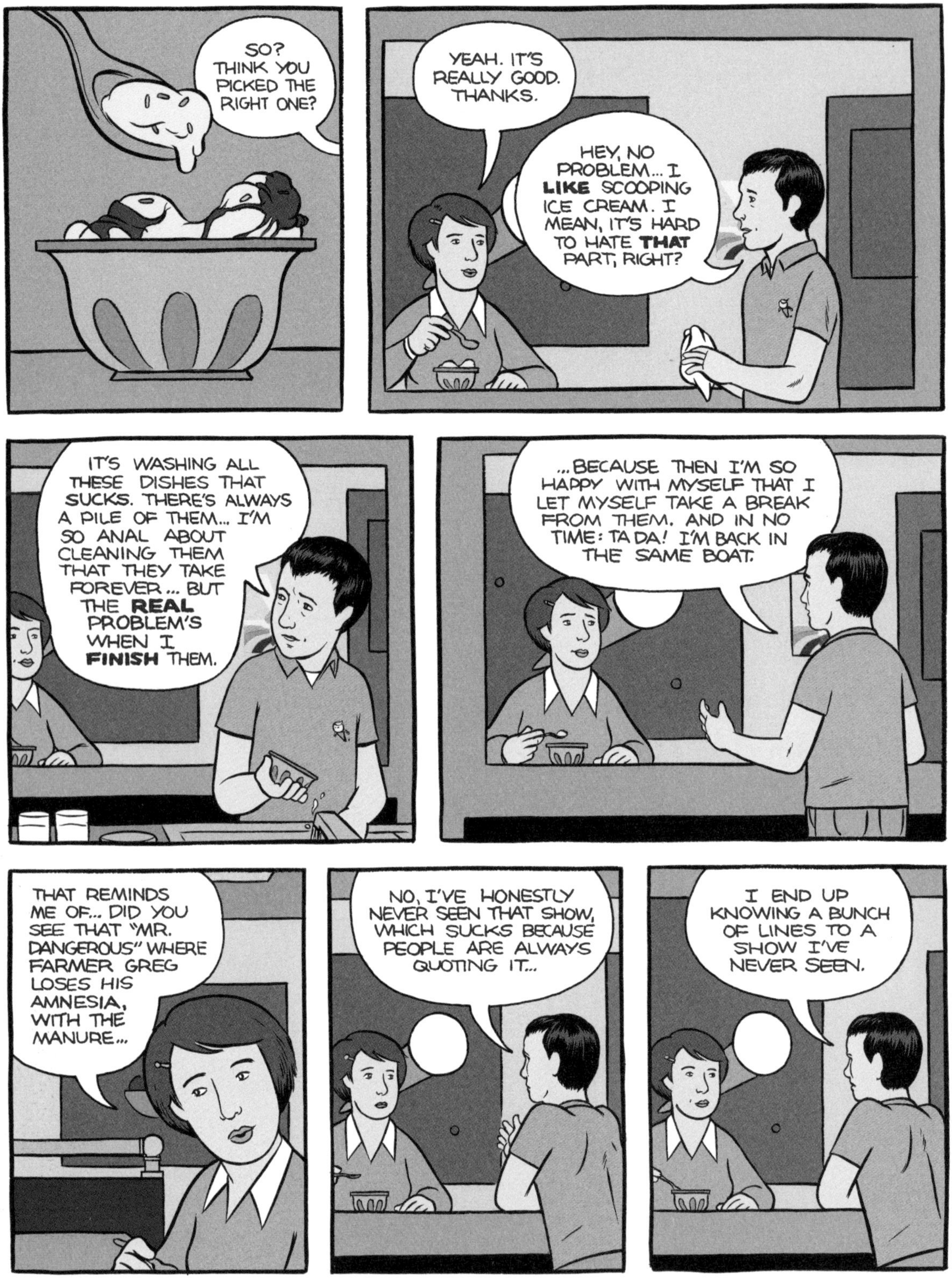
SO? THINK YOU PICKED THE RIGHT ONE?
YEAH. IT'S REALLY GOOD. THANKS.
HEY, NO PROBLEM... I **LIKE** SCOOPING ICE CREAM. I MEAN, IT'S HARD TO HATE **THAT** PART, RIGHT?
IT'S WASHING ALL THESE DISHES THAT SUCKS. THERE'S ALWAYS A PILE OF THEM... I'M SO ANAL ABOUT CLEANING THEM THAT THEY TAKE FOREVER... BUT THE **REAL** PROBLEM'S WHEN I **FINISH** THEM.
...BECAUSE THEN I'M SO HAPPY WITH MYSELF THAT I LET MYSELF TAKE A BREAK FROM THEM. AND IN NO TIME: TA DA! I'M BACK IN THE SAME BOAT.
THAT REMINDS ME OF... DID YOU SEE THAT "MR. DANGEROUS" WHERE FARMER GREG LOSES HIS AMNESIA, WITH THE MANURE...
NO, I'VE HONESTLY NEVER SEEN THAT SHOW, WHICH SUCKS BECAUSE PEOPLE ARE ALWAYS QUOTING IT...
I END UP KNOWING A BUNCH OF LINES TO A SHOW I'VE NEVER SEEN.

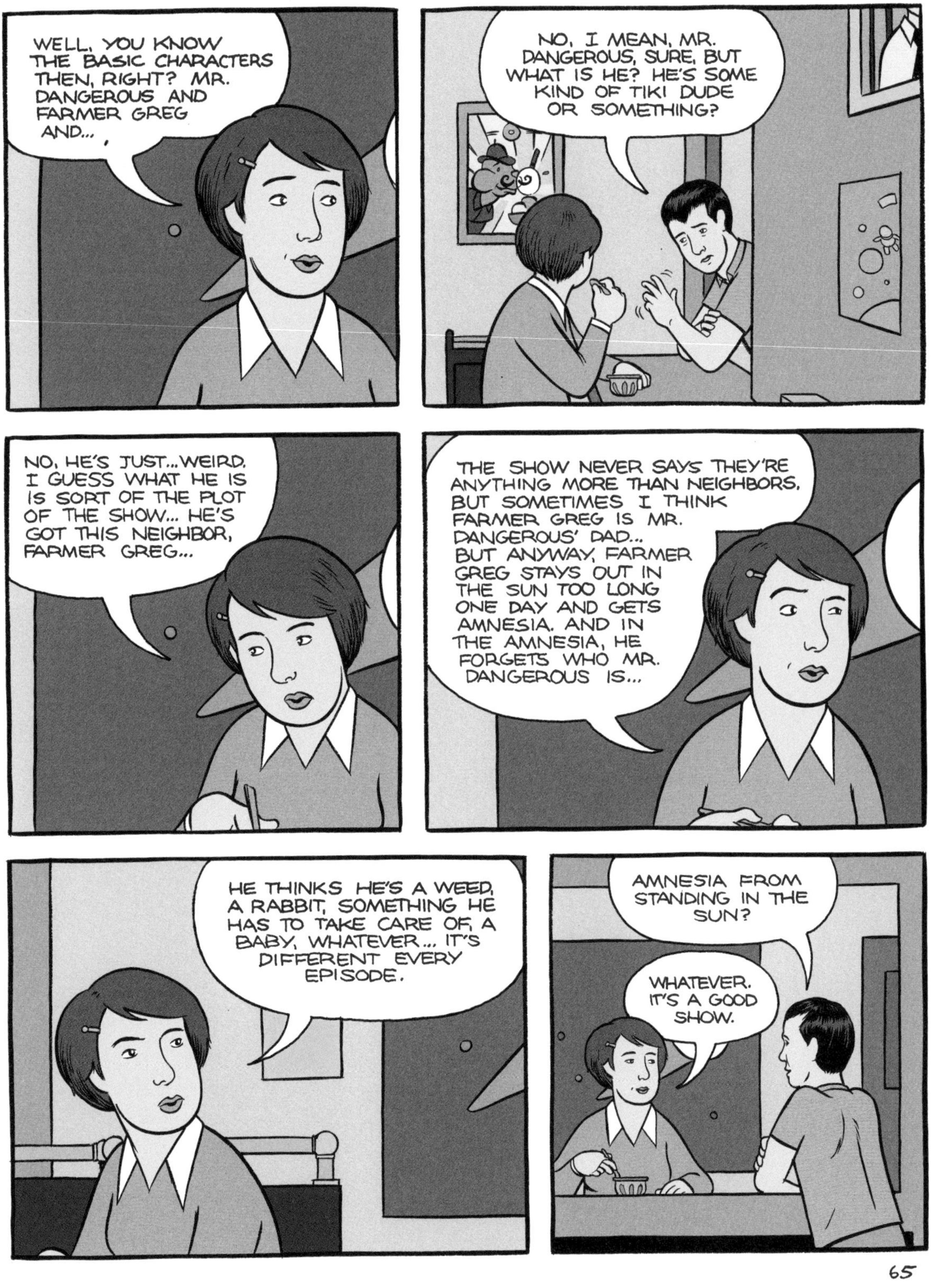
WELL, YOU KNOW THE BASIC CHARACTERS THEN, RIGHT? MR. DANGEROUS AND FARMER GREG AND...
NO, I MEAN, MR. DANGEROUS, SURE, BUT WHAT IS HE? HE'S SOME KIND OF TIKI DUDE OR SOMETHING?
NO, HE'S JUST...WEIRD. I GUESS WHAT HE IS IS SORT OF THE PLOT OF THE SHOW... HE'S GOT THIS NEIGHBOR, FARMER GREG...
THE SHOW NEVER SAYS THEY'RE ANYTHING MORE THAN NEIGHBORS, BUT SOMETIMES I THINK FARMER GREG IS MR. DANGEROUS' DAD... BUT ANYWAY, FARMER GREG STAYS OUT IN THE SUN TOO LONG ONE DAY AND GETS AMNESIA. AND IN THE AMNESIA, HE FORGETS WHO MR. DANGEROUS IS...
HE THINKS HE'S A WEED, A RABBIT, SOMETHING HE HAS TO TAKE CARE OF, A BABY, WHATEVER... IT'S DIFFERENT EVERY EPISODE.
AMNESIA FROM STANDING IN THE SUN?
WHATEVER. IT'S A GOOD SHOW.

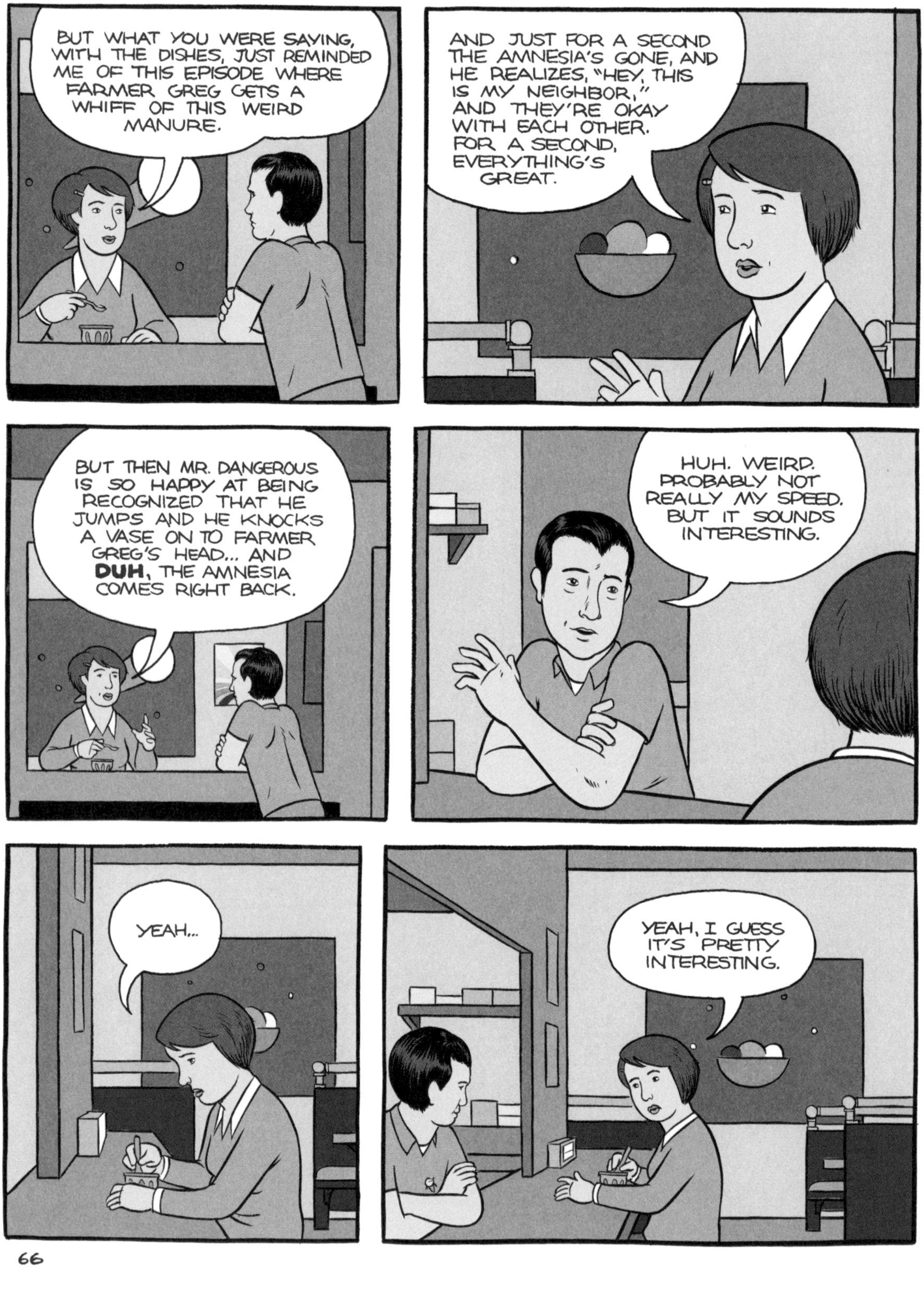
BUT WHAT YOU WERE SAYING, WITH THE DISHES, JUST REMINDED ME OF THIS EPISODE WHERE FARMER GREG GETS A WHIFF OF THIS WEIRD MANURE.
AND JUST FOR A SECOND THE AMNESIA'S GONE, AND HE REALIZES, "HEY, THIS IS MY NEIGHBOR," AND THEY'RE OKAY WITH EACH OTHER. FOR A SECOND, EVERYTHING'S GREAT.
BUT THEN MR. DANGEROUS IS SO HAPPY AT BEING RECOGNIZED THAT HE JUMPS AND HE KNOCKS A VASE ON TO FARMER GREG'S HEAD... AND **DUH**, THE AMNESIA COMES RIGHT BACK.
HUH. WEIRD. PROBABLY NOT REALLY MY SPEED. BUT IT SOUNDS INTERESTING.
YEAH...
YEAH, I GUESS IT'S PRETTY INTERESTING.

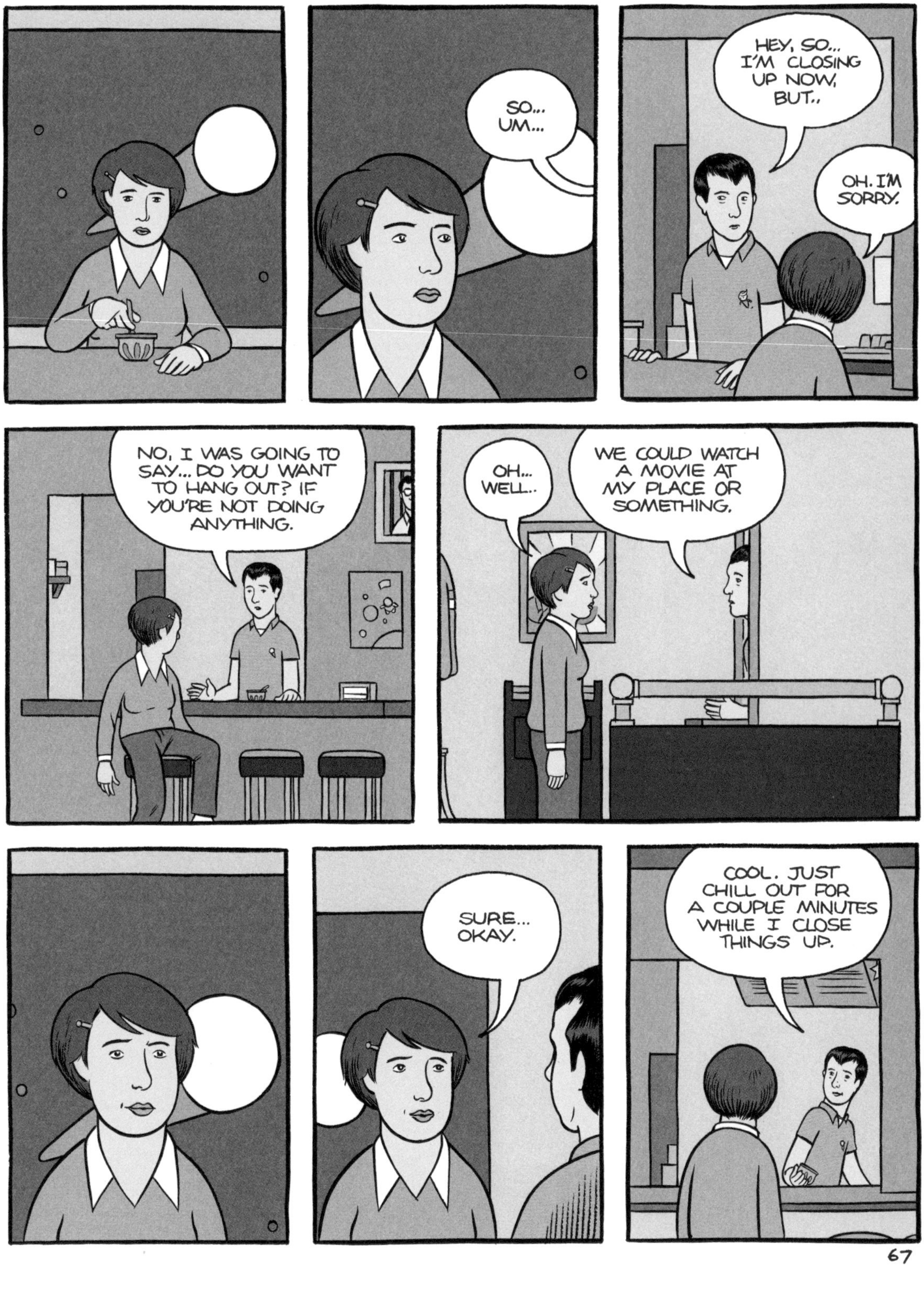
SO... UM...
HEY, SO... I'M CLOSING UP NOW, BUT..
OH. I'M SORRY.
NO, I WAS GOING TO SAY... DO YOU WANT TO HANG OUT? IF YOU'RE NOT DOING ANYTHING.
OH... WELL...
WE COULD WATCH A MOVIE AT MY PLACE OR SOMETHING.
SURE... OKAY.
COOL. JUST CHILL OUT FOR A COUPLE MINUTES WHILE I CLOSE THINGS UP.

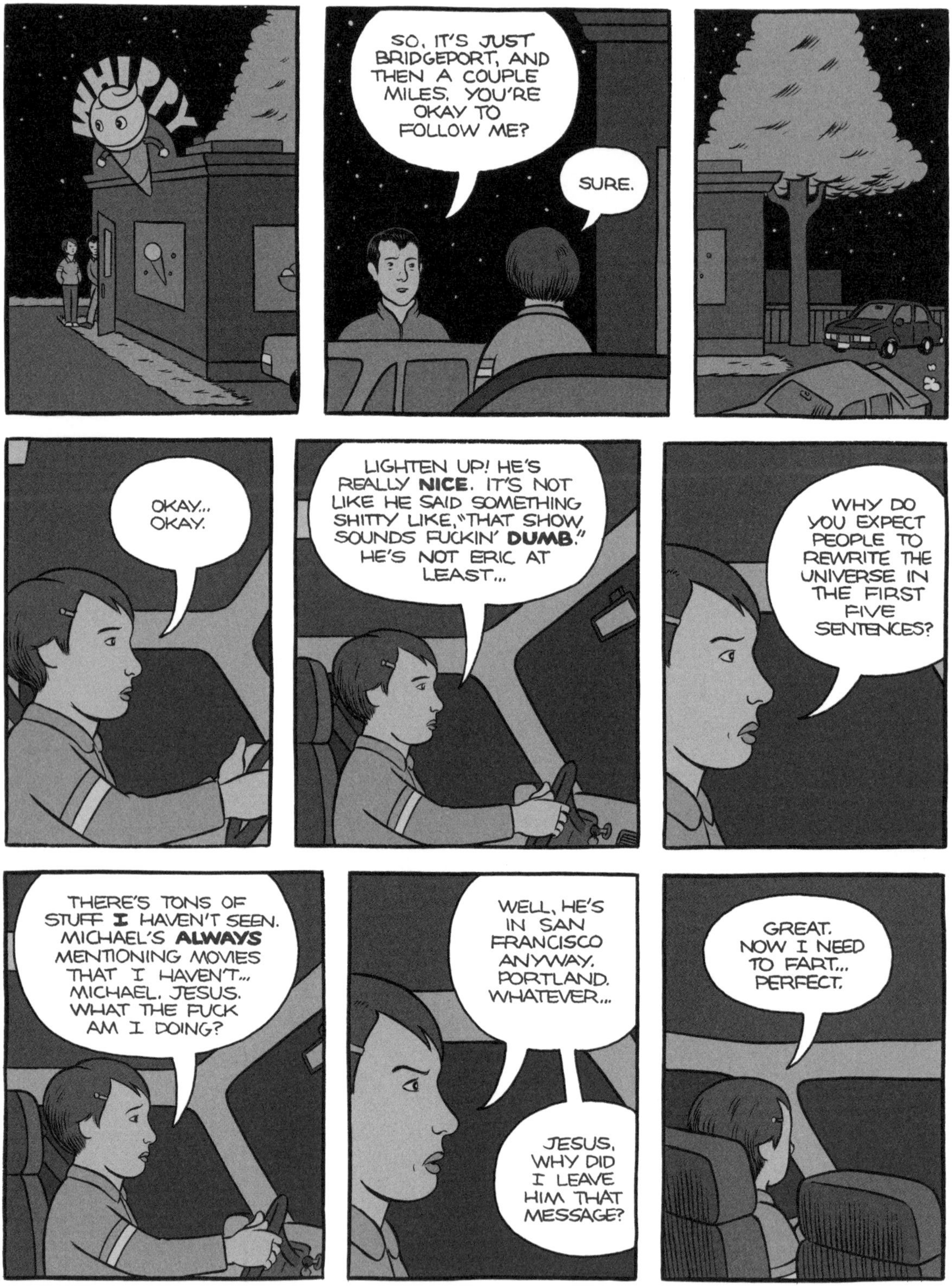
WHIPPY
SO, IT'S JUST BRIDGEPORT, AND THEN A COUPLE MILES. YOU'RE OKAY TO FOLLOW ME?
SURE.
OKAY... OKAY.
LIGHTEN UP! HE'S REALLY **NICE**. IT'S NOT LIKE HE SAID SOMETHING SHITTY LIKE, "THAT SHOW SOUNDS FUCKIN' **DUMB**." HE'S NOT ERIC AT LEAST...
WHY DO YOU EXPECT PEOPLE TO REWRITE THE UNIVERSE IN THE FIRST FIVE SENTENCES?
THERE'S TONS OF STUFF **I** HAVEN'T SEEN. MICHAEL'S **ALWAYS** MENTIONING MOVIES THAT I HAVEN'T... MICHAEL. JESUS. WHAT THE FUCK AM I DOING?
WELL, HE'S IN SAN FRANCISCO ANYWAY. PORTLAND. WHATEVER...
JESUS, WHY DID I LEAVE HIM THAT MESSAGE?
GREAT. NOW I NEED TO FART... PERFECT.

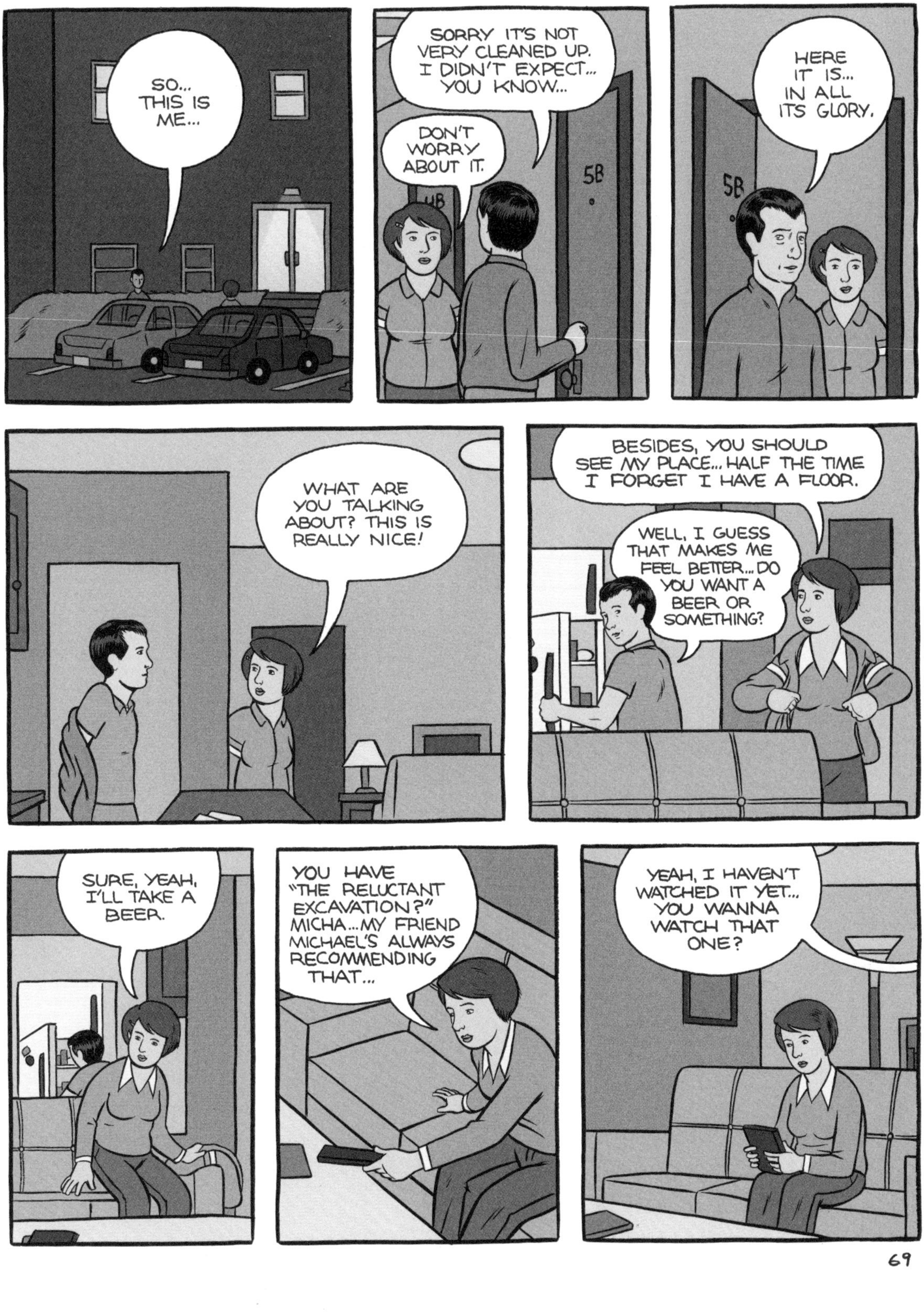
SO... THIS IS ME...
SORRY IT'S NOT VERY CLEANED UP. I DIDN'T EXPECT... YOU KNOW...
DON'T WORRY ABOUT IT.
5B
HERE IT IS... IN ALL ITS GLORY.
WHAT ARE YOU TALKING ABOUT? THIS IS REALLY NICE!
BESIDES, YOU SHOULD SEE MY PLACE... HALF THE TIME I FORGET I HAVE A FLOOR.
WELL, I GUESS THAT MAKES ME FEEL BETTER... DO YOU WANT A BEER OR SOMETHING?
SURE, YEAH, I'LL TAKE A BEER.
YOU HAVE "THE RELUCTANT EXCAVATION?" MICHA... MY FRIEND MICHAEL'S ALWAYS RECOMMENDING THAT...
YEAH, I HAVEN'T WATCHED IT YET... YOU WANNA WATCH THAT ONE?

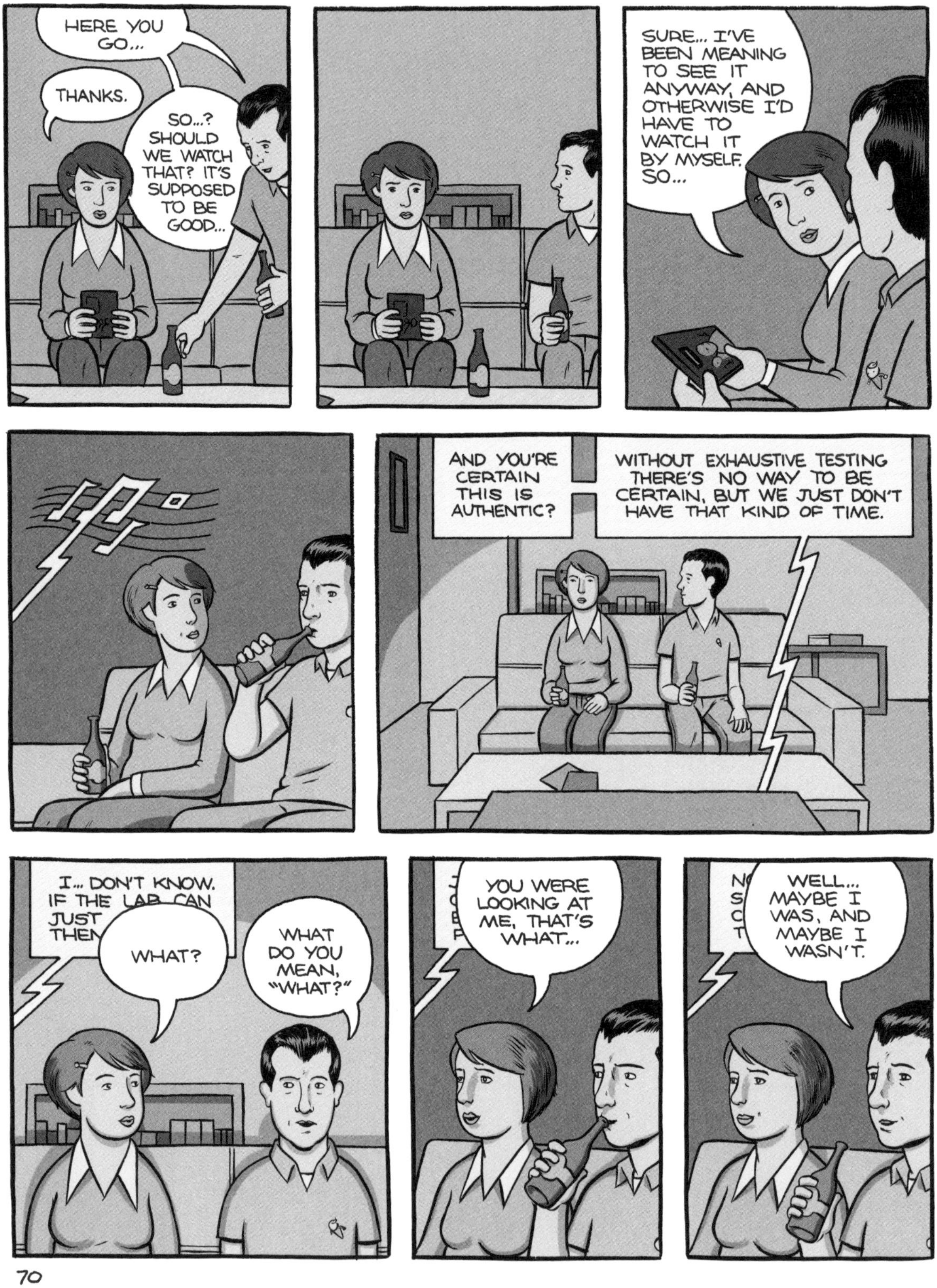
HERE YOU GO...
THANKS.
SO...? SHOULD WE WATCH THAT? IT'S SUPPOSED TO BE GOOD...
SURE... I'VE BEEN MEANING TO SEE IT ANYWAY, AND OTHERWISE I'D HAVE TO WATCH IT BY MYSELF. SO...
AND YOU'RE CERTAIN THIS IS AUTHENTIC?
WITHOUT EXHAUSTIVE TESTING THERE'S NO WAY TO BE CERTAIN, BUT WE JUST DON'T HAVE THAT KIND OF TIME.
I... DON'T KNOW. IF THE LAB CAN JUST
WHAT?
WHAT DO YOU MEAN, "WHAT?"
YOU WERE LOOKING AT ME, THAT'S WHAT...
WELL... MAYBE I WAS, AND MAYBE I WASN'T.

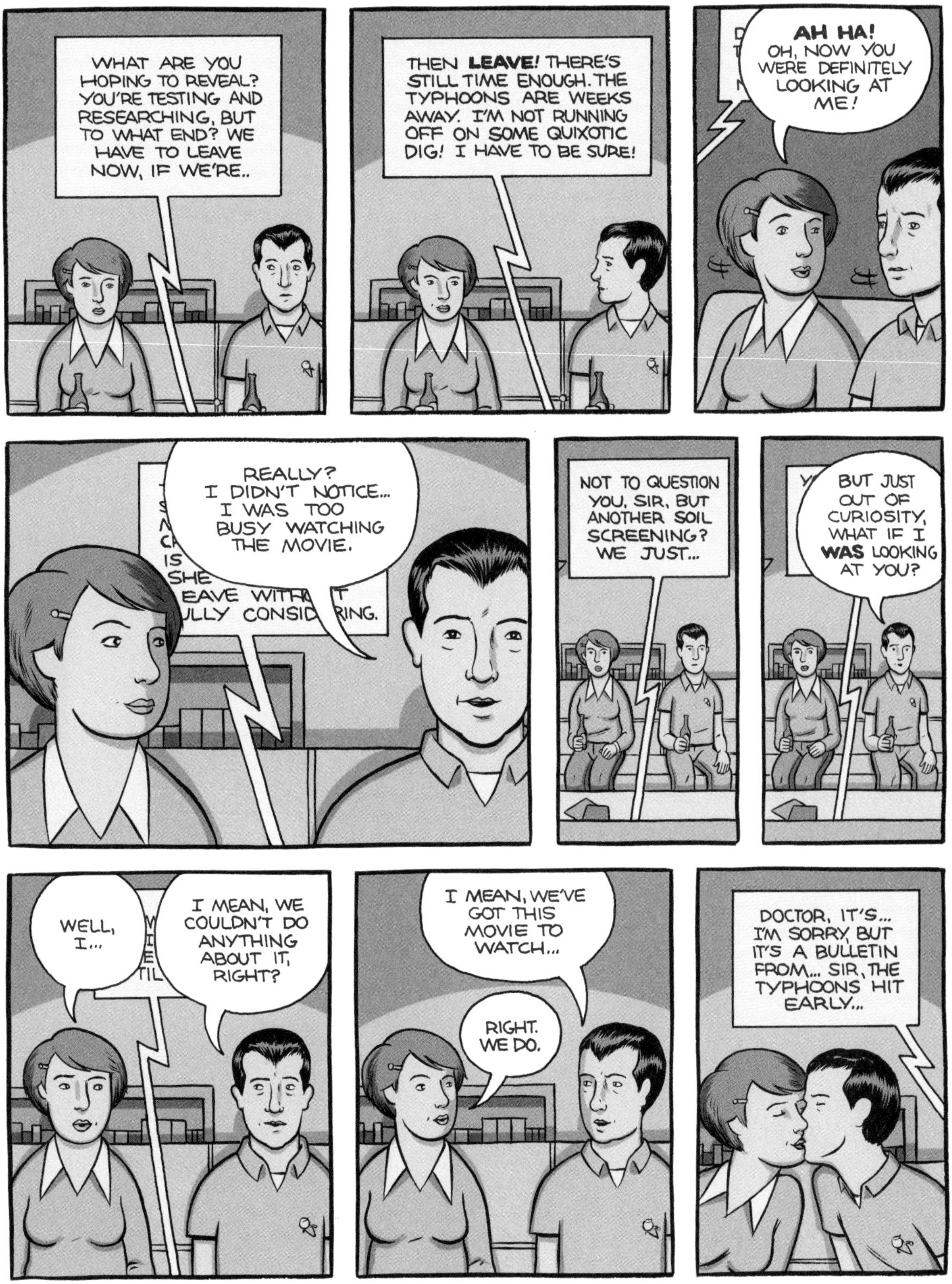
WHAT ARE YOU HOPING TO REVEAL? YOU'RE TESTING AND RESEARCHING, BUT TO WHAT END? WE HAVE TO LEAVE NOW, IF WE'RE..
THEN LEAVE! THERE'S STILL TIME ENOUGH. THE TYPHOONS ARE WEEKS AWAY. I'M NOT RUNNING OFF ON SOME QUIXOTIC DIG! I HAVE TO BE SURE!
AH HA! OH, NOW YOU WERE DEFINITELY LOOKING AT ME!
REALLY? I DIDN'T NOTICE... I WAS TOO BUSY WATCHING THE MOVIE.
NOT TO QUESTION YOU, SIR, BUT ANOTHER SOIL SCREENING? WE JUST...
BUT JUST OUT OF CURIOSITY, WHAT IF I WAS LOOKING AT YOU?
WELL, I...
I MEAN, WE COULDN'T DO ANYTHING ABOUT IT, RIGHT?
I MEAN, WE'VE GOT THIS MOVIE TO WATCH...
RIGHT. WE DO.
DOCTOR, IT'S... I'M SORRY, BUT IT'S A BULLETIN FROM... SIR, THE TYPHOONS HIT EARLY...

GET EVERYTHING ON TO THE BOAT. WHAT ABOUT COMMUNICATIONS? HAVE YOU TRIED CONTACTING...

I TRIED, SIR. THERE'S NO SIGNAL. THE LAST WE HEARD FROM HER WAS DAYS AGO, WHEN WE RELAYED YOUR LAST MESSAGE.

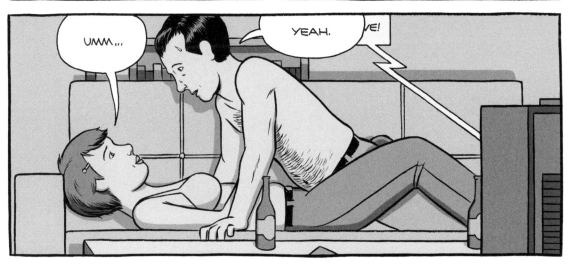

UMM...

YEAH.

VE!

DO YOU WANNA GO TO THE BEDROOM?

YEAH...

WH
HAVE
BEEN DOING
WIT
RE
B

72

WOW...

SORRY, I'M JUST GONNA THROW THIS OUT.

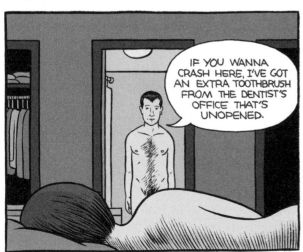

IF YOU WANNA CRASH HERE, I'VE GOT AN EXTRA TOOTHBRUSH FROM THE DENTIST'S OFFICE THAT'S UNOPENED.

DO YOU NEED ANYTHING? SOME WATER? OR..

NO, I'M FINE, THANKS.

WELL, GOOD NIGHT.

:SMK:

GOOD NIGHT.

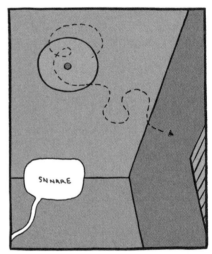

SNNRRE

SNNNRE

SNNRRE SNNRRE

SNNRRRE

I'M SORRY

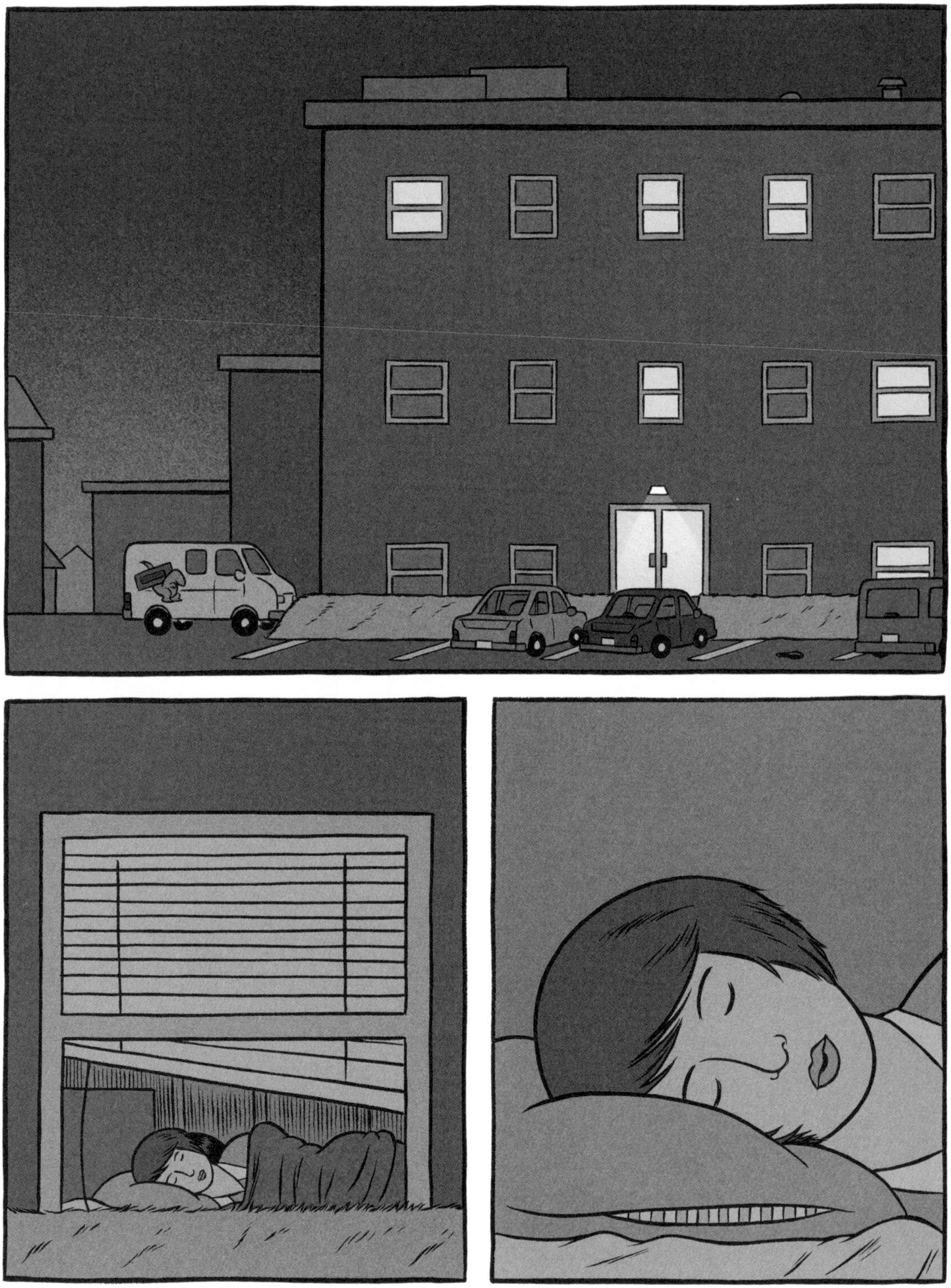

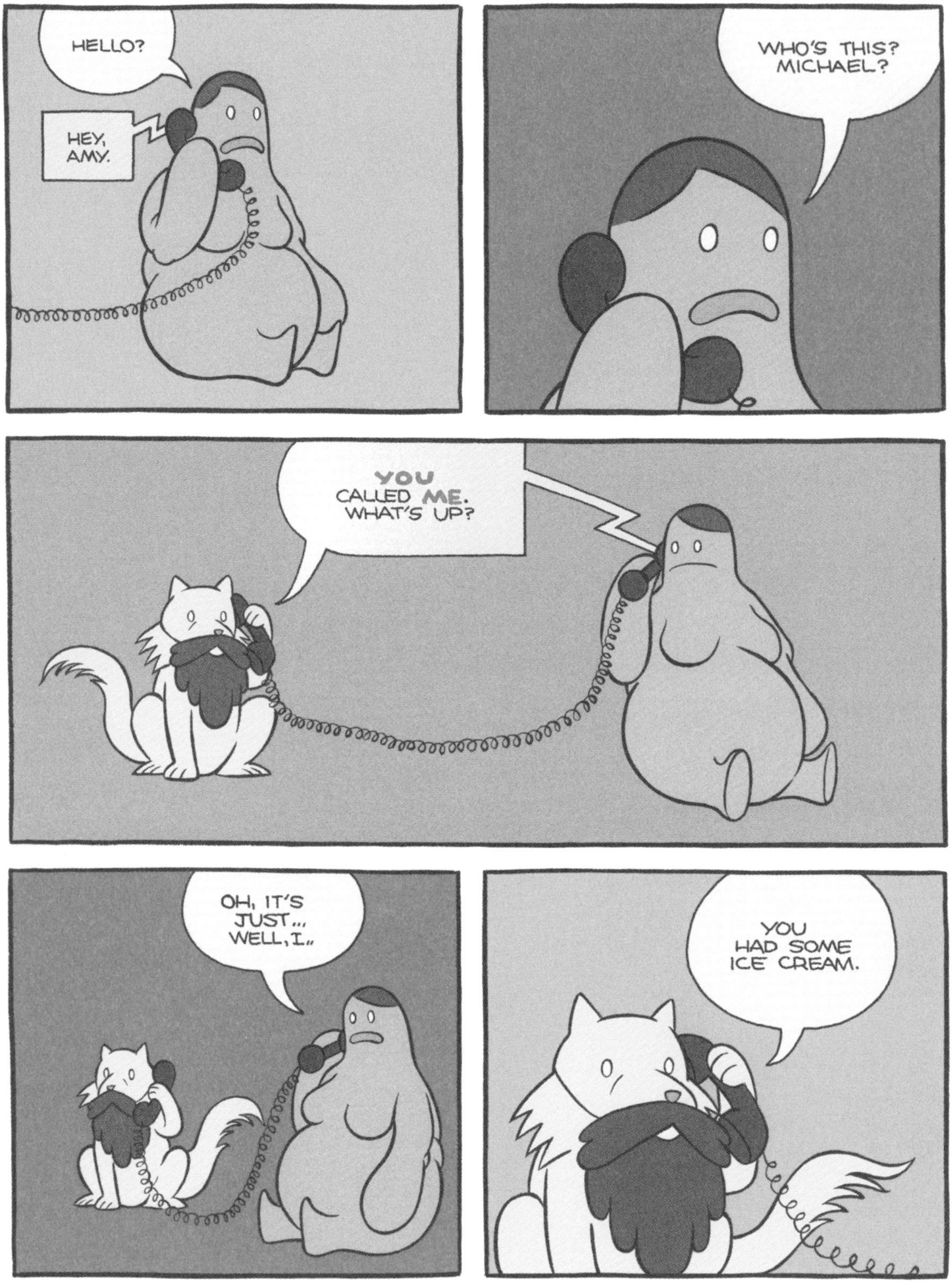
HELLO?
HEY, AMY.
WHO'S THIS? MICHAEL?
YOU CALLED ME. WHAT'S UP?
OH, IT'S JUST... WELL, I..
YOU HAD SOME ICE CREAM.

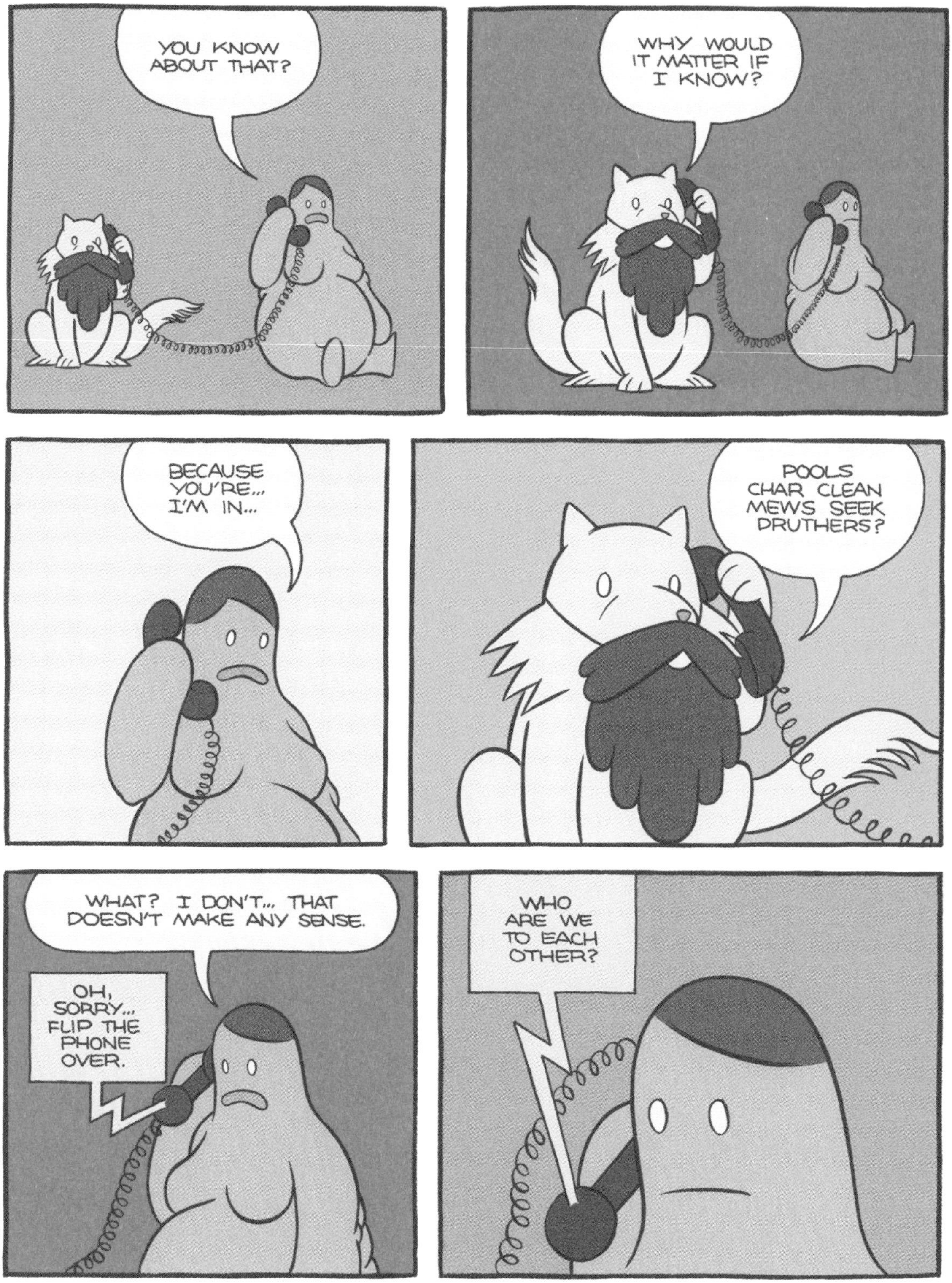
YOU KNOW ABOUT THAT?
WHY WOULD IT MATTER IF I KNOW?
BECAUSE YOU'RE... I'M IN...
POOLS CHAR CLEAN MEWS SEEK DRUTHERS?
WHAT? I DON'T... THAT DOESN'T MAKE ANY SENSE.
OH, SORRY... FLIP THE PHONE OVER.
WHO ARE WE TO EACH OTHER?

6
The Details
of the Morning

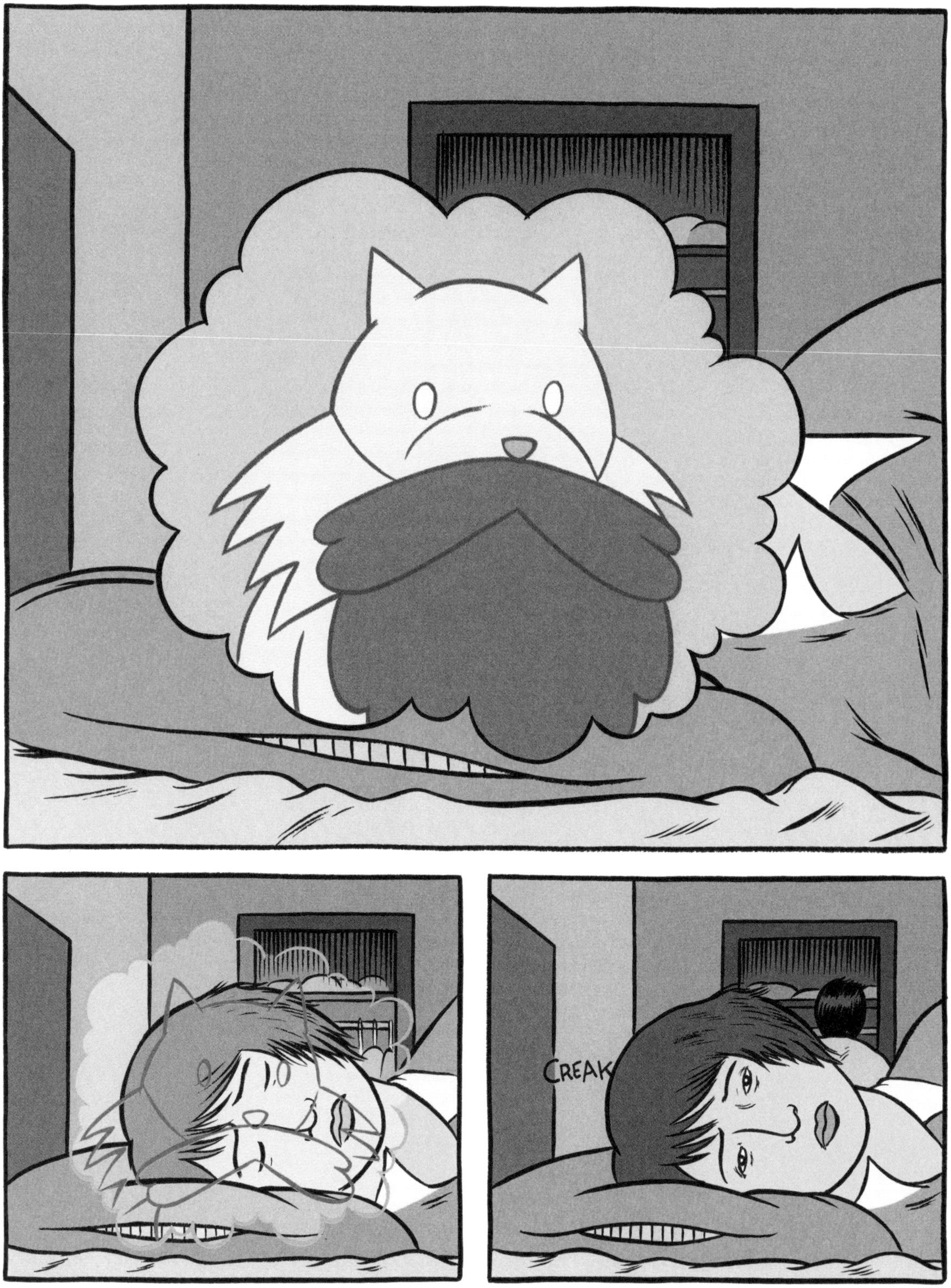
CREAK

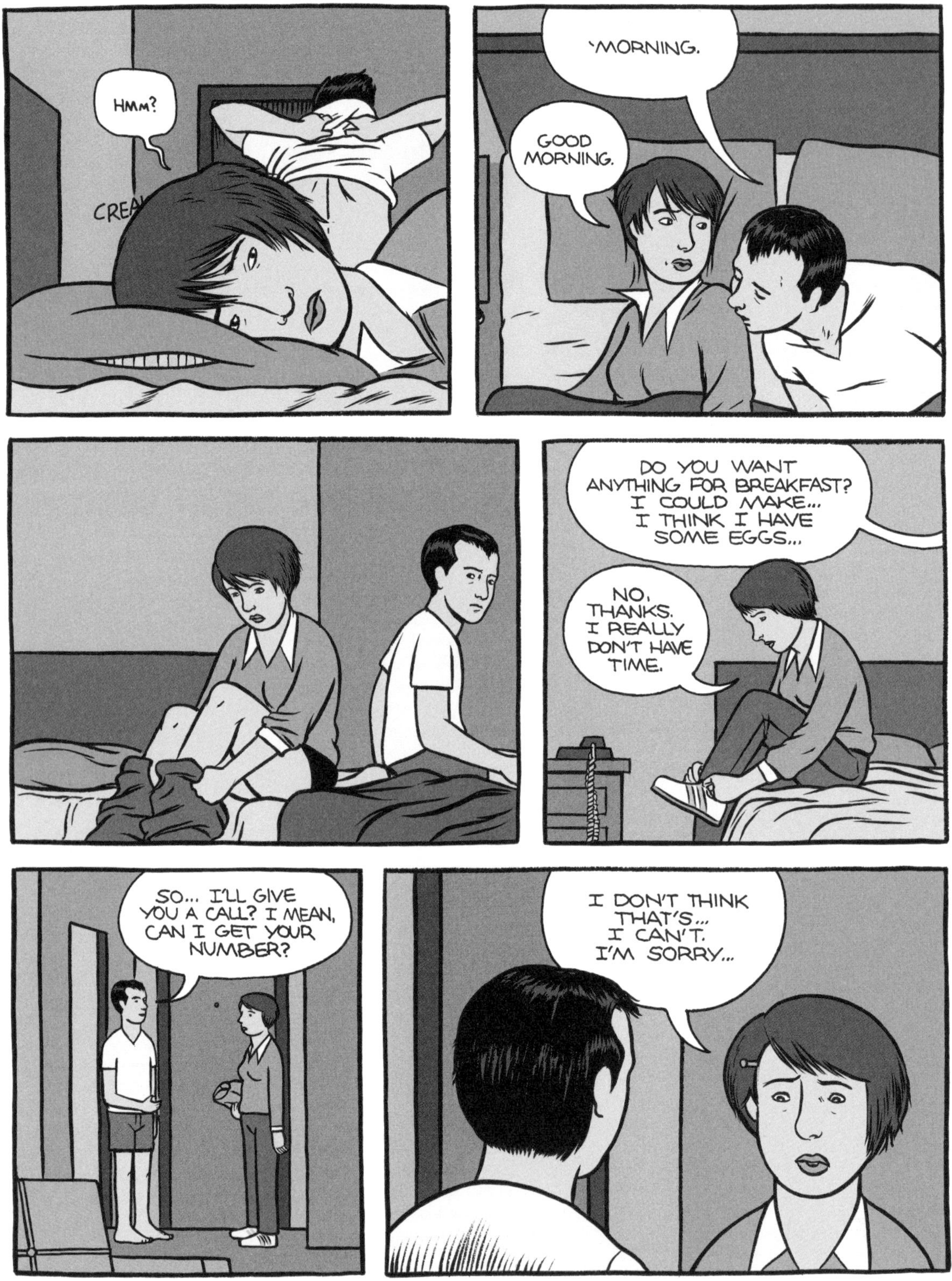
HMM?
CREAK
'MORNING.
GOOD MORNING.
DO YOU WANT ANYTHING FOR BREAKFAST? I COULD MAKE... I THINK I HAVE SOME EGGS...
NO, THANKS. I REALLY DON'T HAVE TIME.
SO... I'LL GIVE YOU A CALL? I MEAN, CAN I GET YOUR NUMBER?
I DON'T THINK THAT'S... I CAN'T. I'M SORRY...

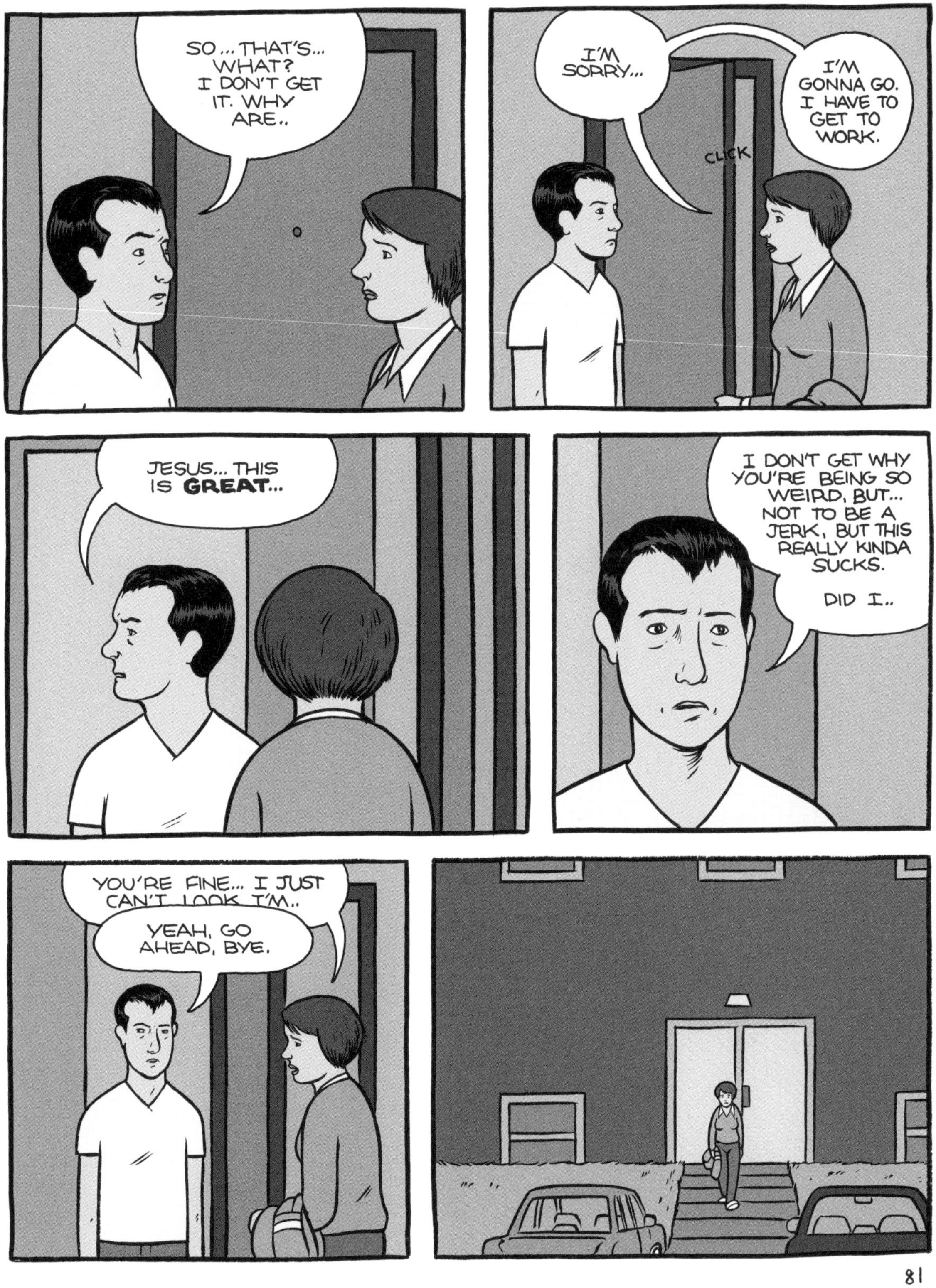
SO... THAT'S... WHAT? I DON'T GET IT. WHY ARE..
I'M SORRY...
I'M GONNA GO. I HAVE TO GET TO WORK.
CLICK
JESUS... THIS IS **GREAT**...
I DON'T GET WHY YOU'RE BEING SO WEIRD, BUT... NOT TO BE A JERK, BUT THIS REALLY KINDA SUCKS.
DID I..
YOU'RE FINE... I JUST CAN'T LOOK I'M..
YEAH, GO AHEAD, BYE.

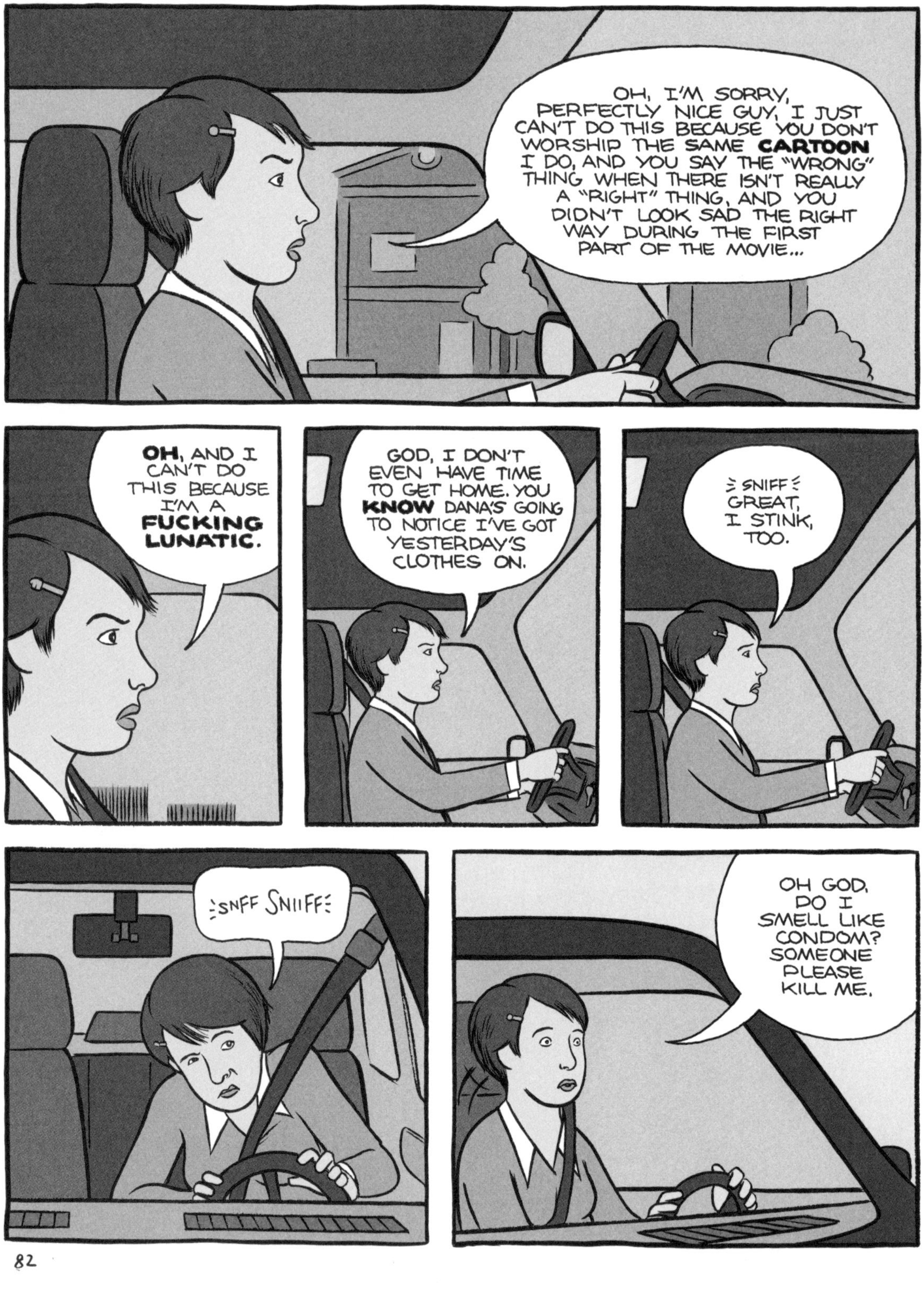
OH, I'M SORRY, PERFECTLY NICE GUY, I JUST CAN'T DO THIS BECAUSE YOU DON'T WORSHIP THE SAME **CARTOON** I DO, AND YOU SAY THE "WRONG" THING WHEN THERE ISN'T REALLY A "RIGHT" THING, AND YOU DIDN'T LOOK SAD THE RIGHT WAY DURING THE FIRST PART OF THE MOVIE...
OH, AND I CAN'T DO THIS BECAUSE I'M A **FUCKING LUNATIC**.
GOD, I DON'T EVEN HAVE TIME TO GET HOME. YOU **KNOW** DANA'S GOING TO NOTICE I'VE GOT YESTERDAY'S CLOTHES ON.
SNIFF GREAT, I STINK, TOO.
SNFF SNIIFF
OH GOD, DO I SMELL LIKE CONDOM? SOMEONE PLEASE KILL ME.

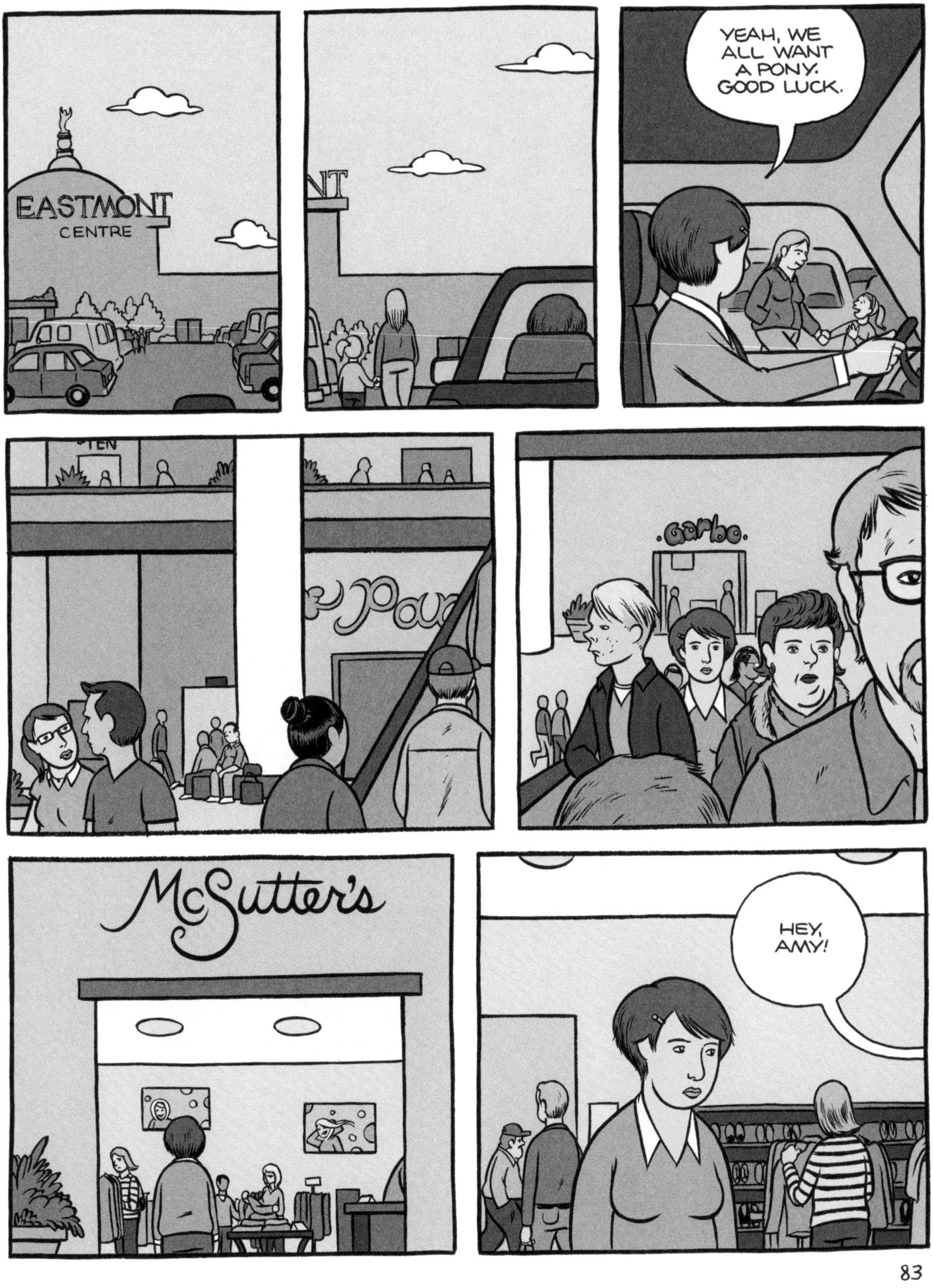
EASTMONT
CENTRE
YEAH, WE ALL WANT A PONY. GOOD LUCK.
TEN
garbo
McSutter's
HEY, AMY!

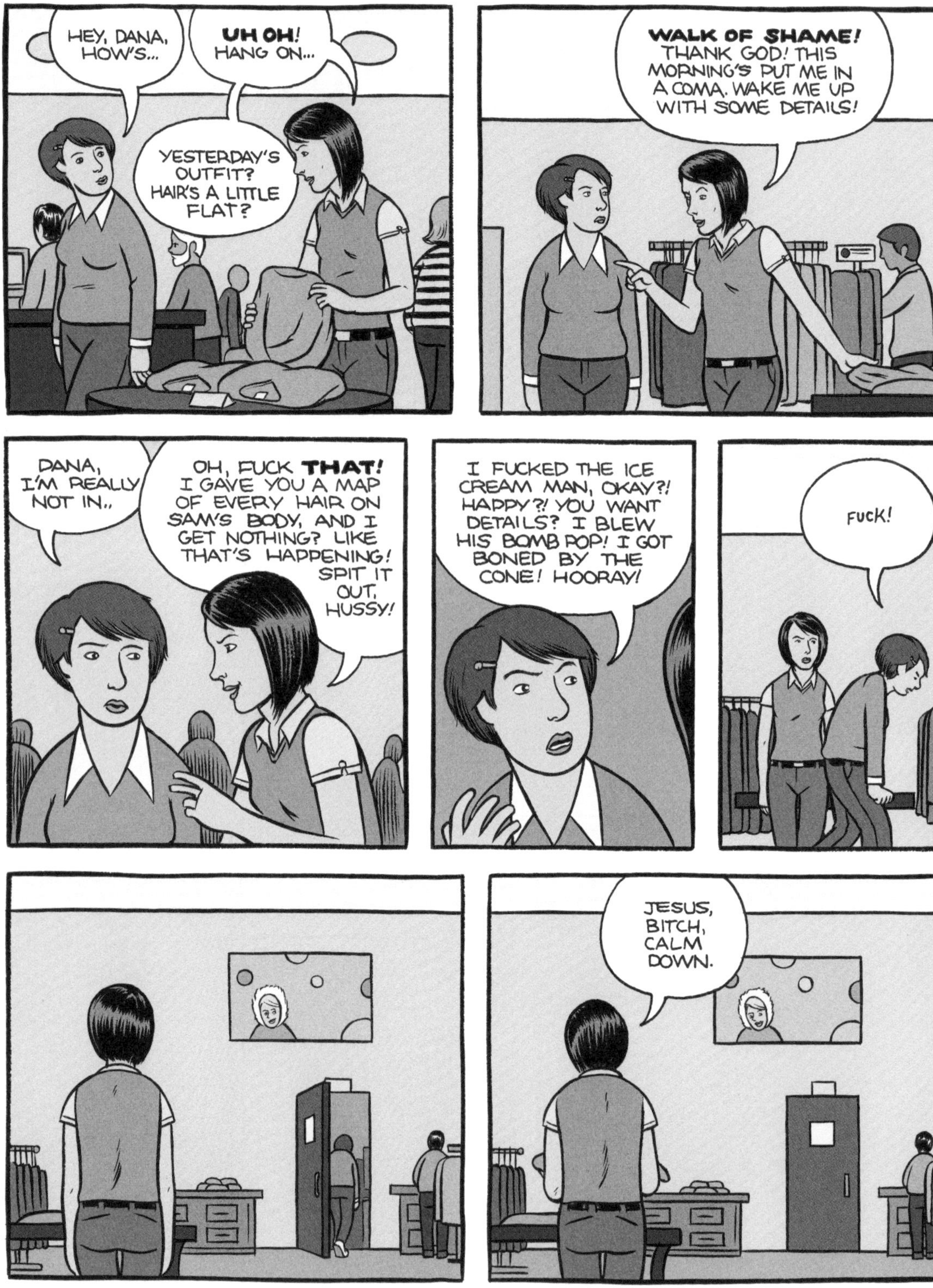
HEY, DANA, HOW'S...
UH OH! HANG ON...
YESTERDAY'S OUTFIT? HAIR'S A LITTLE FLAT?
WALK OF SHAME! THANK GOD! THIS MORNING'S PUT ME IN A COMA. WAKE ME UP WITH SOME DETAILS!
DANA, I'M REALLY NOT IN..
OH, FUCK THAT! I GAVE YOU A MAP OF EVERY HAIR ON SAM'S BODY, AND I GET NOTHING? LIKE THAT'S HAPPENING! SPIT IT OUT, HUSSY!
I FUCKED THE ICE CREAM MAN, OKAY?! HAPPY?! YOU WANT DETAILS? I BLEW HIS BOMB POP! I GOT BONED BY THE CONE! HOORAY!
FUCK!
JESUS, BITCH, CALM DOWN.

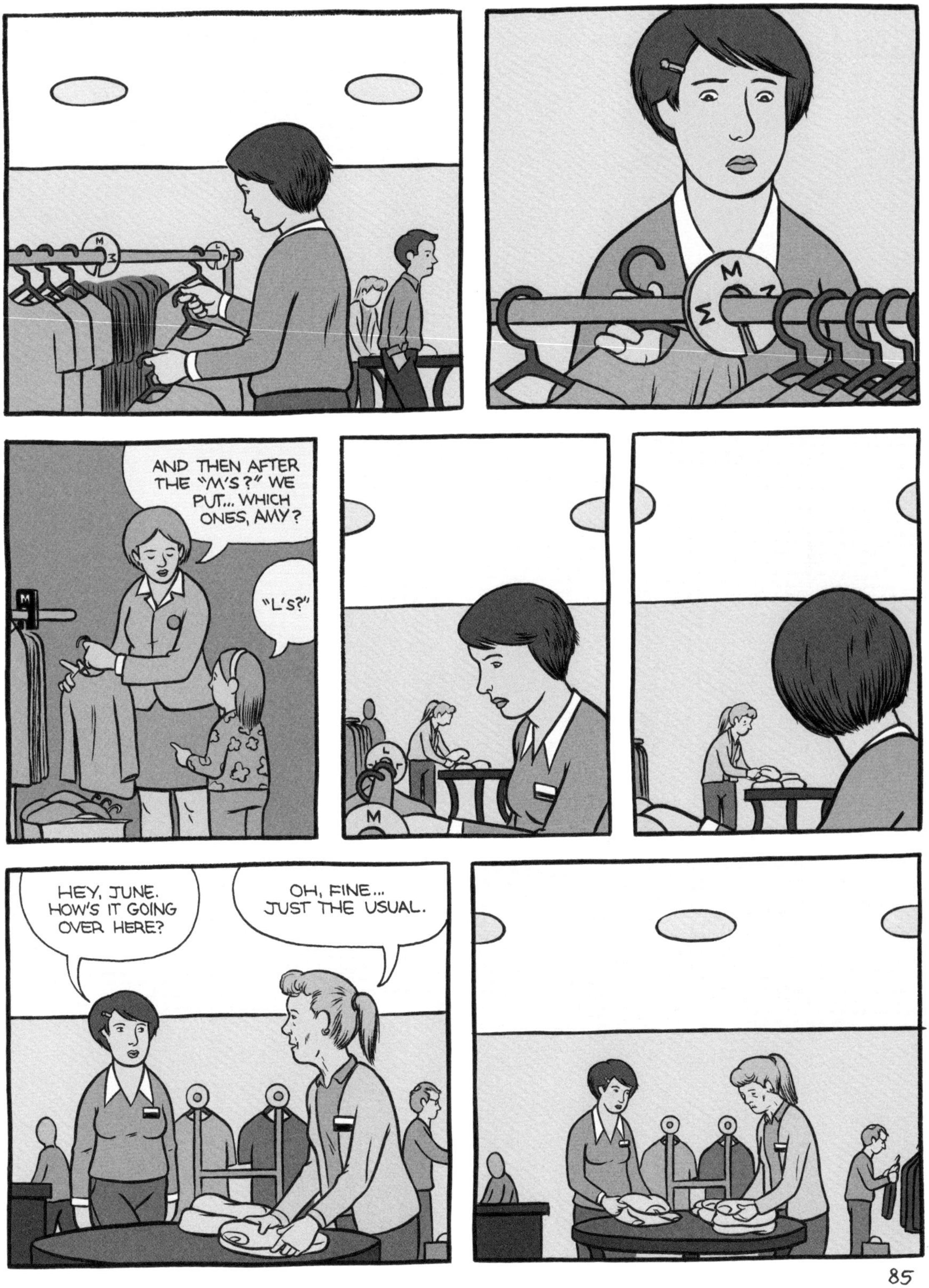
AND THEN AFTER THE "M'S?" WE PUT... WHICH ONES, AMY?
"L'S?"
HEY, JUNE. HOW'S IT GOING OVER HERE?
OH, FINE... JUST THE USUAL.

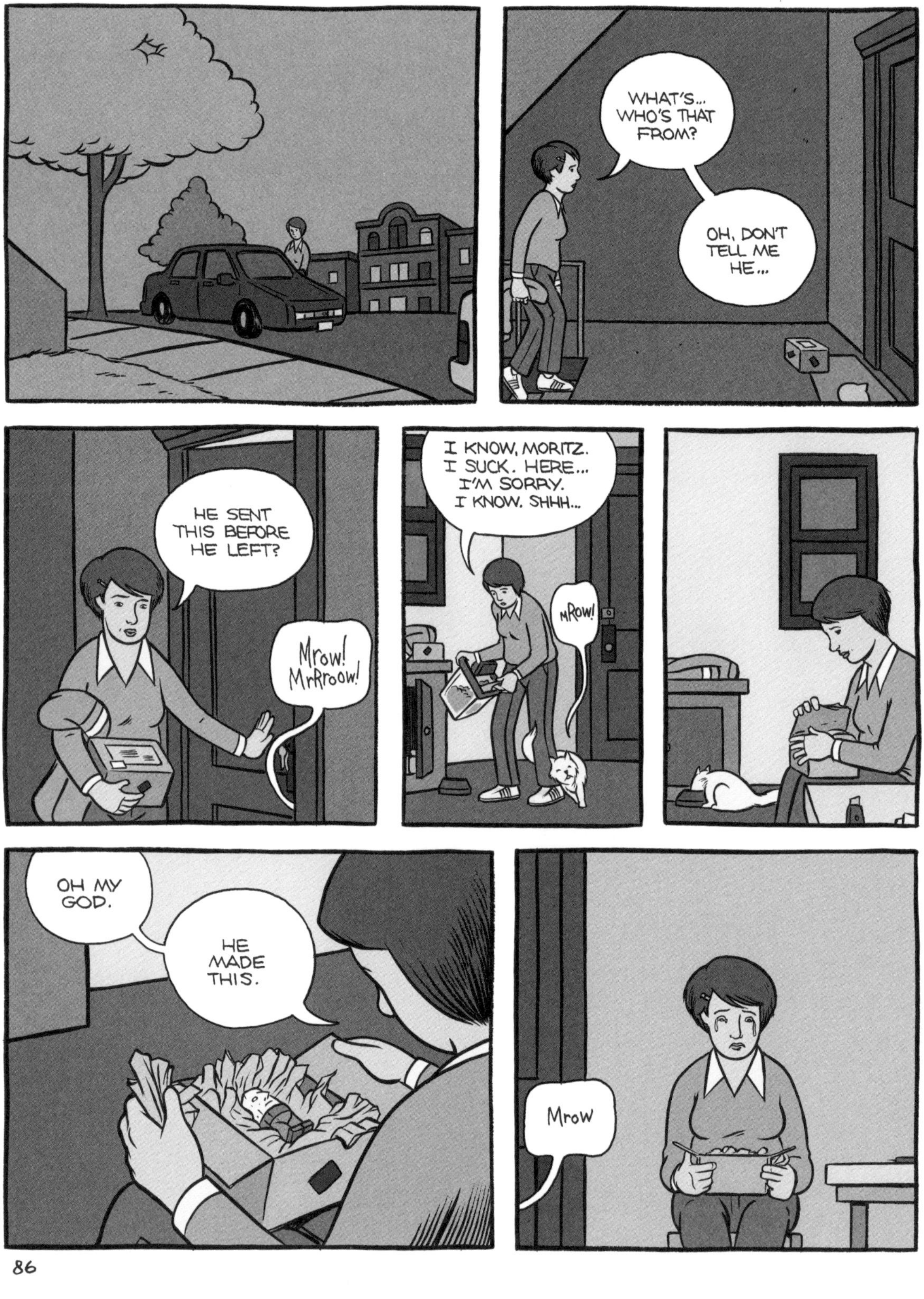
WHAT'S... WHO'S THAT FROM?
OH, DON'T TELL ME HE...
HE SENT THIS BEFORE HE LEFT?
Mrow! MrRroow!
I KNOW, MORITZ. I SUCK. HERE... I'M SORRY. I KNOW. SHHH...
MROW!
OH MY GOD.
HE MADE THIS.
Mrow

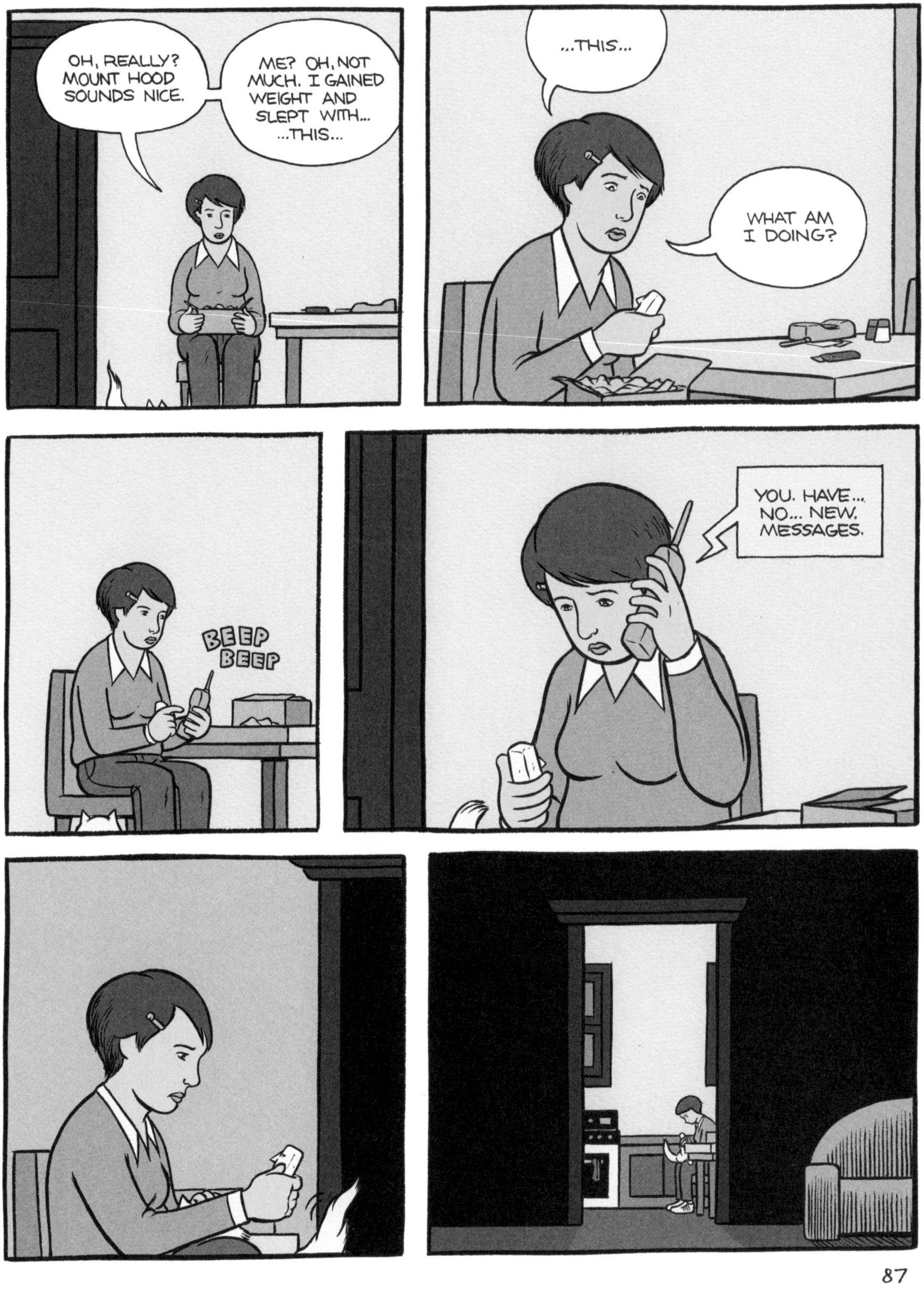
OH, REALLY? MOUNT HOOD SOUNDS NICE.
ME? OH, NOT MUCH. I GAINED WEIGHT AND SLEPT WITH... ...THIS...
...THIS...
WHAT AM I DOING?
BEEP BEEP
YOU. HAVE... NO... NEW. MESSAGES.

7
I Have to Be
Somewhere

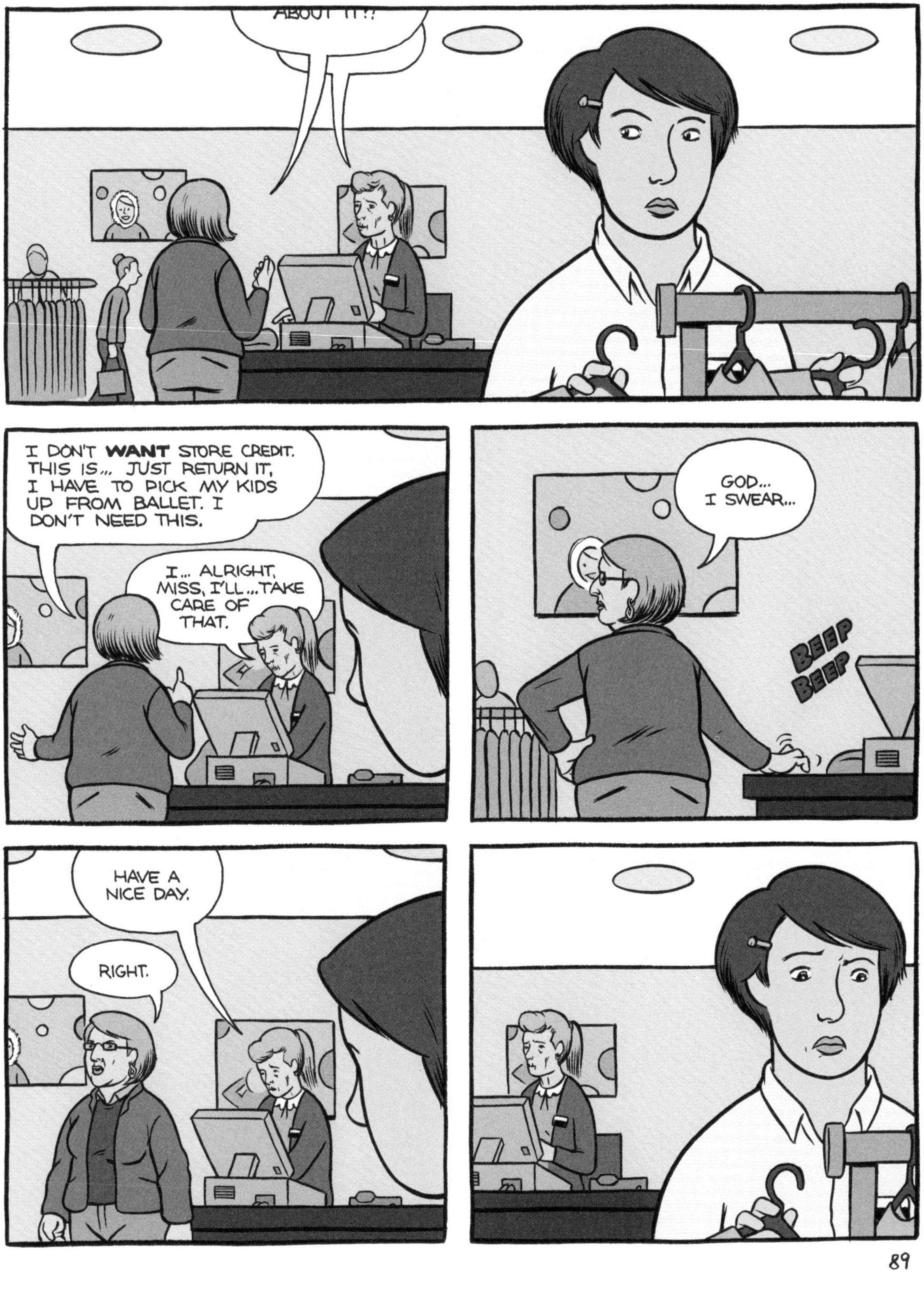
ABOUT IT!?
I DON'T WANT STORE CREDIT. THIS IS... JUST RETURN IT, I HAVE TO PICK MY KIDS UP FROM BALLET. I DON'T NEED THIS.
I... ALRIGHT, MISS, I'LL...TAKE CARE OF THAT.
GOD... I SWEAR...
BEEP BEEP
HAVE A NICE DAY.
RIGHT.

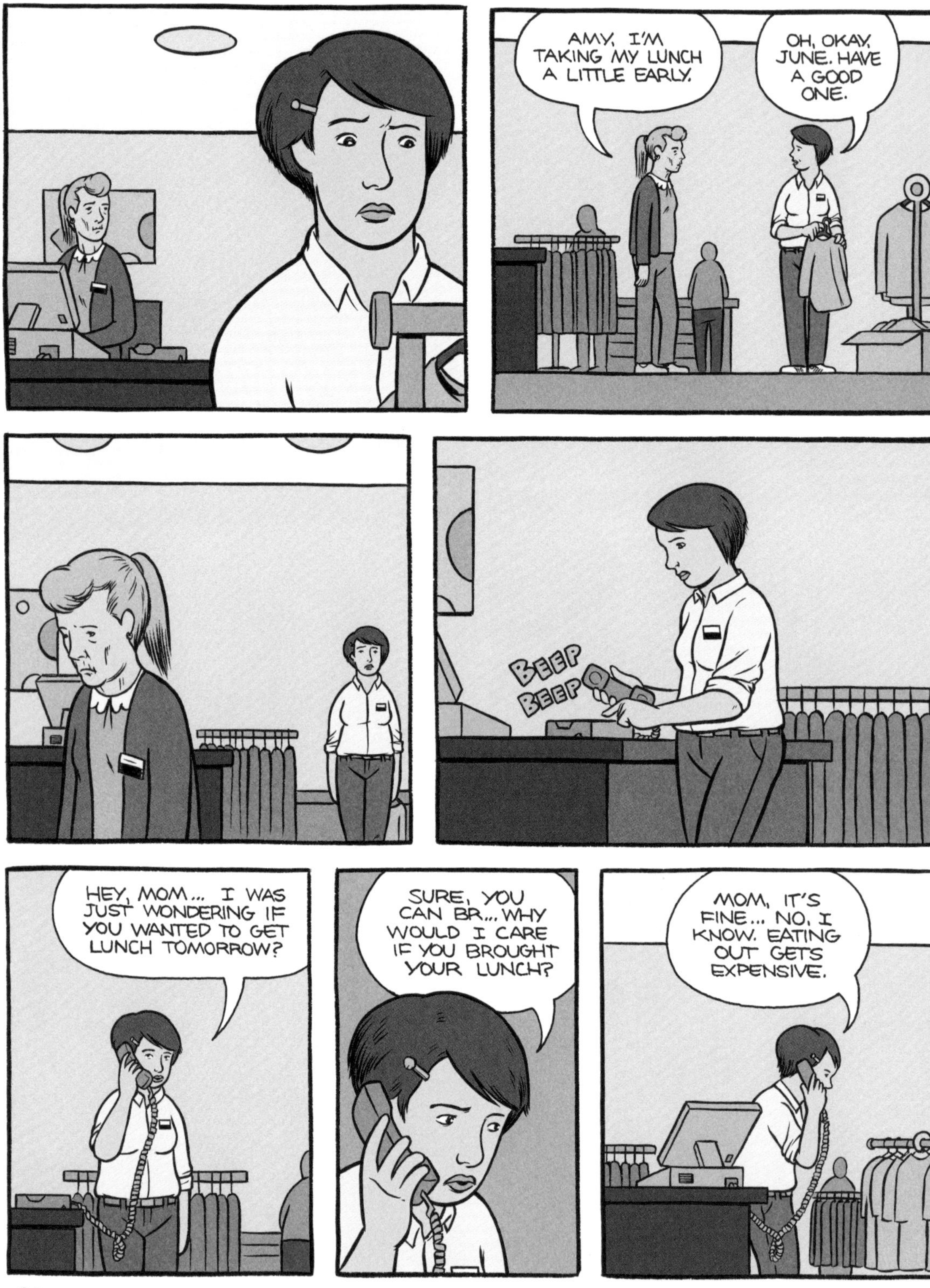
AMY, I'M TAKING MY LUNCH A LITTLE EARLY.
OH, OKAY, JUNE. HAVE A GOOD ONE.
BEEP BEEP
HEY, MOM... I WAS JUST WONDERING IF YOU WANTED TO GET LUNCH TOMORROW?
SURE, YOU CAN BR... WHY WOULD I CARE IF YOU BROUGHT YOUR LUNCH?
MOM, IT'S FINE... NO, I KNOW. EATING OUT GETS EXPENSIVE.

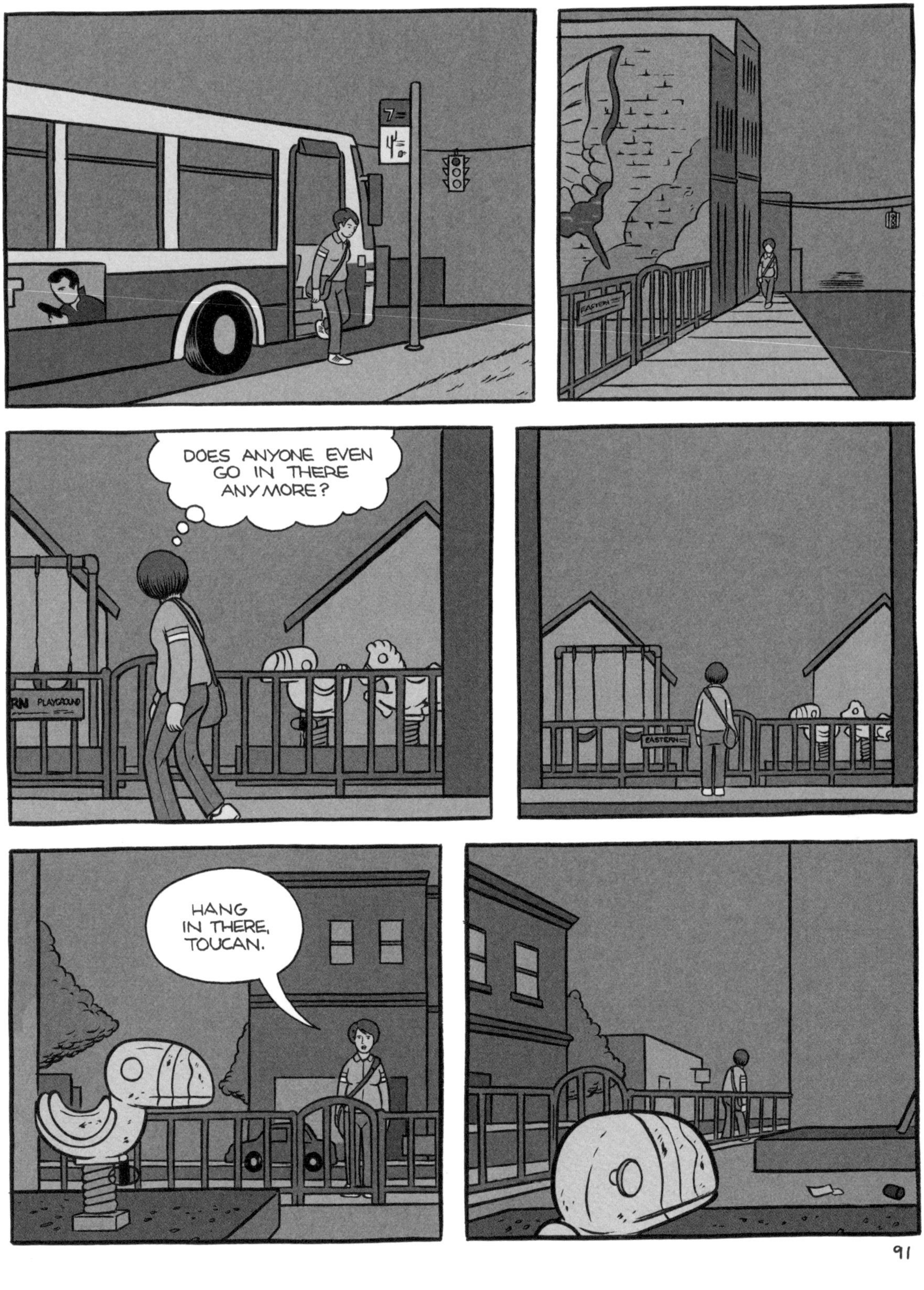
7
EASTERN
DOES ANYONE EVEN GO IN THERE ANYMORE?
PLAYGROUND
EASTERN
HANG IN THERE, TOUCAN.

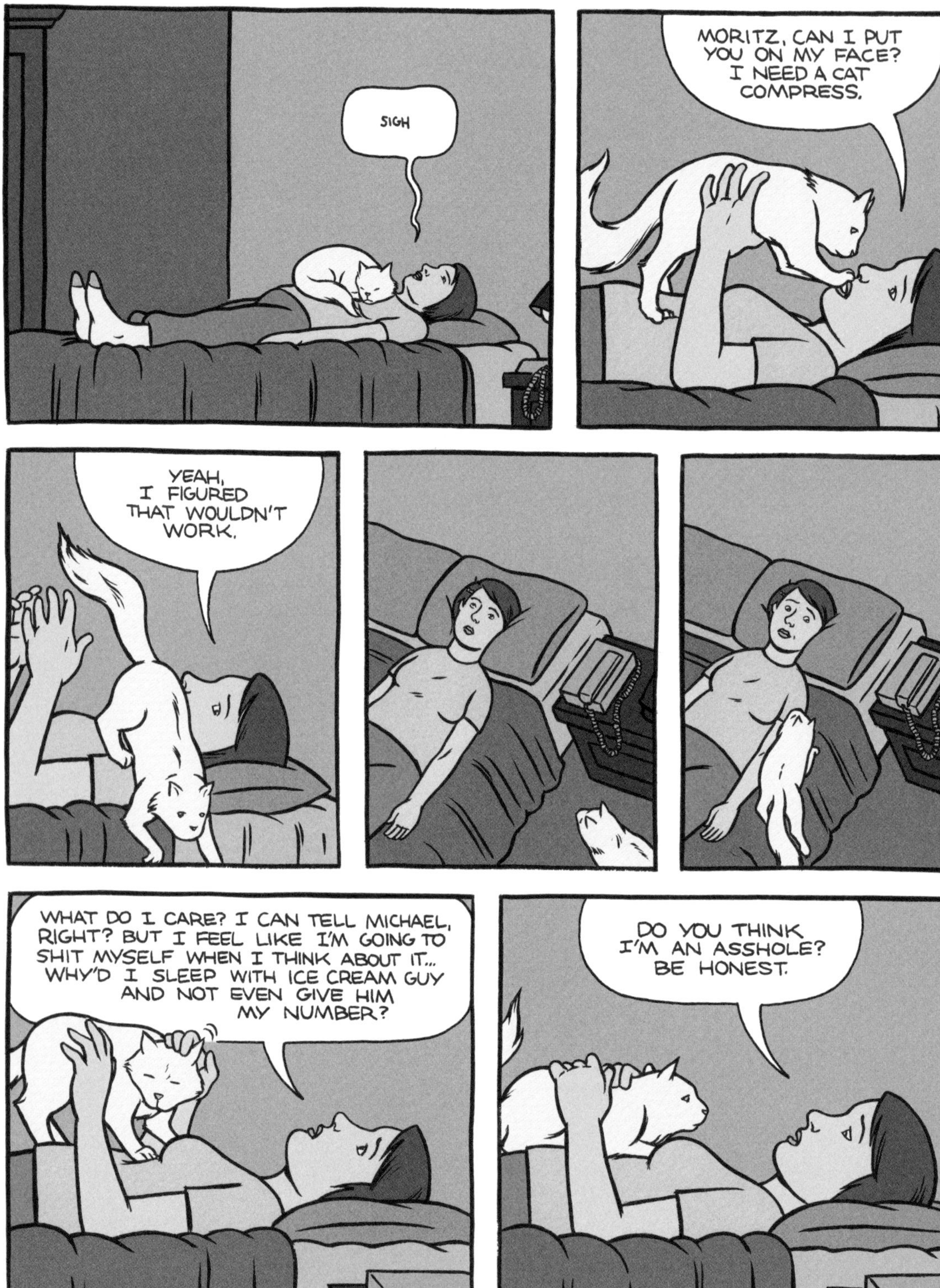
SIGH
MORITZ, CAN I PUT YOU ON MY FACE? I NEED A CAT COMPRESS.
YEAH, I FIGURED THAT WOULDN'T WORK.
WHAT DO I CARE? I CAN TELL MICHAEL, RIGHT? BUT I FEEL LIKE I'M GOING TO SHIT MYSELF WHEN I THINK ABOUT IT... WHY'D I SLEEP WITH ICE CREAM GUY AND NOT EVEN GIVE HIM MY NUMBER?
DO YOU THINK I'M AN ASSHOLE? BE HONEST.

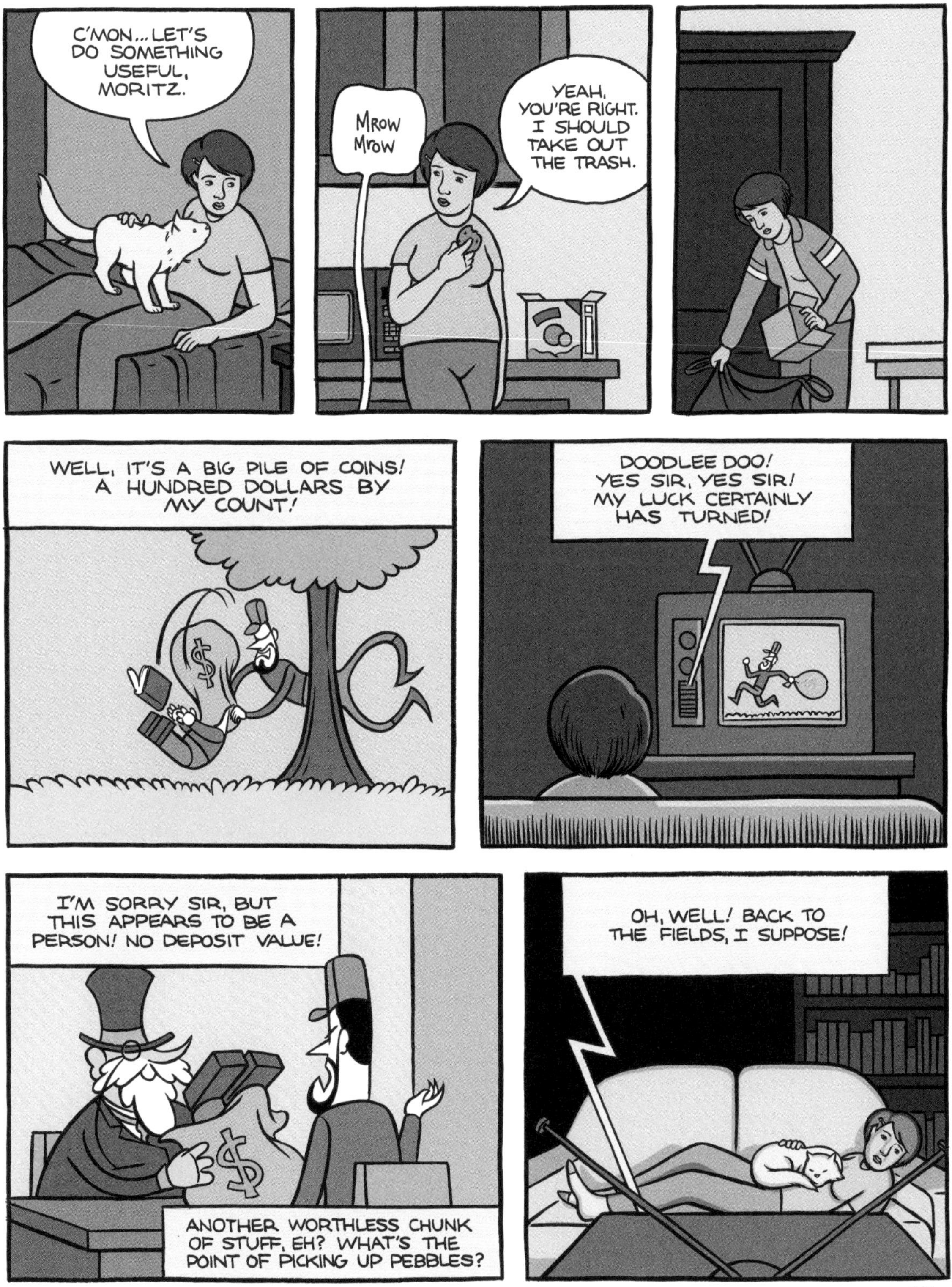

C'MON... LET'S DO SOMETHING USEFUL, MORITZ.
MROW MROW
YEAH, YOU'RE RIGHT. I SHOULD TAKE OUT THE TRASH.
WELL, IT'S A BIG PILE OF COINS! A HUNDRED DOLLARS BY MY COUNT!
DOODLEE DOO! YES SIR, YES SIR! MY LUCK CERTAINLY HAS TURNED!
I'M SORRY SIR, BUT THIS APPEARS TO BE A PERSON! NO DEPOSIT VALUE!
ANOTHER WORTHLESS CHUNK OF STUFF, EH? WHAT'S THE POINT OF PICKING UP PEBBLES?
OH, WELL! BACK TO THE FIELDS, I SUPPOSE!

8
Lunch Dates, Lost Notes

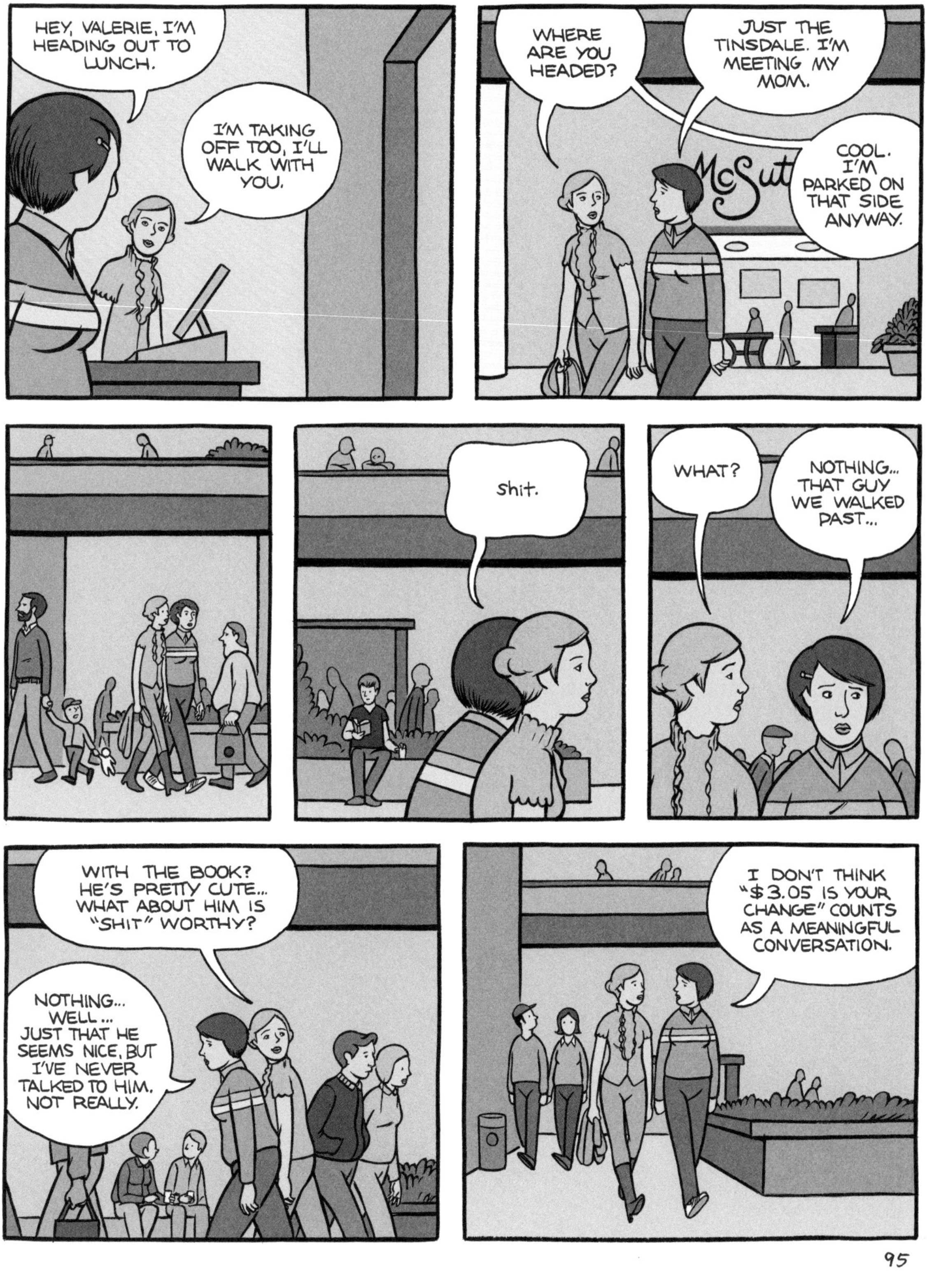
HEY, VALERIE, I'M HEADING OUT TO LUNCH.
I'M TAKING OFF TOO, I'LL WALK WITH YOU.
WHERE ARE YOU HEADED?
JUST THE TINSDALE. I'M MEETING MY MOM.
McSut
COOL. I'M PARKED ON THAT SIDE ANYWAY.
shit.
WHAT?
NOTHING... THAT GUY WE WALKED PAST...
WITH THE BOOK? HE'S PRETTY CUTE... WHAT ABOUT HIM IS "SHIT" WORTHY?
NOTHING... WELL... JUST THAT HE SEEMS NICE, BUT I'VE NEVER TALKED TO HIM. NOT REALLY.
I DON'T THINK "$3.05 IS YOUR CHANGE" COUNTS AS A MEANINGFUL CONVERSATION.

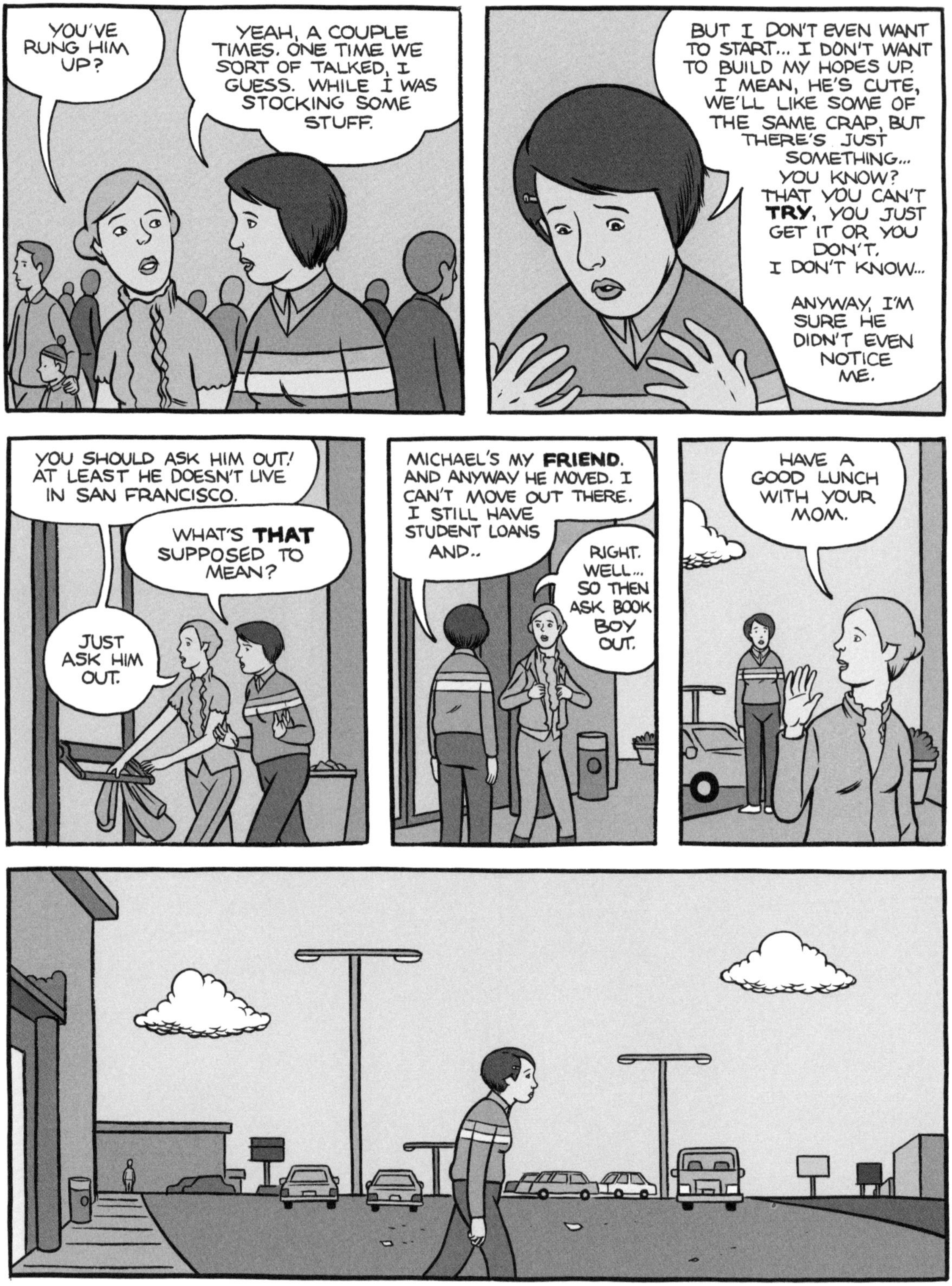
YOU'VE RUNG HIM UP?
YEAH, A COUPLE TIMES. ONE TIME WE SORT OF TALKED, I GUESS. WHILE I WAS STOCKING SOME STUFF.
BUT I DON'T EVEN WANT TO START... I DON'T WANT TO BUILD MY HOPES UP. I MEAN, HE'S CUTE, WE'LL LIKE SOME OF THE SAME CRAP, BUT THERE'S JUST SOMETHING... YOU KNOW? THAT YOU CAN'T TRY, YOU JUST GET IT OR YOU DON'T. I DON'T KNOW...
ANYWAY, I'M SURE HE DIDN'T EVEN NOTICE ME.
YOU SHOULD ASK HIM OUT! AT LEAST HE DOESN'T LIVE IN SAN FRANCISCO.
WHAT'S THAT SUPPOSED TO MEAN?
JUST ASK HIM OUT.
MICHAEL'S MY FRIEND. AND ANYWAY HE MOVED. I CAN'T MOVE OUT THERE. I STILL HAVE STUDENT LOANS AND..
RIGHT. WELL... SO THEN ASK BOOK BOY OUT.
HAVE A GOOD LUNCH WITH YOUR MOM.

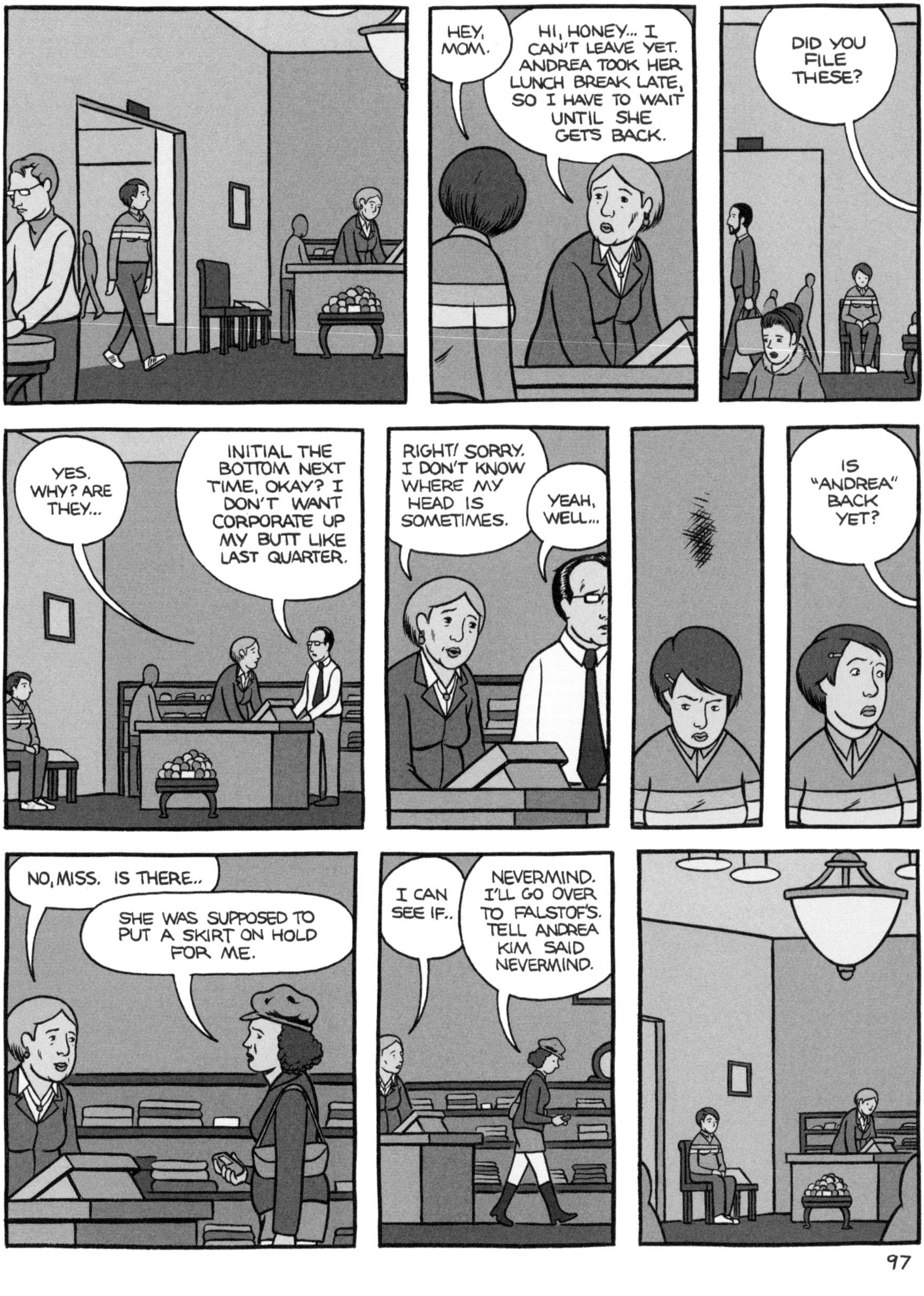
HEY, MOM.
HI, HONEY... I CAN'T LEAVE YET. ANDREA TOOK HER LUNCH BREAK LATE, SO I HAVE TO WAIT UNTIL SHE GETS BACK.
DID YOU FILE THESE?
YES. WHY? ARE THEY...
INITIAL THE BOTTOM NEXT TIME, OKAY? I DON'T WANT CORPORATE UP MY BUTT LIKE LAST QUARTER.
RIGHT! SORRY. I DON'T KNOW WHERE MY HEAD IS SOMETIMES.
YEAH, WELL...
IS "ANDREA" BACK YET?
NO, MISS. IS THERE..
SHE WAS SUPPOSED TO PUT A SKIRT ON HOLD FOR ME.
I CAN SEE IF..
NEVERMIND. I'LL GO OVER TO FALSTOF'S. TELL ANDREA KIM SAID NEVERMIND.

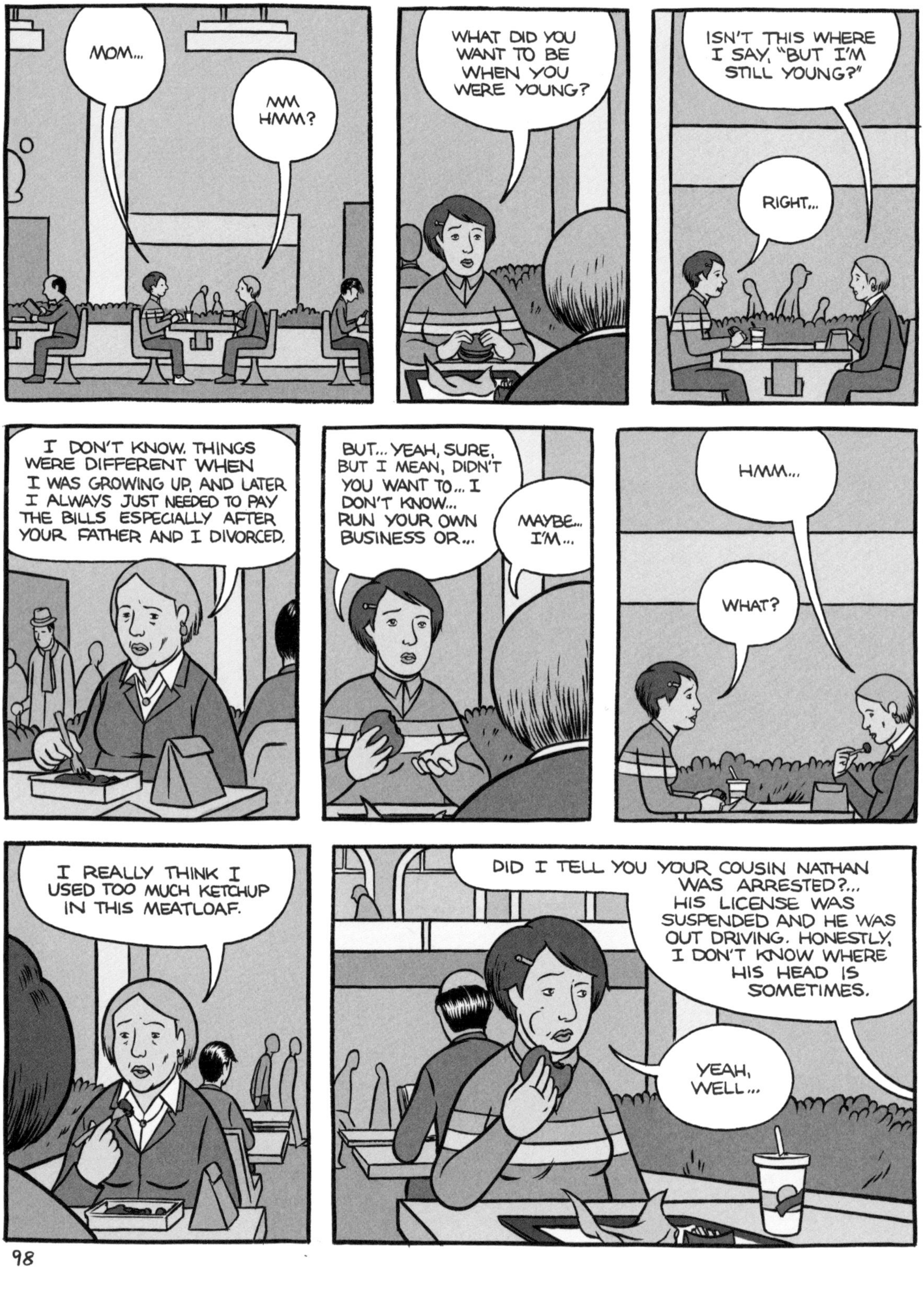
MOM...
MM HMM?
WHAT DID YOU WANT TO BE WHEN YOU WERE YOUNG?
ISN'T THIS WHERE I SAY, "BUT I'M STILL YOUNG?"
RIGHT...
I DON'T KNOW. THINGS WERE DIFFERENT WHEN I WAS GROWING UP, AND LATER I ALWAYS JUST NEEDED TO PAY THE BILLS ESPECIALLY AFTER YOUR FATHER AND I DIVORCED.
BUT... YEAH, SURE, BUT I MEAN, DIDN'T YOU WANT TO... I DON'T KNOW... RUN YOUR OWN BUSINESS OR...
MAYBE... I'M...
HMM...
WHAT?
I REALLY THINK I USED TOO MUCH KETCHUP IN THIS MEATLOAF.
DID I TELL YOU YOUR COUSIN NATHAN WAS ARRESTED?... HIS LICENSE WAS SUSPENDED AND HE WAS OUT DRIVING. HONESTLY, I DON'T KNOW WHERE HIS HEAD IS SOMETIMES.
YEAH, WELL...

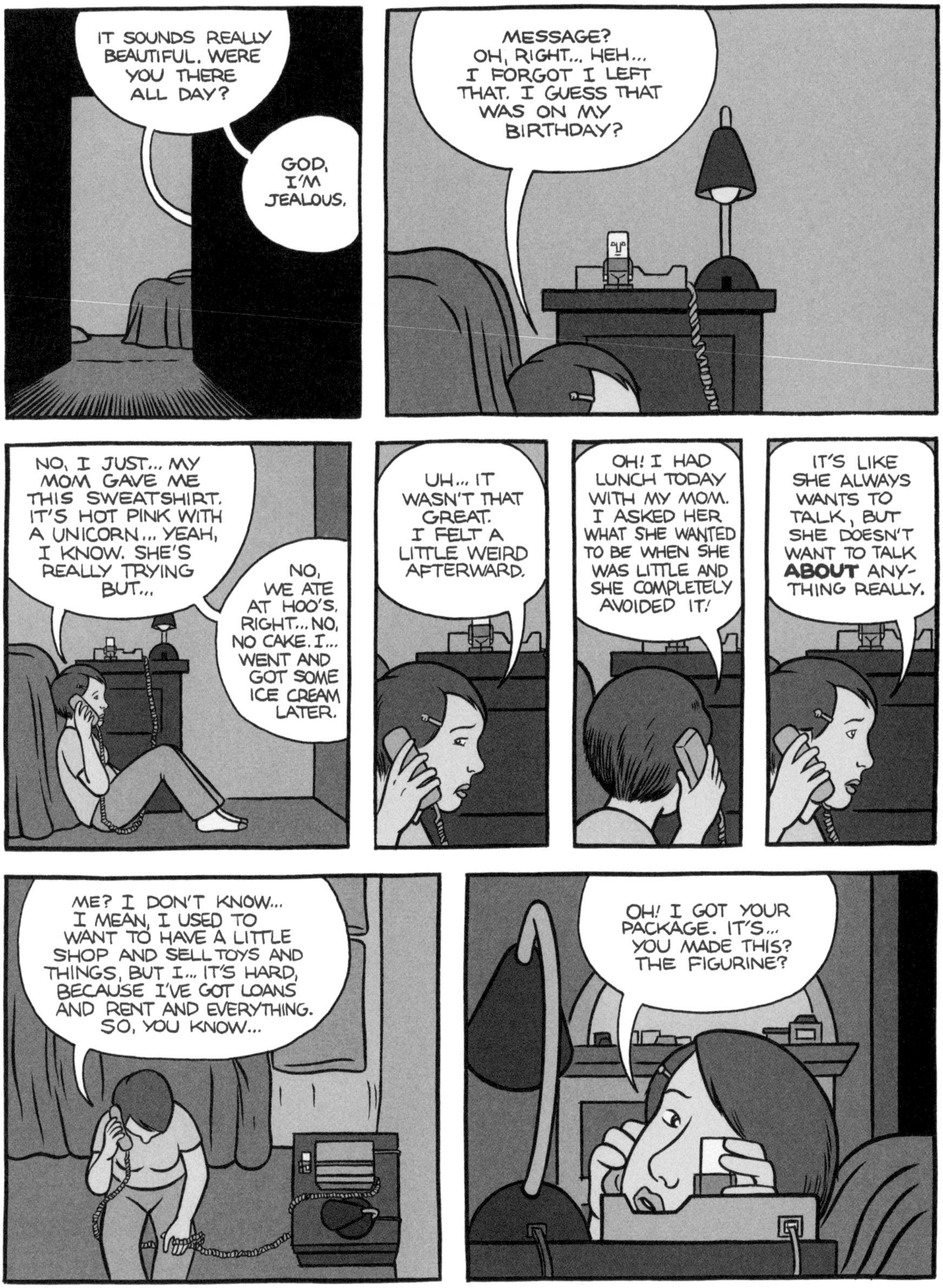
IT SOUNDS REALLY BEAUTIFUL. WERE YOU THERE ALL DAY?
GOD, I'M JEALOUS.
MESSAGE? OH, RIGHT... HEH... I FORGOT I LEFT THAT. I GUESS THAT WAS ON MY BIRTHDAY?
NO, I JUST... MY MOM GAVE ME THIS SWEATSHIRT. IT'S HOT PINK WITH A UNICORN... YEAH, I KNOW. SHE'S REALLY TRYING BUT...
NO, WE ATE AT HOO'S. RIGHT... NO, NO CAKE. I... WENT AND GOT SOME ICE CREAM LATER.
UH... IT WASN'T THAT GREAT. I FELT A LITTLE WEIRD AFTERWARD.
OH! I HAD LUNCH TODAY WITH MY MOM. I ASKED HER WHAT SHE WANTED TO BE WHEN SHE WAS LITTLE AND SHE COMPLETELY AVOIDED IT!
IT'S LIKE SHE ALWAYS WANTS TO TALK, BUT SHE DOESN'T WANT TO TALK **ABOUT** ANYTHING REALLY.
ME? I DON'T KNOW... I MEAN, I USED TO WANT TO HAVE A LITTLE SHOP AND SELL TOYS AND THINGS, BUT I... IT'S HARD, BECAUSE I'VE GOT LOANS AND RENT AND EVERYTHING. SO, YOU KNOW...
OH! I GOT YOUR PACKAGE. IT'S... YOU MADE THIS? THE FIGURINE?

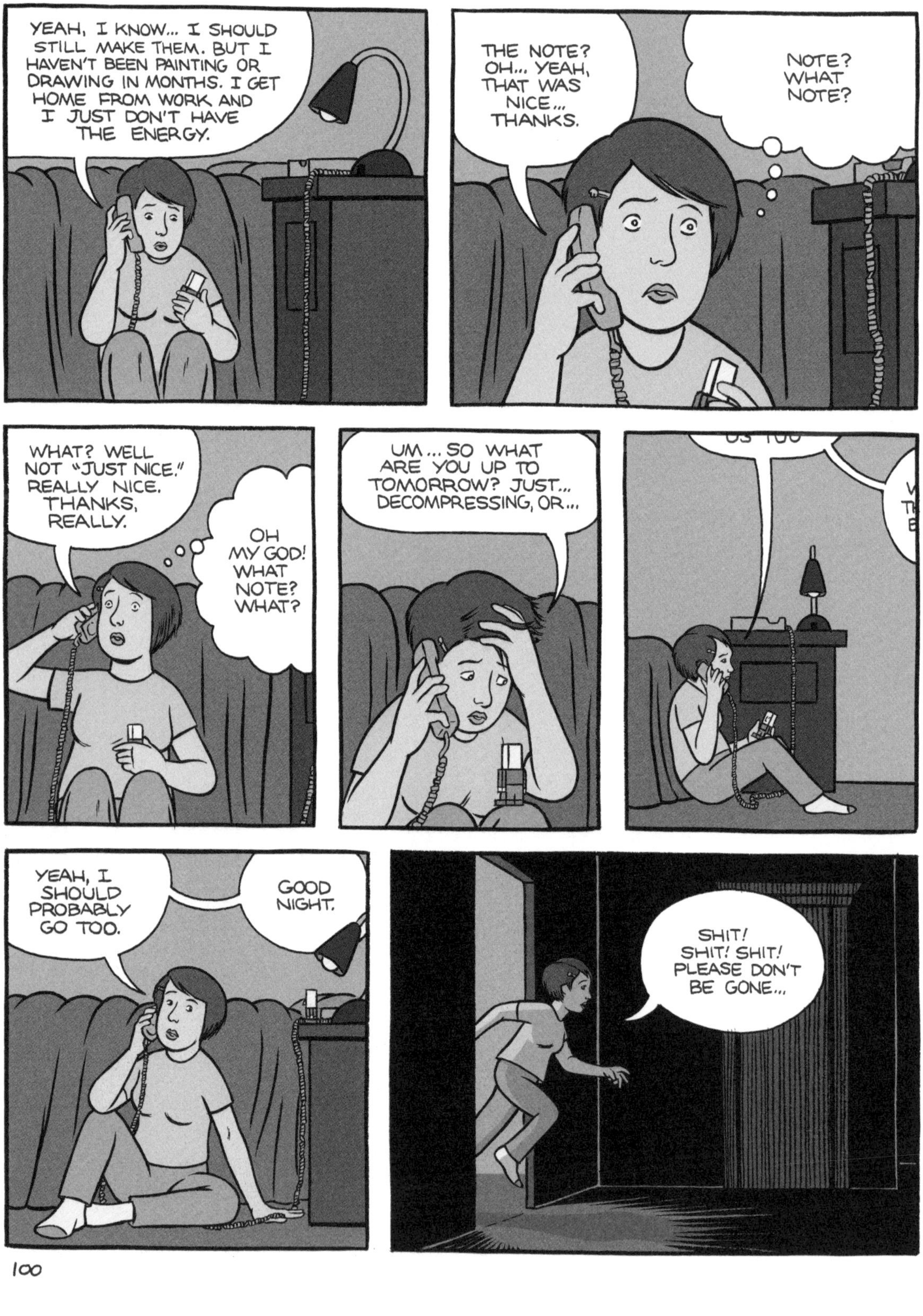
YEAH, I KNOW... I SHOULD STILL MAKE THEM. BUT I HAVEN'T BEEN PAINTING OR DRAWING IN MONTHS. I GET HOME FROM WORK AND I JUST DON'T HAVE THE ENERGY.
THE NOTE? OH... YEAH, THAT WAS NICE... THANKS.
NOTE? WHAT NOTE?
WHAT? WELL NOT "JUST NICE." REALLY NICE. THANKS, REALLY.
OH MY GOD! WHAT NOTE? WHAT?
UM... SO WHAT ARE YOU UP TO TOMORROW? JUST... DECOMPRESSING, OR...
YEAH, I SHOULD PROBABLY GO TOO.
GOOD NIGHT.
SHIT! SHIT! SHIT! PLEASE DON'T BE GONE...

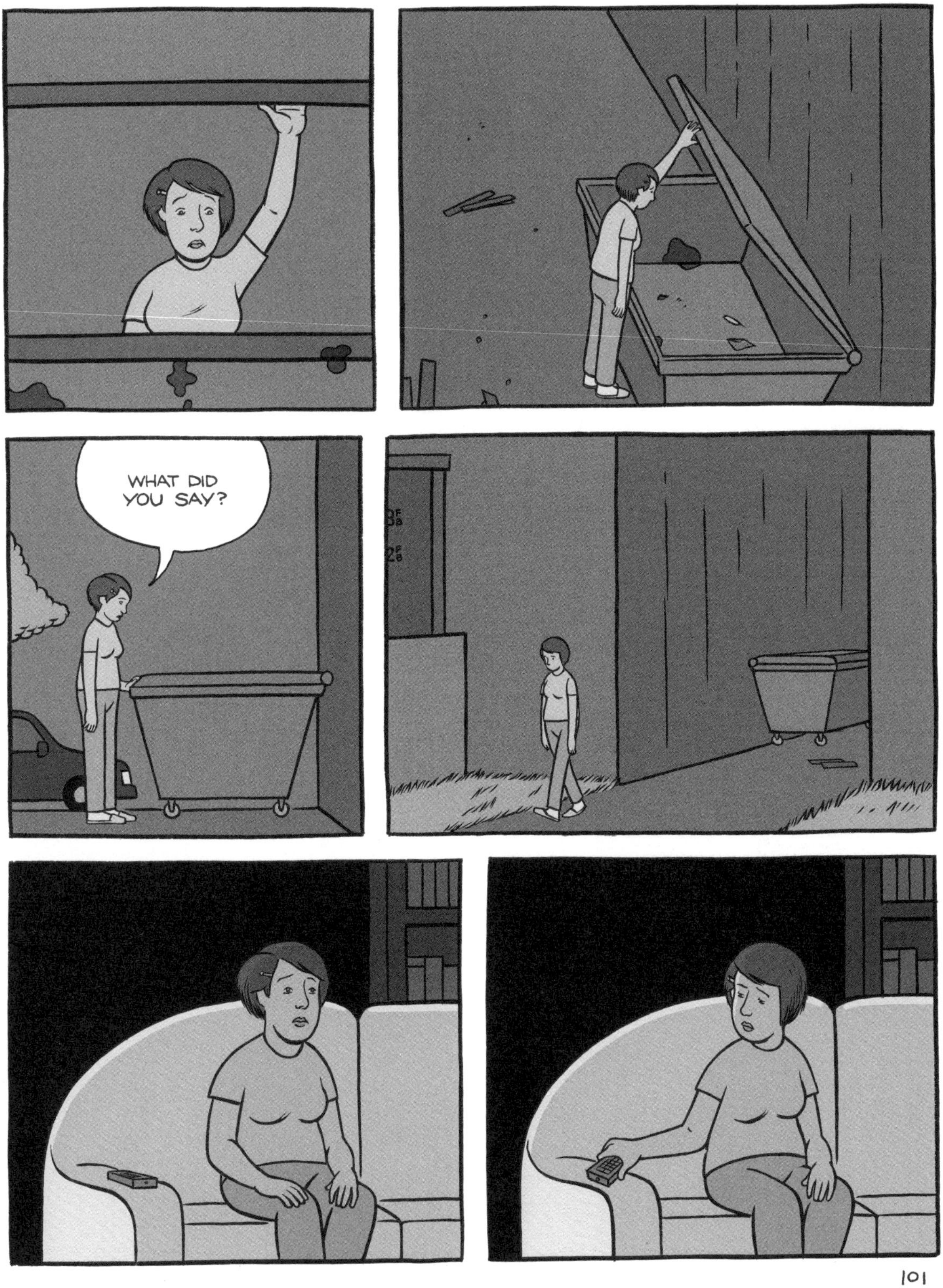
WHAT DID YOU SAY?

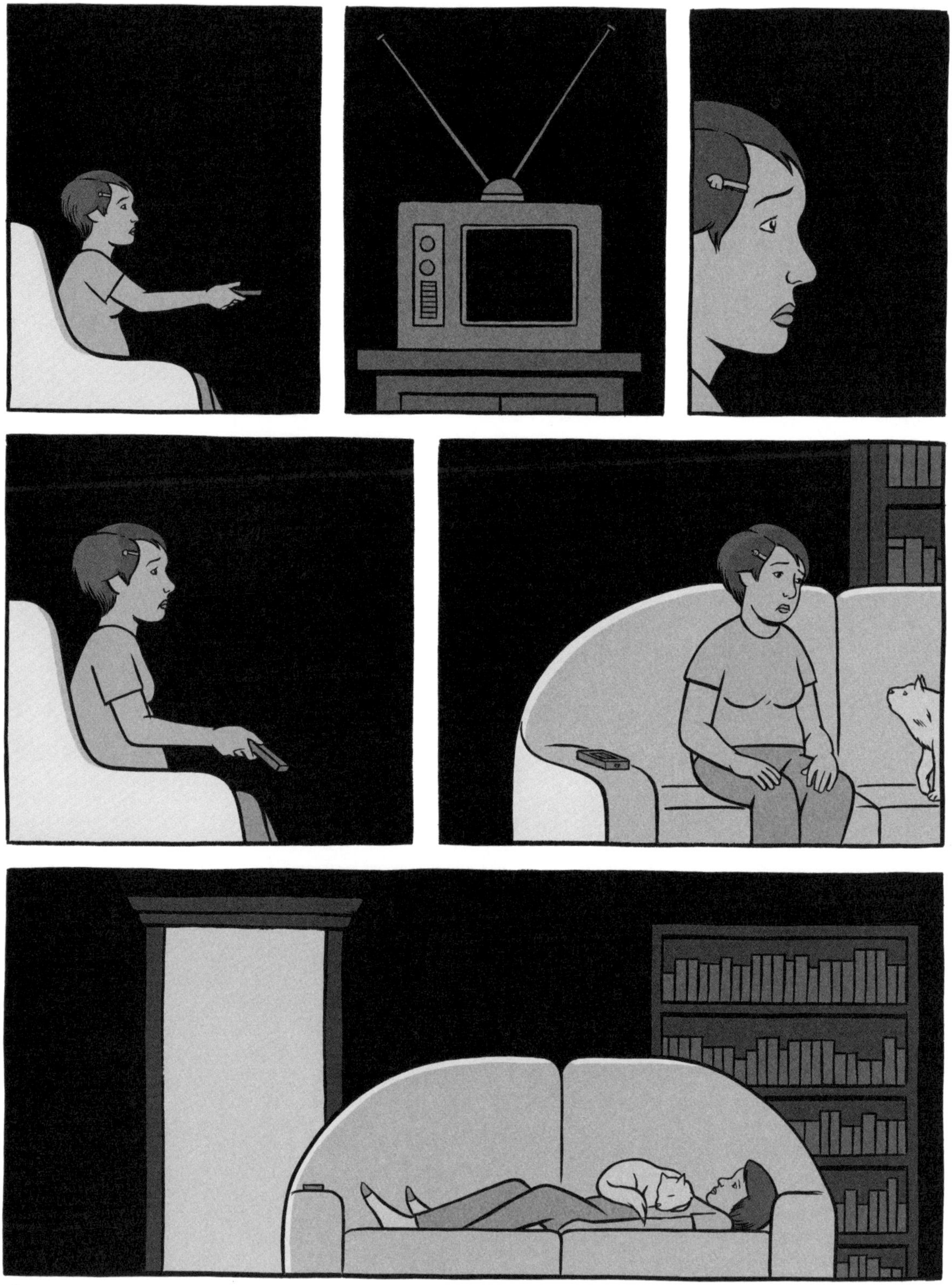

9
Boy of a
Thousand Faces

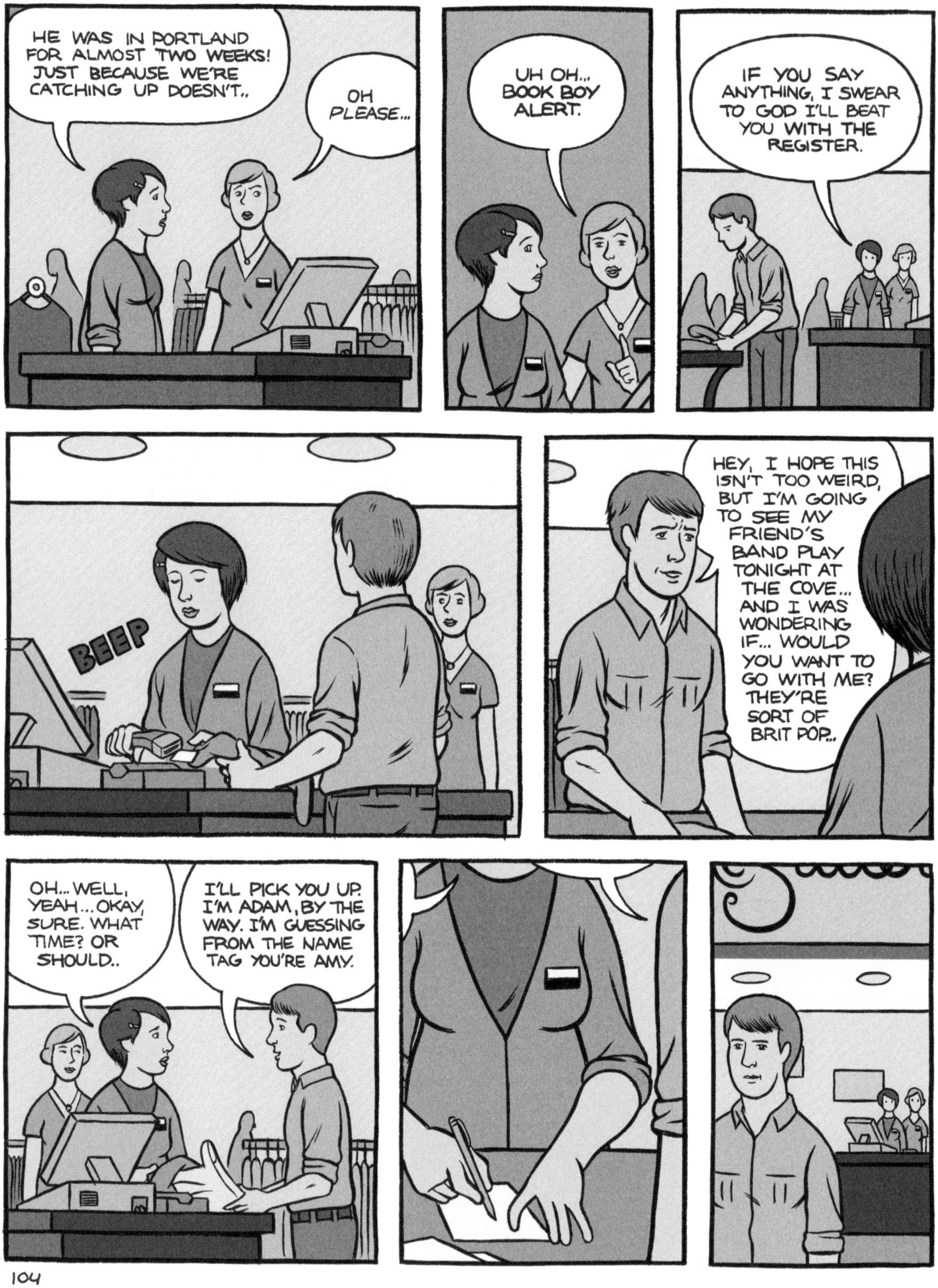
HE WAS IN PORTLAND FOR ALMOST TWO WEEKS! JUST BECAUSE WE'RE CATCHING UP DOESN'T..
OH PLEASE...
UH OH... BOOK BOY ALERT.
IF YOU SAY ANYTHING, I SWEAR TO GOD I'LL BEAT YOU WITH THE REGISTER.
BEEP
HEY, I HOPE THIS ISN'T TOO WEIRD, BUT I'M GOING TO SEE MY FRIEND'S BAND PLAY TONIGHT AT THE COVE... AND I WAS WONDERING IF... WOULD YOU WANT TO GO WITH ME? THEY'RE SORT OF BRIT POP...
OH... WELL, YEAH... OKAY, SURE. WHAT TIME? OR SHOULD..
I'LL PICK YOU UP. I'M ADAM, BY THE WAY. I'M GUESSING FROM THE NAME TAG YOU'RE AMY.

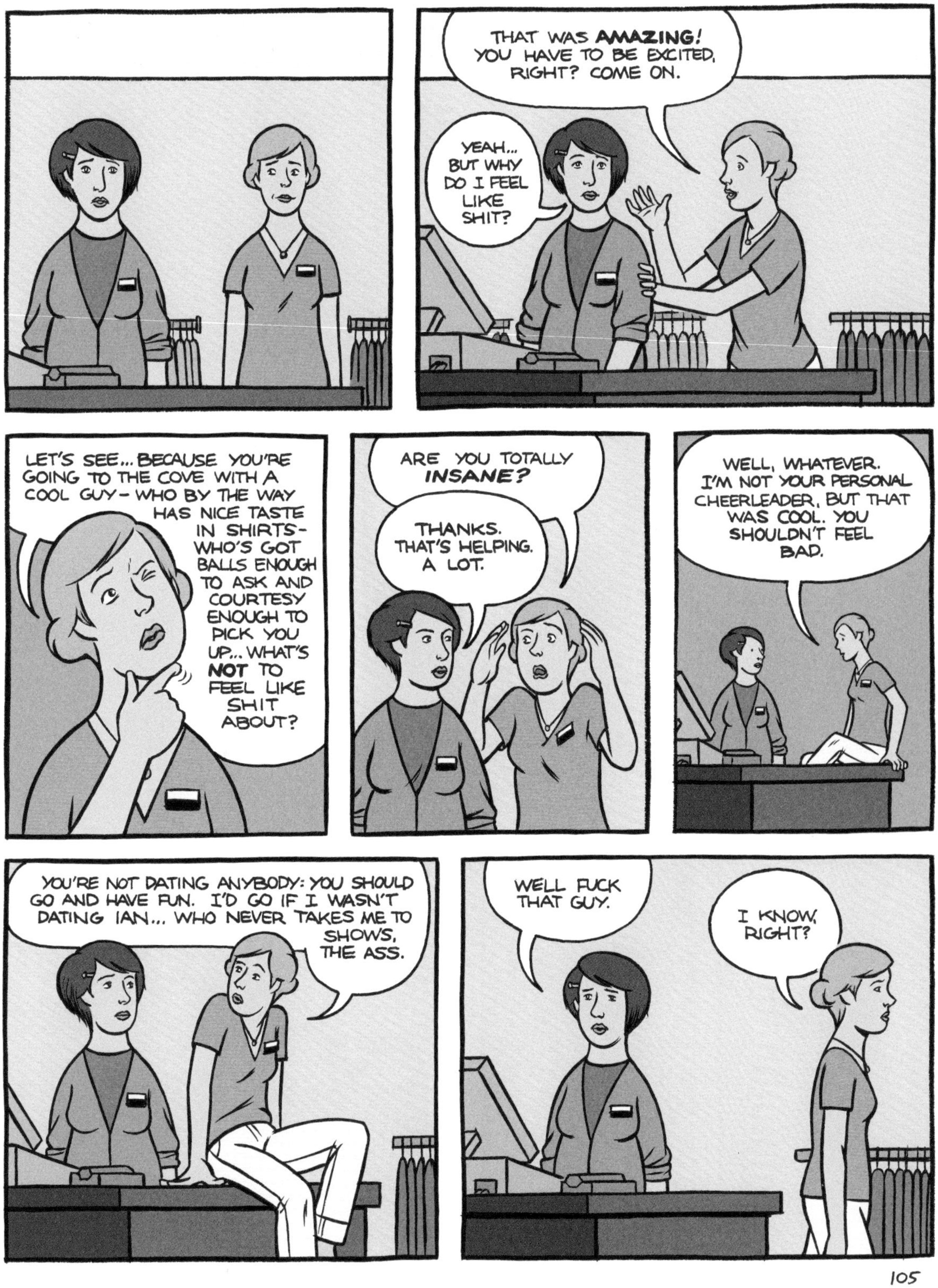
THAT WAS **AMAZING!** YOU HAVE TO BE EXCITED, RIGHT? COME ON.
YEAH... BUT WHY DO I FEEL LIKE SHIT?
LET'S SEE... BECAUSE YOU'RE GOING TO THE COVE WITH A COOL GUY- WHO BY THE WAY HAS NICE TASTE IN SHIRTS- WHO'S GOT BALLS ENOUGH TO ASK AND COURTESY ENOUGH TO PICK YOU UP... WHAT'S **NOT** TO FEEL LIKE SHIT ABOUT?
ARE YOU TOTALLY ***INSANE?***
THANKS. THAT'S HELPING. A LOT.
WELL, WHATEVER. I'M NOT YOUR PERSONAL CHEERLEADER, BUT THAT WAS COOL. YOU SHOULDN'T FEEL BAD.
YOU'RE NOT DATING ANYBODY: YOU SHOULD GO AND HAVE FUN. I'D GO IF I WASN'T DATING IAN... WHO NEVER TAKES ME TO SHOWS, THE ASS.
WELL FUCK THAT GUY.
I KNOW, RIGHT?

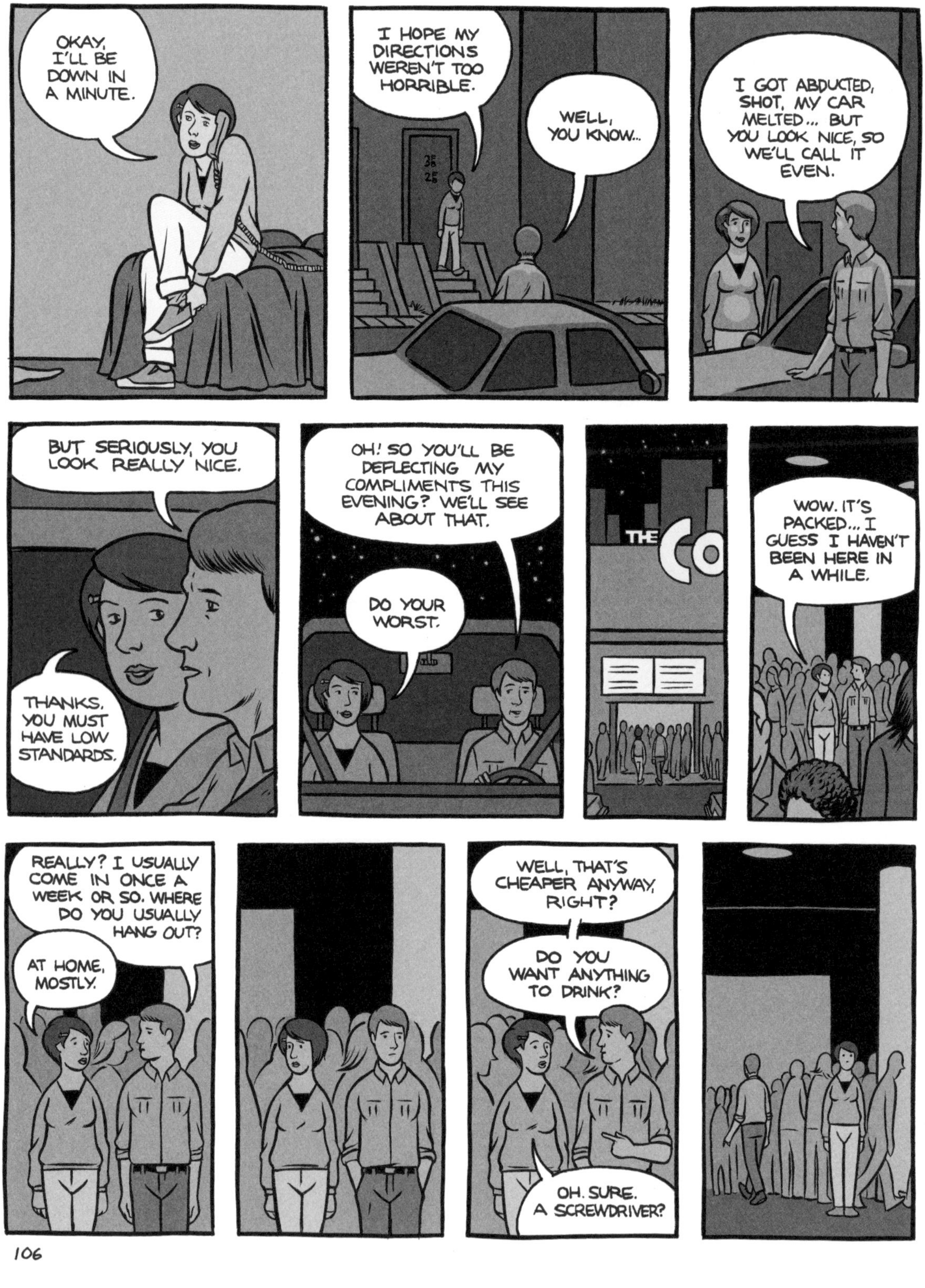
OKAY, I'LL BE DOWN IN A MINUTE.
I HOPE MY DIRECTIONS WEREN'T TOO HORRIBLE.
WELL, YOU KNOW...
I GOT ABDUCTED, SHOT, MY CAR MELTED... BUT YOU LOOK NICE, SO WE'LL CALL IT EVEN.
BUT SERIOUSLY, YOU LOOK REALLY NICE.
THANKS. YOU MUST HAVE LOW STANDARDS.
OH! SO YOU'LL BE DEFLECTING MY COMPLIMENTS THIS EVENING? WE'LL SEE ABOUT THAT.
DO YOUR WORST.
THE CO
WOW. IT'S PACKED... I GUESS I HAVEN'T BEEN HERE IN A WHILE.
REALLY? I USUALLY COME IN ONCE A WEEK OR SO. WHERE DO YOU USUALLY HANG OUT?
AT HOME, MOSTLY.
WELL, THAT'S CHEAPER ANYWAY, RIGHT?
DO YOU WANT ANYTHING TO DRINK?
OH. SURE. A SCREWDRIVER?

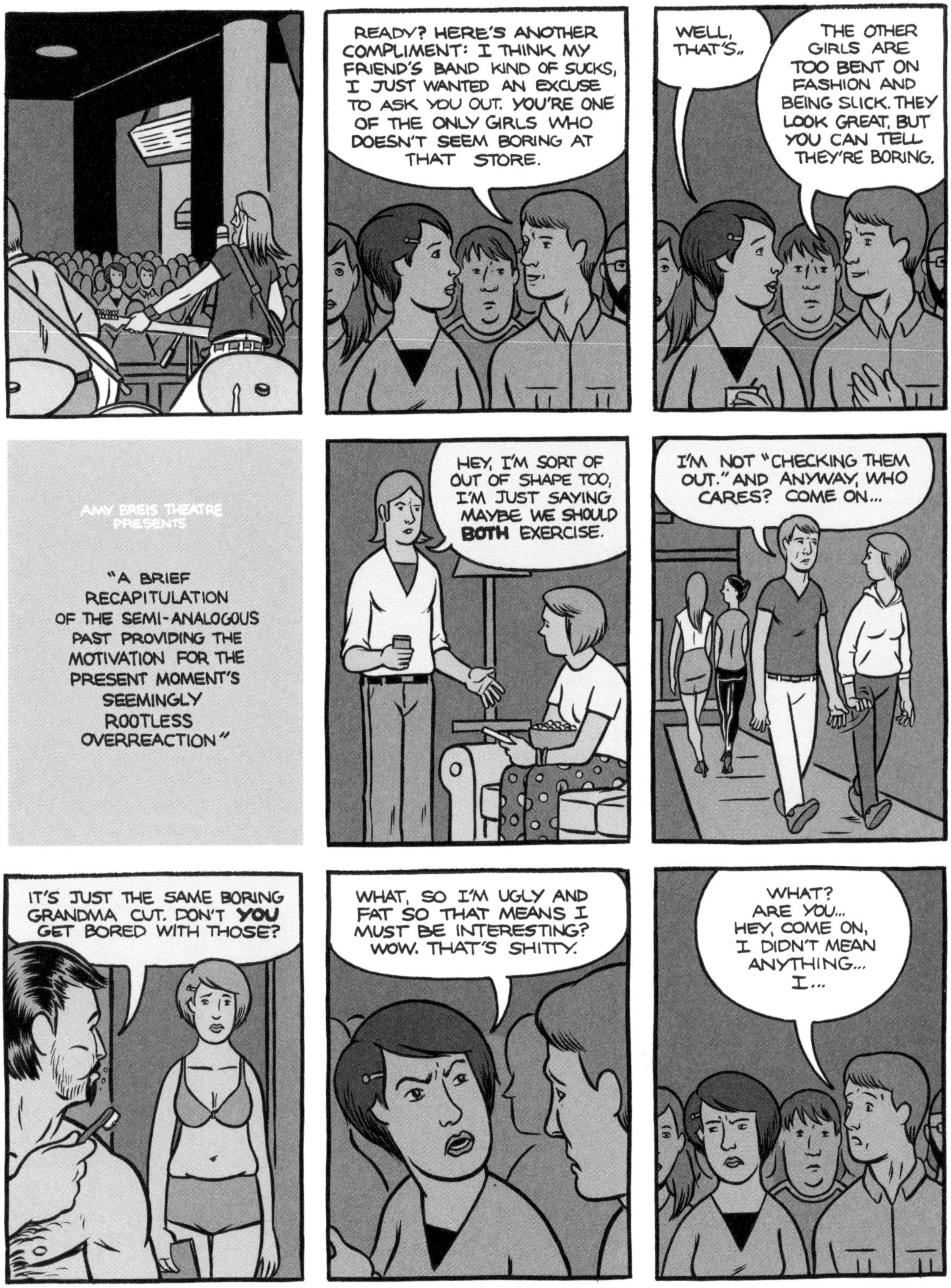
READY? HERE'S ANOTHER COMPLIMENT: I THINK MY FRIEND'S BAND KIND OF SUCKS, I JUST WANTED AN EXCUSE TO ASK YOU OUT. YOU'RE ONE OF THE ONLY GIRLS WHO DOESN'T SEEM BORING AT THAT STORE.
WELL, THAT'S..
THE OTHER GIRLS ARE TOO BENT ON FASHION AND BEING SLICK. THEY LOOK GREAT, BUT YOU CAN TELL THEY'RE BORING.
AMY BREIS THEATRE PRESENTS
"A BRIEF RECAPITULATION OF THE SEMI-ANALOGOUS PAST PROVIDING THE MOTIVATION FOR THE PRESENT MOMENT'S SEEMINGLY ROOTLESS OVERREACTION"
HEY, I'M SORT OF OUT OF SHAPE TOO, I'M JUST SAYING MAYBE WE SHOULD BOTH EXERCISE.
I'M NOT "CHECKING THEM OUT." AND ANYWAY, WHO CARES? COME ON...
IT'S JUST THE SAME BORING GRANDMA CUT. DON'T YOU GET BORED WITH THOSE?
WHAT, SO I'M UGLY AND FAT SO THAT MEANS I MUST BE INTERESTING? WOW. THAT'S SHITTY.
WHAT? ARE YOU... HEY, COME ON, I DIDN'T MEAN ANYTHING... I...

HA! GOT YA! DEFLECTED YOUR COMPLIMENT! ...I WAS JUST KIDDING.

JESUS, I THOUGHT YOU WERE HONESTLY PISSED... WOW.

DO YOU WANT TO COME OVER TO MY PLACE? WE COULD RENT A MOVIE OR SOMETHING.

S UNGLU IGLOO	M THE B'S
4 YER KNACK	O Q.SANSWER
S TEN 3 UP	T WOLF FIT
N HOPPLATE	E THEMES

HOW COULD IT HIT THIS FAR INLAND? AND THIS SOON?

WHERE WAS SHE LAST SEEN?

IS THIS ALL THAT'S LEFT? THESE FRAGMENTS...

IS THIS PLANE

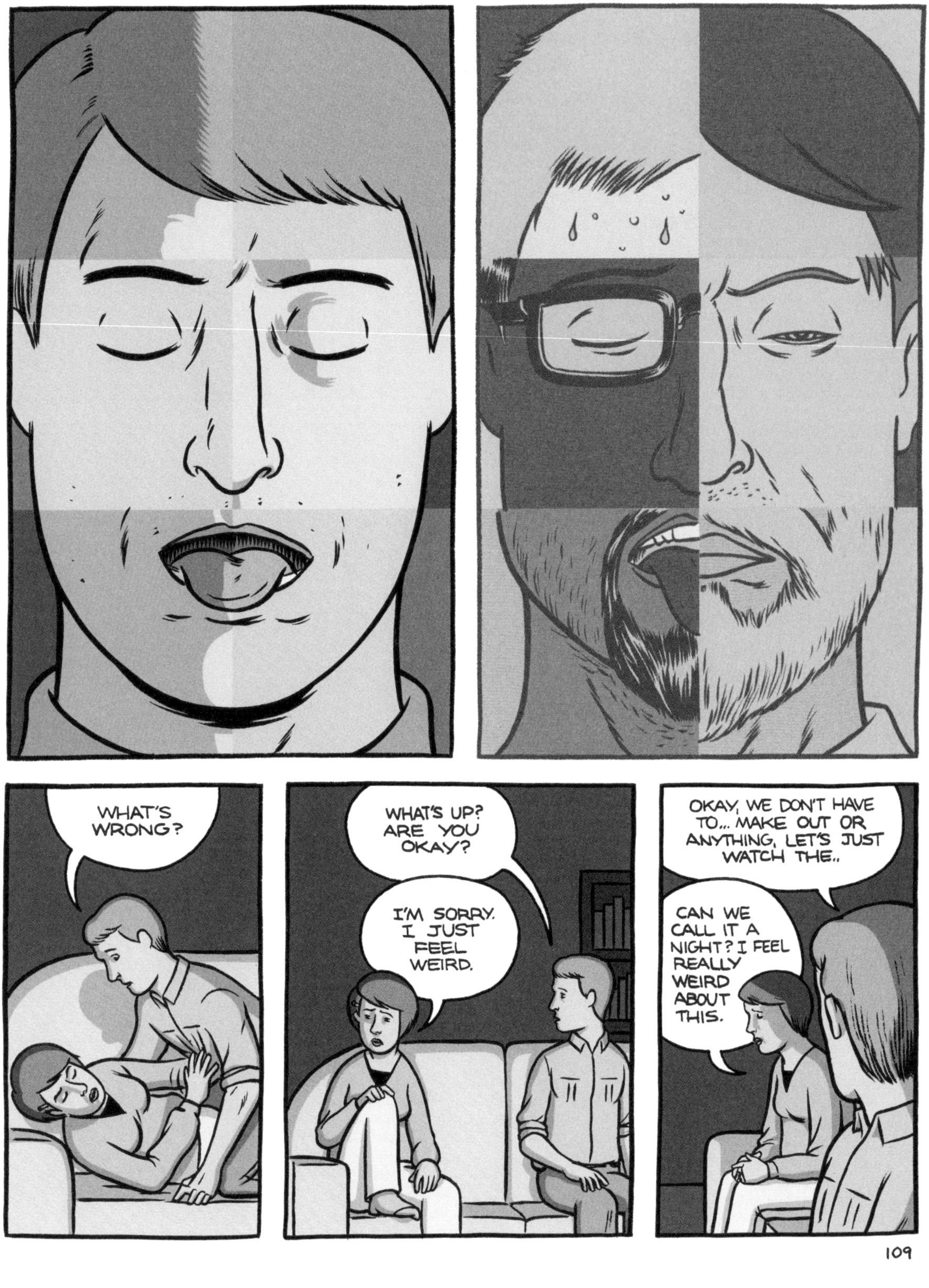
WHAT'S WRONG?
WHAT'S UP? ARE YOU OKAY?
I'M SORRY. I JUST FEEL WEIRD.
OKAY, WE DON'T HAVE TO... MAKE OUT OR ANYTHING, LET'S JUST WATCH THE..
CAN WE CALL IT A NIGHT? I FEEL REALLY WEIRD ABOUT THIS.

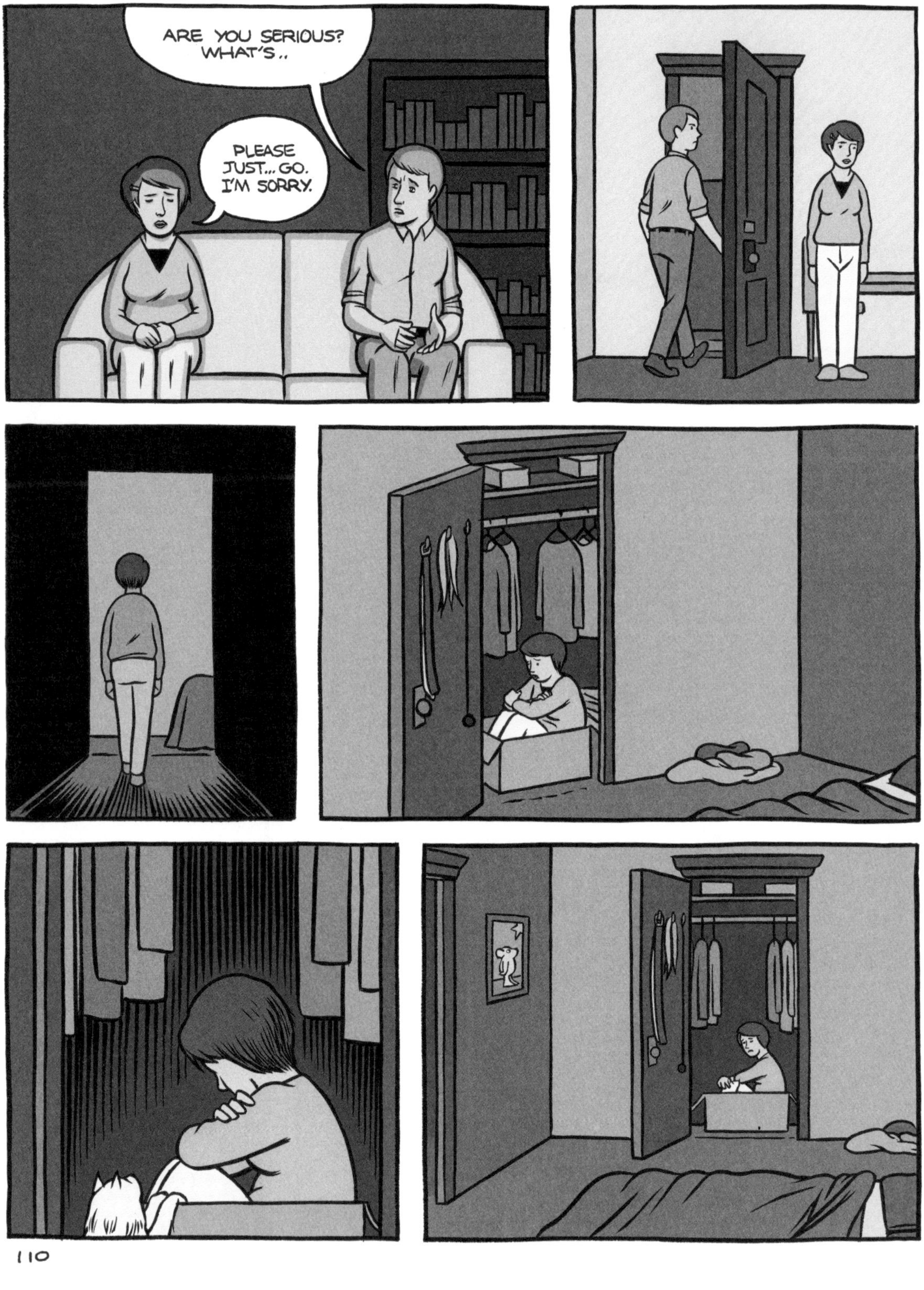
ARE YOU SERIOUS? WHAT'S..
PLEASE JUST... GO. I'M SORRY.

10
Photo-Rays from
the Future

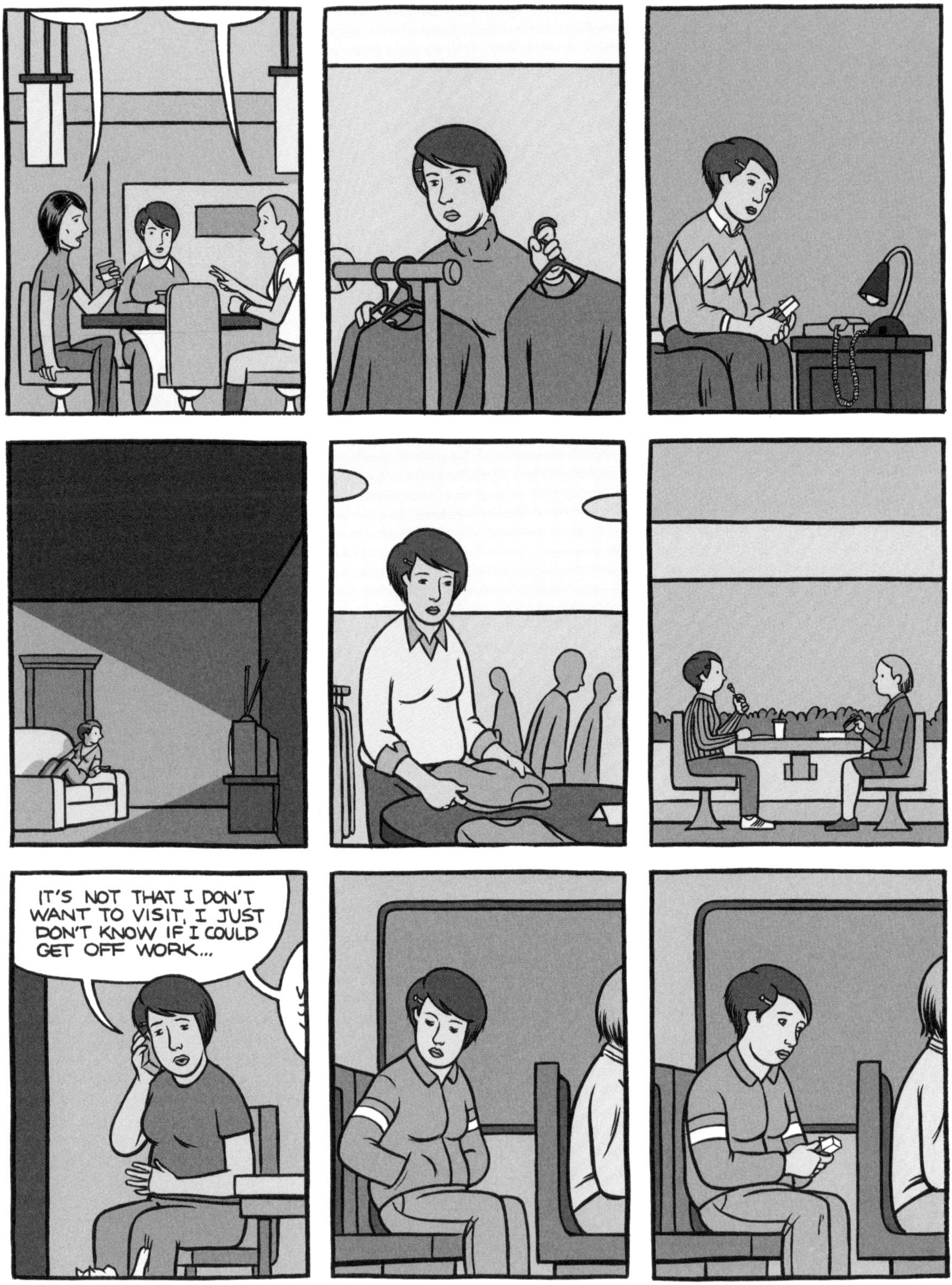
IT'S NOT THAT I DON'T WANT TO VISIT, I JUST DON'T KNOW IF I COULD GET OFF WORK...

ANOTHER ONE?

WHAT DID YOU DO THIS TIME?

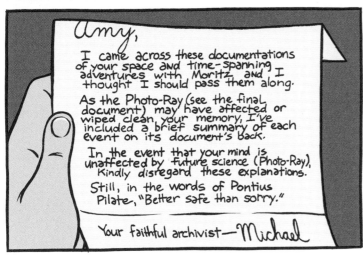

Amy,

I came across these documentations of your space and time-spanning adventures with Moritz, and I thought I should pass them along.

As the Photo-Ray (see the final document) may have affected or wiped clean your memory, I've included a brief summary of each event on its document's back.

In the event that your mind is unaffected by future science (Photo-Ray), kindly disregard these explanations.

Still, in the words of Pontius Pilate, "Better safe than sorry."

Your faithful archivist—Michael

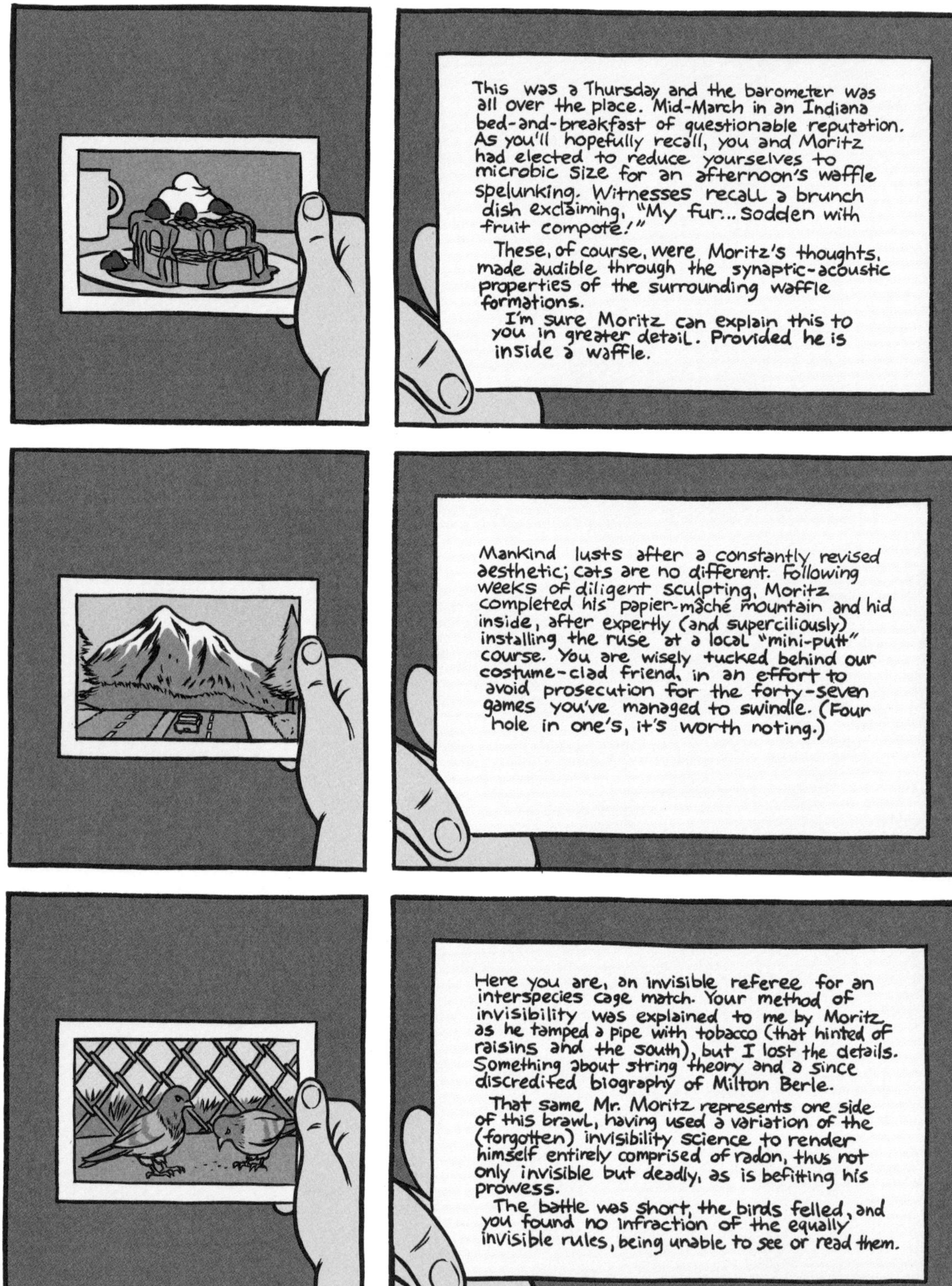
This was a Thursday and the barometer was all over the place. Mid-March in an Indiana bed-and-breakfast of questionable reputation. As you'll hopefully recall, you and Moritz had elected to reduce yourselves to microbic size for an afternoon's waffle spelunking. Witnesses recall a brunch dish exclaiming, "My fur... sodden with fruit compote!"
These, of course, were Moritz's thoughts, made audible through the synaptic-acoustic properties of the surrounding waffle formations.
I'm sure Moritz can explain this to you in greater detail. Provided he is inside a waffle.
Mankind lusts after a constantly revised aesthetic; cats are no different. Following weeks of diligent sculpting, Moritz completed his papier-mâché mountain and hid inside, after expertly (and superciliously) installing the ruse at a local "mini-putt" course. You are wisely tucked behind our costume-clad friend, in an effort to avoid prosecution for the forty-seven games you've managed to swindle. (Four hole in one's, it's worth noting.)
Here you are, an invisible referee for an interspecies cage match. Your method of invisibility was explained to me by Moritz as he tamped a pipe with tobacco (that hinted of raisins and the south), but I lost the details. Something about string theory and a since discredited biography of Milton Berle.
That same Mr. Moritz represents one side of this brawl, having used a variation of the (forgotten) invisibility science to render himself entirely comprised of radon, thus not only invisible but deadly, as is befitting his prowess.
The battle was short, the birds felled, and you found no infraction of the equally invisible rules, being unable to see or read them.

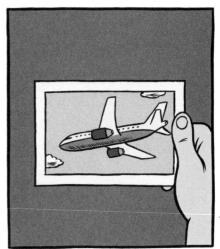

This one's hearsay: this one's a picture Photo-Rayed to me from the future. It may still contain Photo-Ray particles; it's hard to tell. The future's difficult that way.

Moritz is waving to you as you board the plane to San Francisco (no worries about leaving him: he has an action-packed week of bathing and sleeping ahead of him in your absence). I failed to write down the date this was taken. When is that trip? I think you'll be getting this in the future, the photo's point of origin, so hopefully you can provide some clarification.

THIS FINE STRAWBERRY GIVES ME AN INSPIRATION! THESE INGREDIENTS IMPLY A FUTURE RICHNESS! IN I DIP A BERRY, INTO THE MAGIC BATTER...

AND OUT COMES THE OUTCOME: BEST CAKE I EVER BAKED!

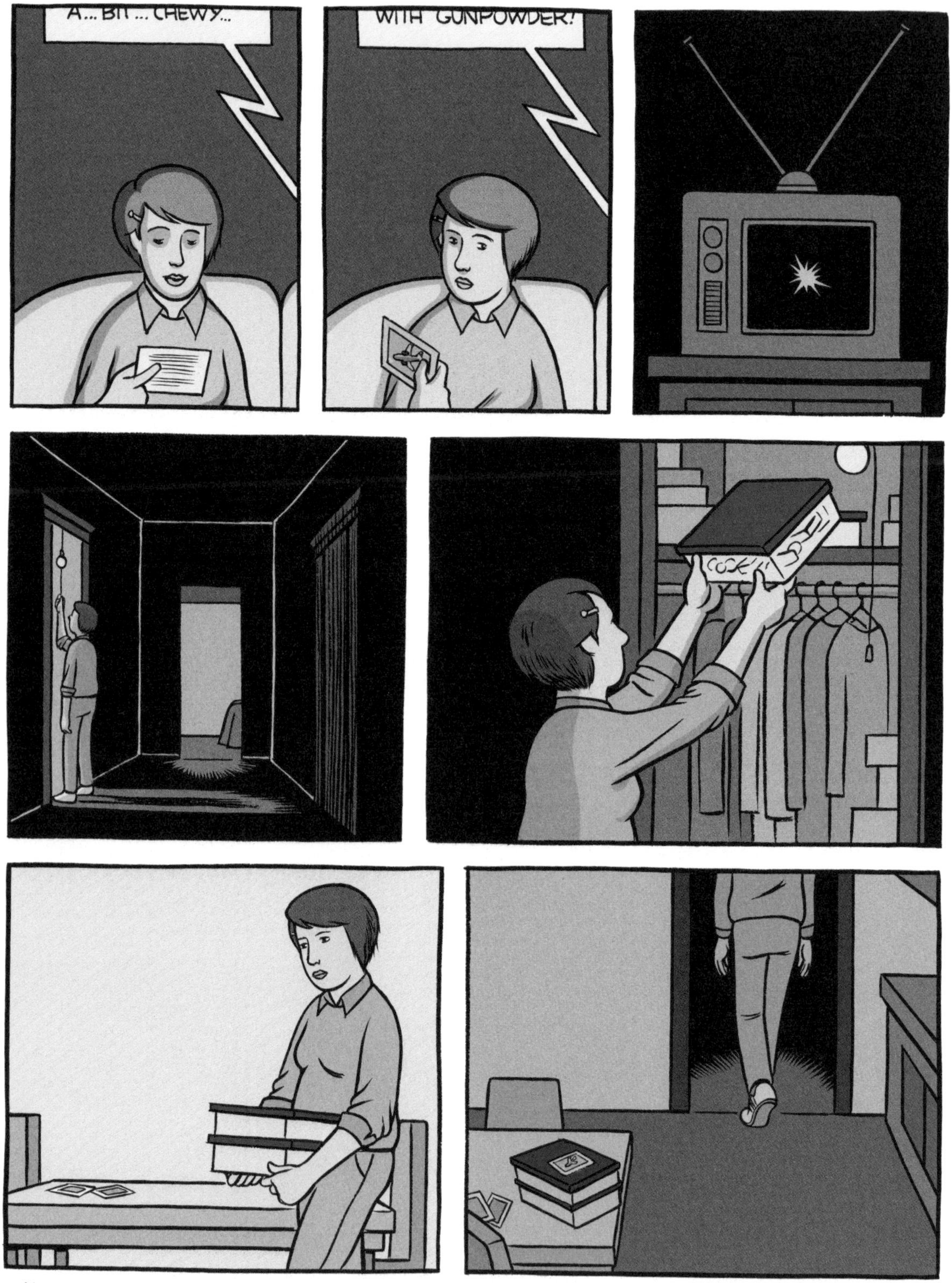
A... BIT ... CHEWY...
WITH GUNPOWDER!

11
Windupless

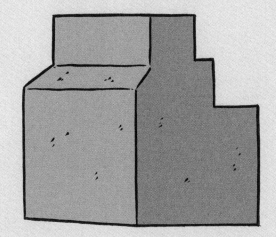

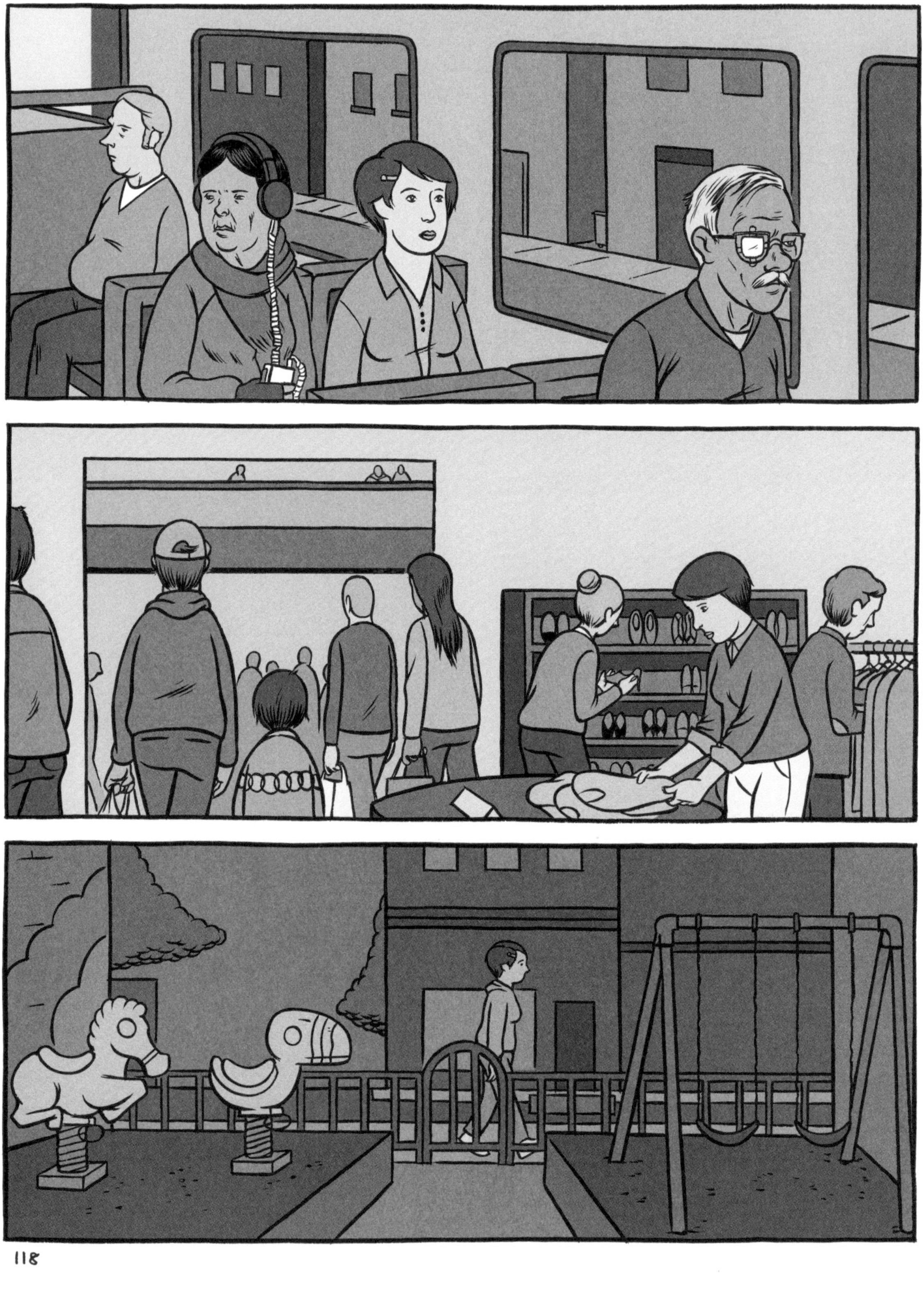

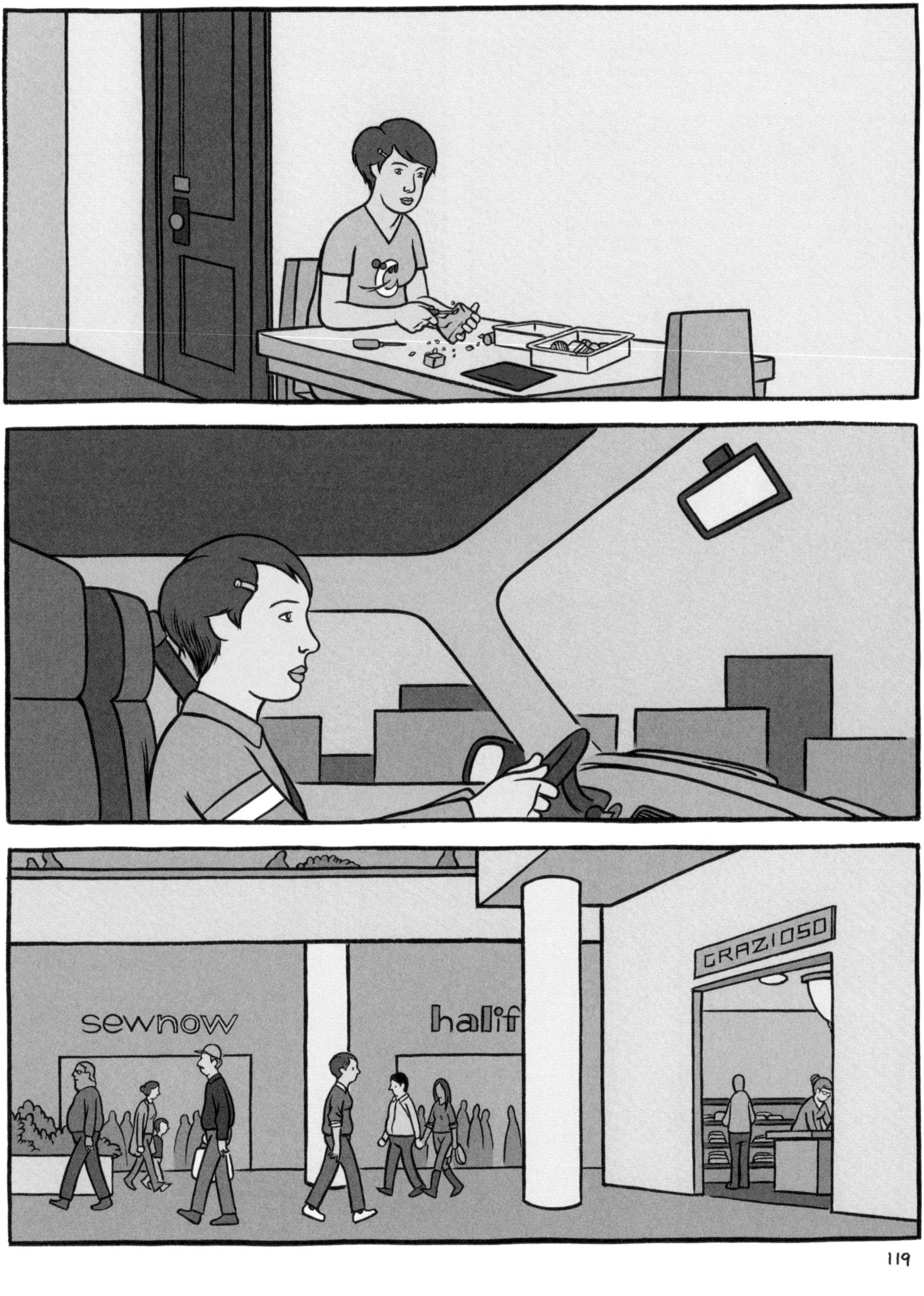

sewnow
halif
GRAZIOSO

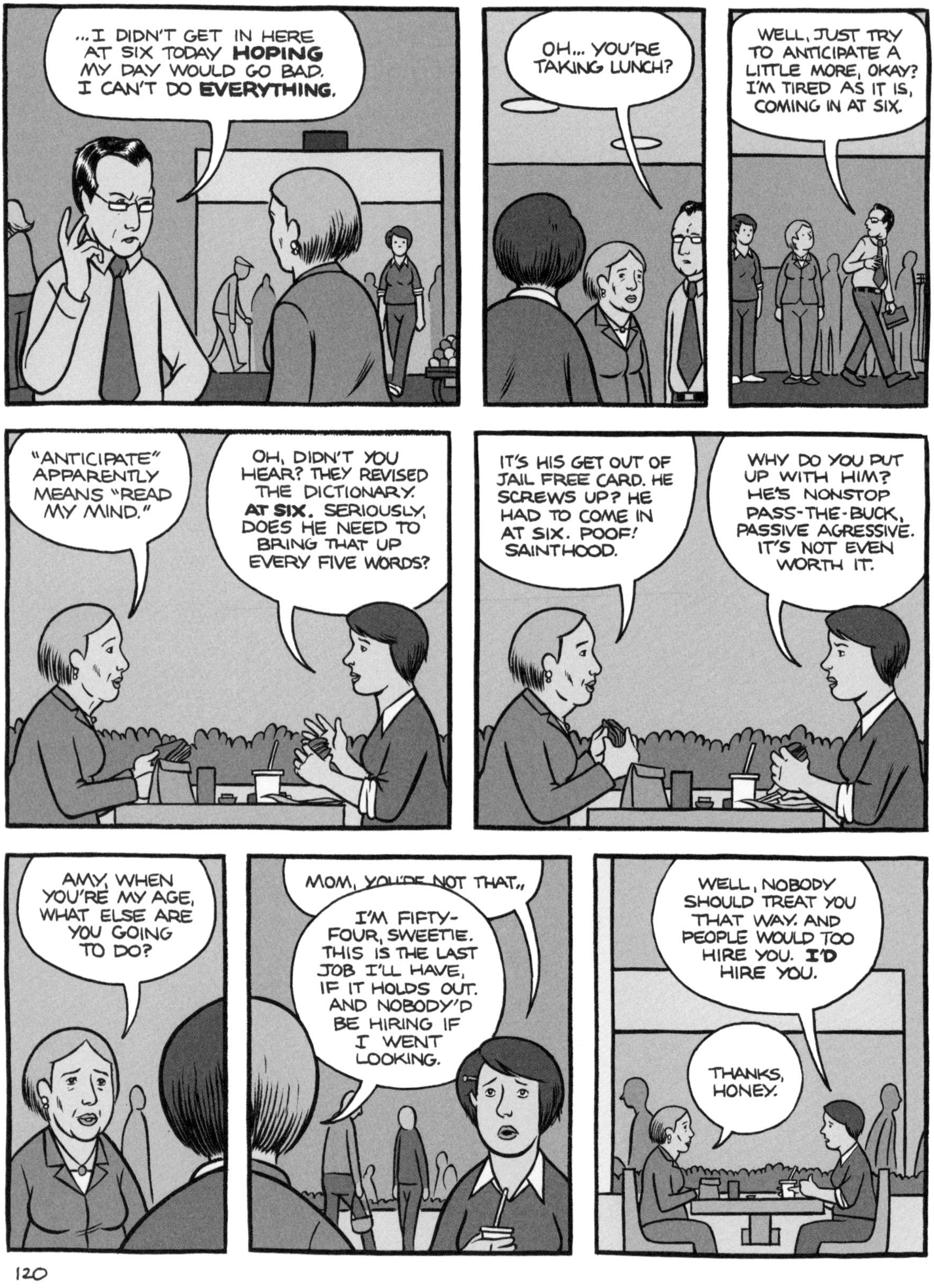
...I DIDN'T GET IN HERE AT SIX TODAY **HOPING** MY DAY WOULD GO BAD. I CAN'T DO **EVERYTHING**.
OH... YOU'RE TAKING LUNCH?
WELL, JUST TRY TO ANTICIPATE A LITTLE MORE, OKAY? I'M TIRED AS IT IS, COMING IN AT SIX.
"ANTICIPATE" APPARENTLY MEANS "READ MY MIND."
OH, DIDN'T YOU HEAR? THEY REVISED THE DICTIONARY. **AT SIX.** SERIOUSLY, DOES HE NEED TO BRING THAT UP EVERY FIVE WORDS?
IT'S HIS GET OUT OF JAIL FREE CARD. HE SCREWS UP? HE HAD TO COME IN AT SIX. POOF! SAINTHOOD.
WHY DO YOU PUT UP WITH HIM? HE'S NONSTOP PASS-THE-BUCK, PASSIVE AGRESSIVE. IT'S NOT EVEN WORTH IT.
AMY, WHEN YOU'RE MY AGE, WHAT ELSE ARE YOU GOING TO DO?
MOM, YOU'RE NOT THAT..
I'M FIFTY-FOUR, SWEETIE. THIS IS THE LAST JOB I'LL HAVE, IF IT HOLDS OUT. AND NOBODY'D BE HIRING IF I WENT LOOKING.
WELL, NOBODY SHOULD TREAT YOU THAT WAY. AND PEOPLE WOULD TOO HIRE YOU. **I'D** HIRE YOU.
THANKS, HONEY.

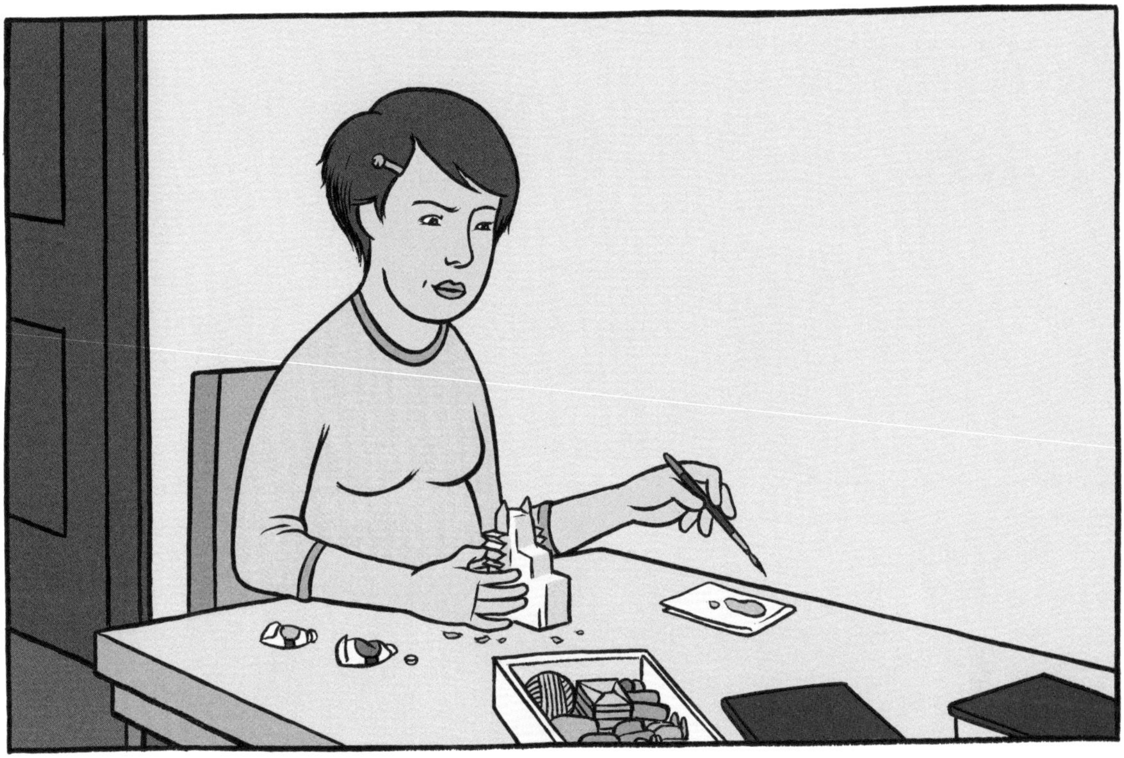

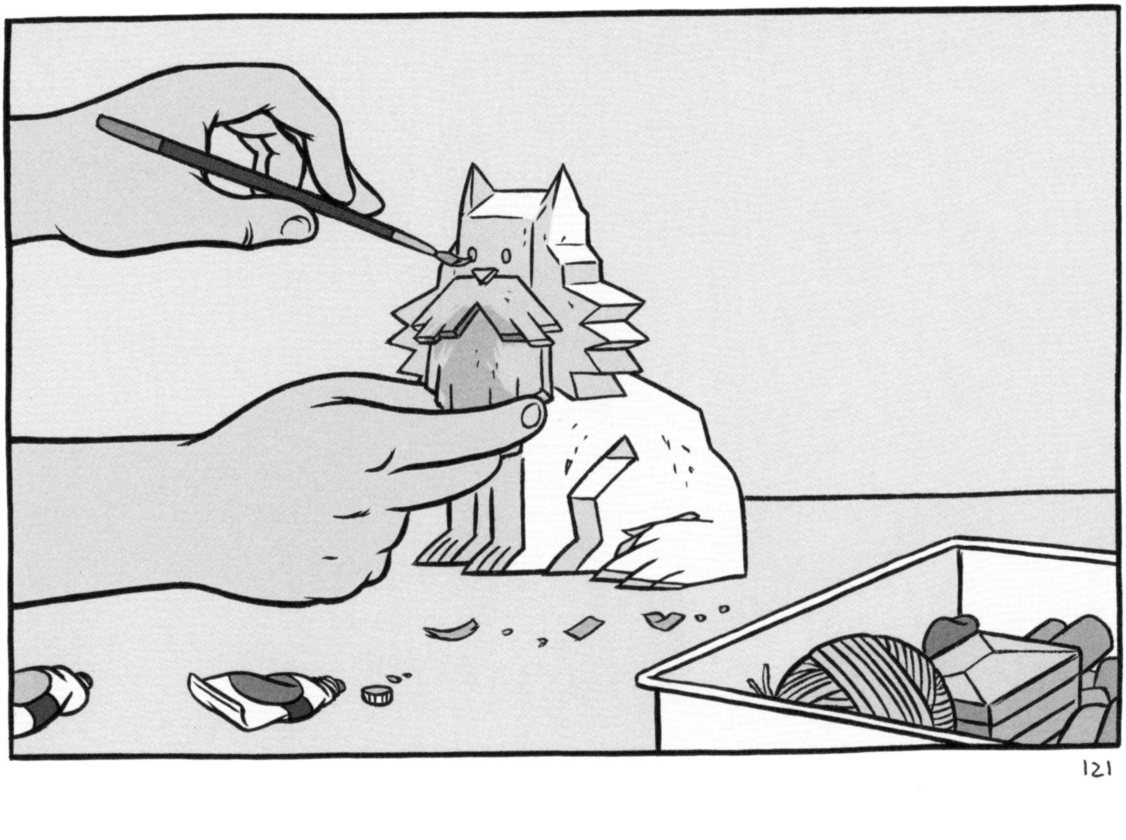

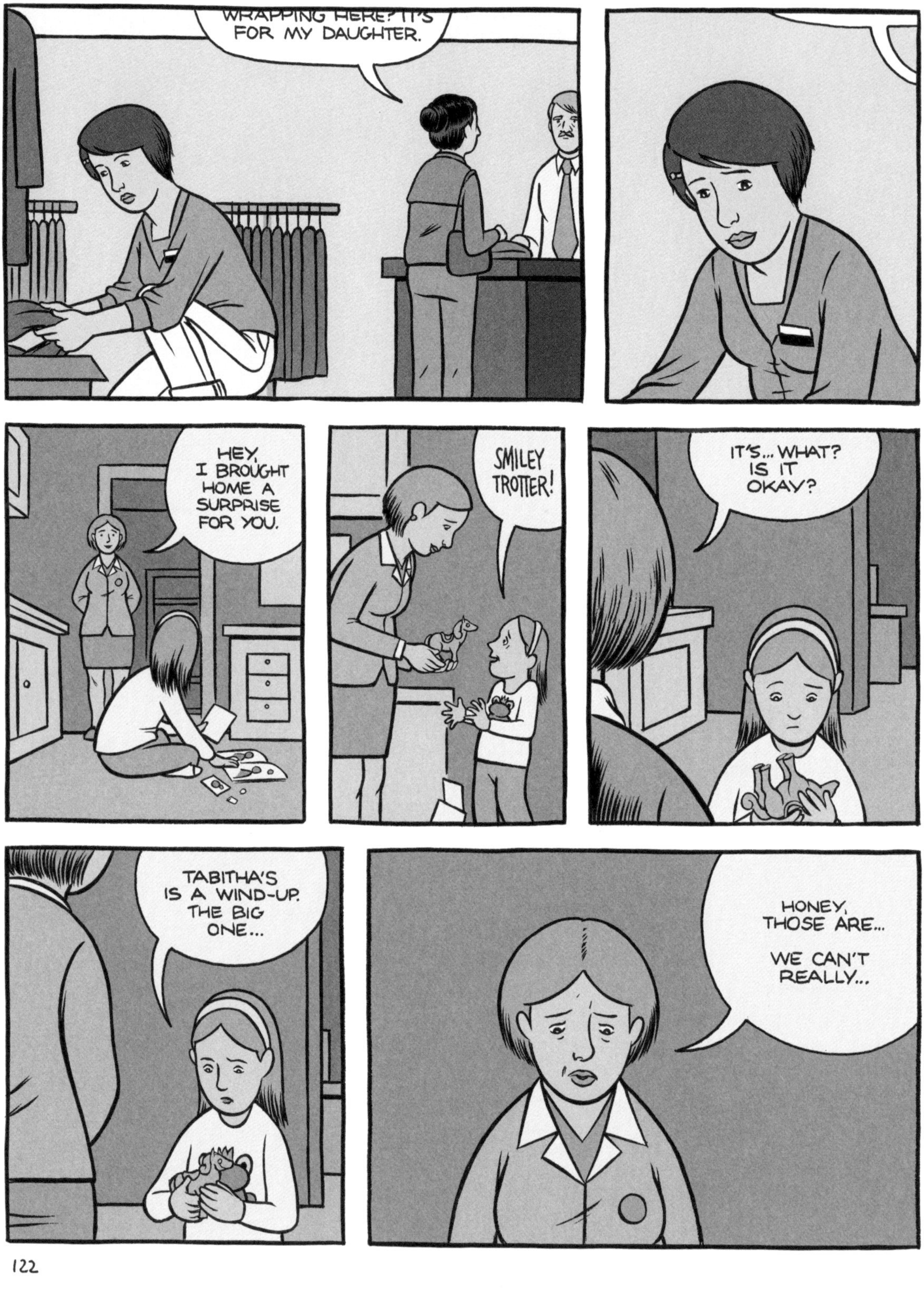
WRAPPING HERE? IT'S FOR MY DAUGHTER.
HEY, I BROUGHT HOME A SURPRISE FOR YOU.
SMILEY TROTTER!
IT'S... WHAT? IS IT OKAY?
TABITHA'S IS A WIND-UP. THE BIG ONE...
HONEY, THOSE ARE...
WE CAN'T REALLY...

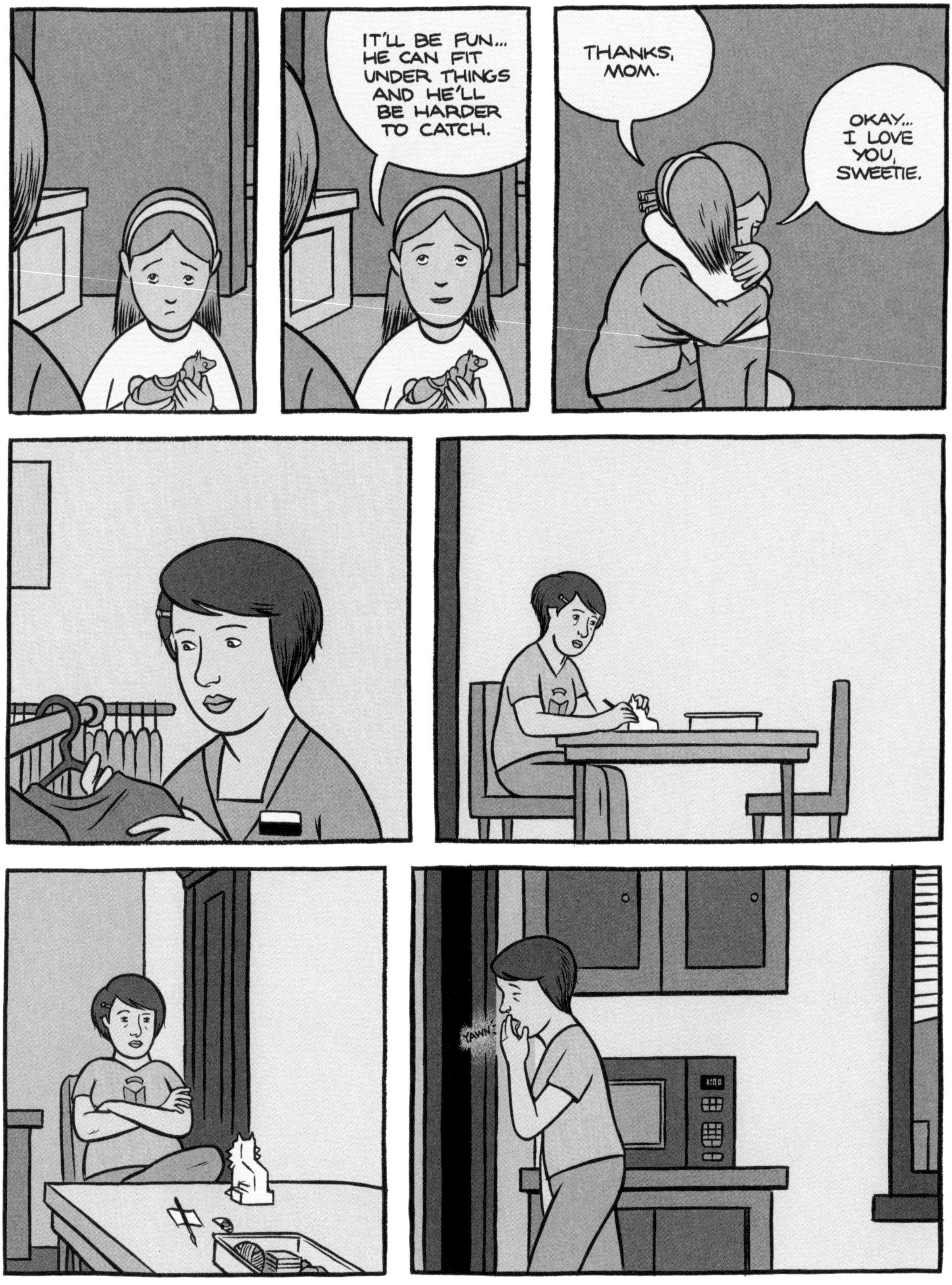
IT'LL BE FUN... HE CAN FIT UNDER THINGS AND HE'LL BE HARDER TO CATCH.
THANKS, MOM.
OKAY... I LOVE YOU, SWEETIE.
YAWN

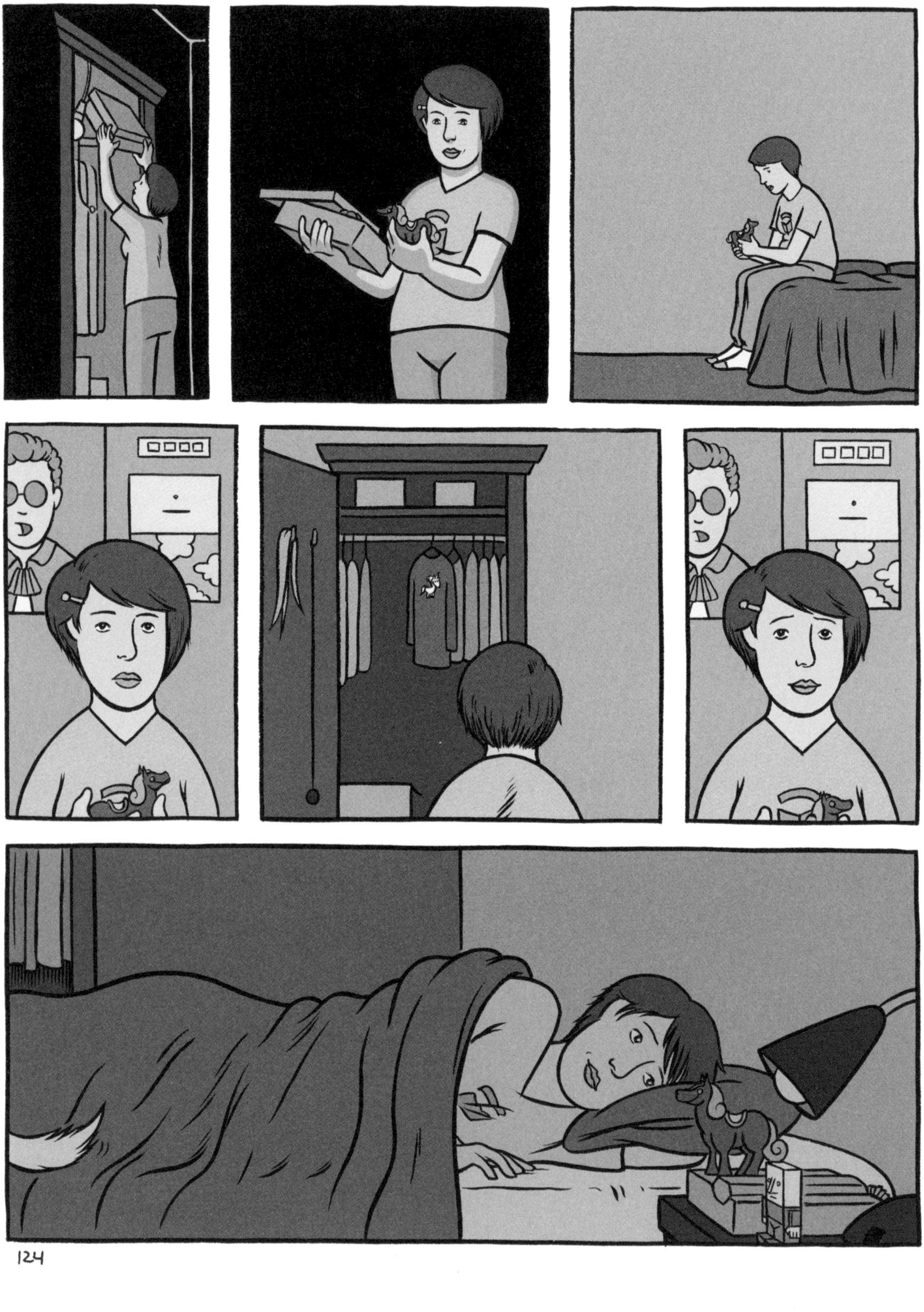

12
Photo-Rays from
the Present

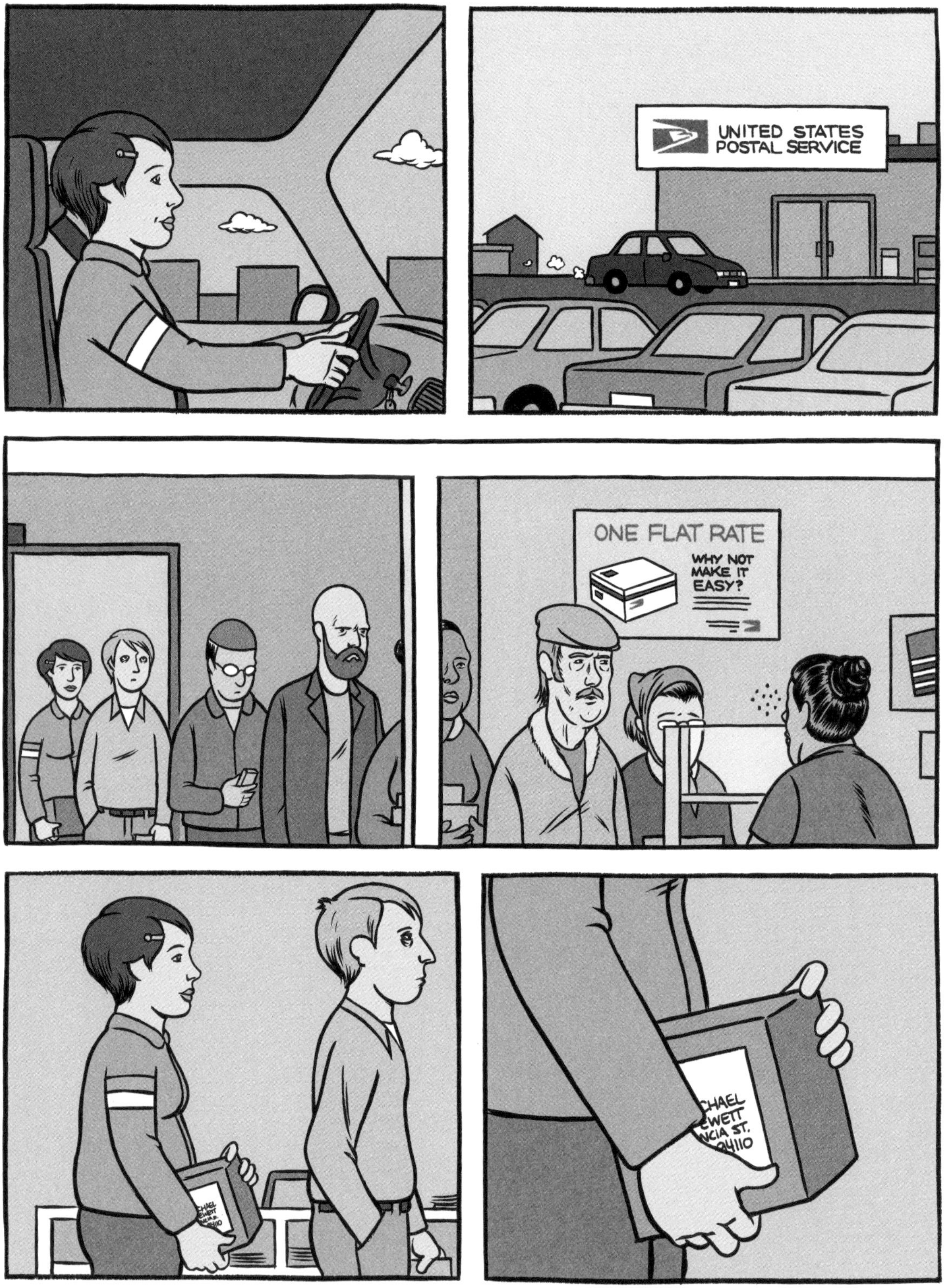
UNITED STATES
POSTAL SERVICE
ONE FLAT RATE
WHY NOT
MAKE IT
EASY?
CHAEL
EWETT
NCIA ST.
94110

13
Call Security

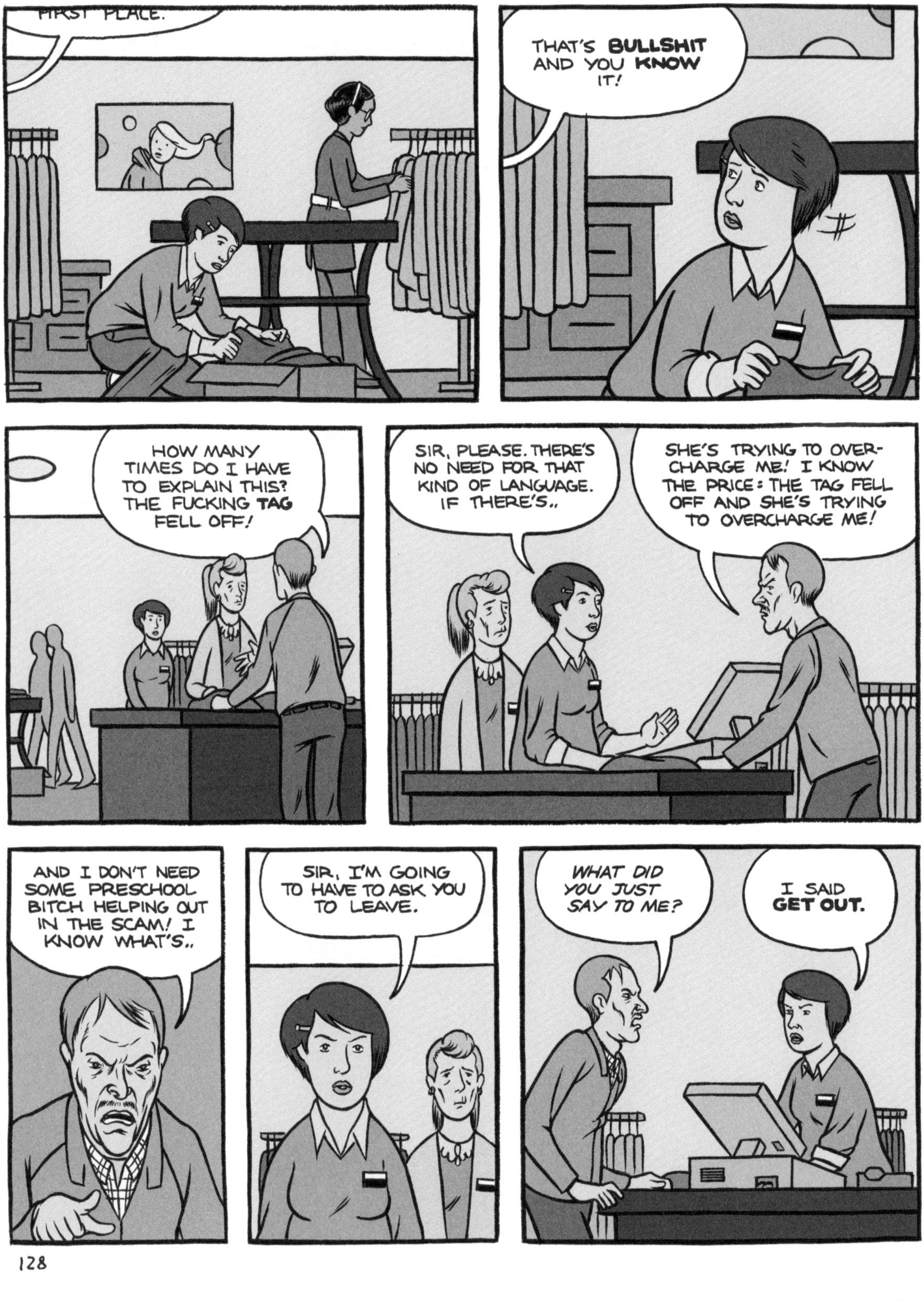
FIRST PLACE.
THAT'S **BULLSHIT** AND YOU **KNOW** IT!
HOW MANY TIMES DO I HAVE TO EXPLAIN THIS? THE FUCKING **TAG** FELL OFF!
SIR, PLEASE. THERE'S NO NEED FOR THAT KIND OF LANGUAGE. IF THERE'S..
SHE'S TRYING TO OVER-CHARGE ME! I KNOW THE PRICE: THE TAG FELL OFF AND SHE'S TRYING TO OVERCHARGE ME!
AND I DON'T NEED SOME PRESCHOOL BITCH HELPING OUT IN THE SCAM! I KNOW WHAT'S..
SIR, I'M GOING TO HAVE TO ASK YOU TO LEAVE.
WHAT DID YOU JUST SAY TO ME?
I SAID **GET OUT.**

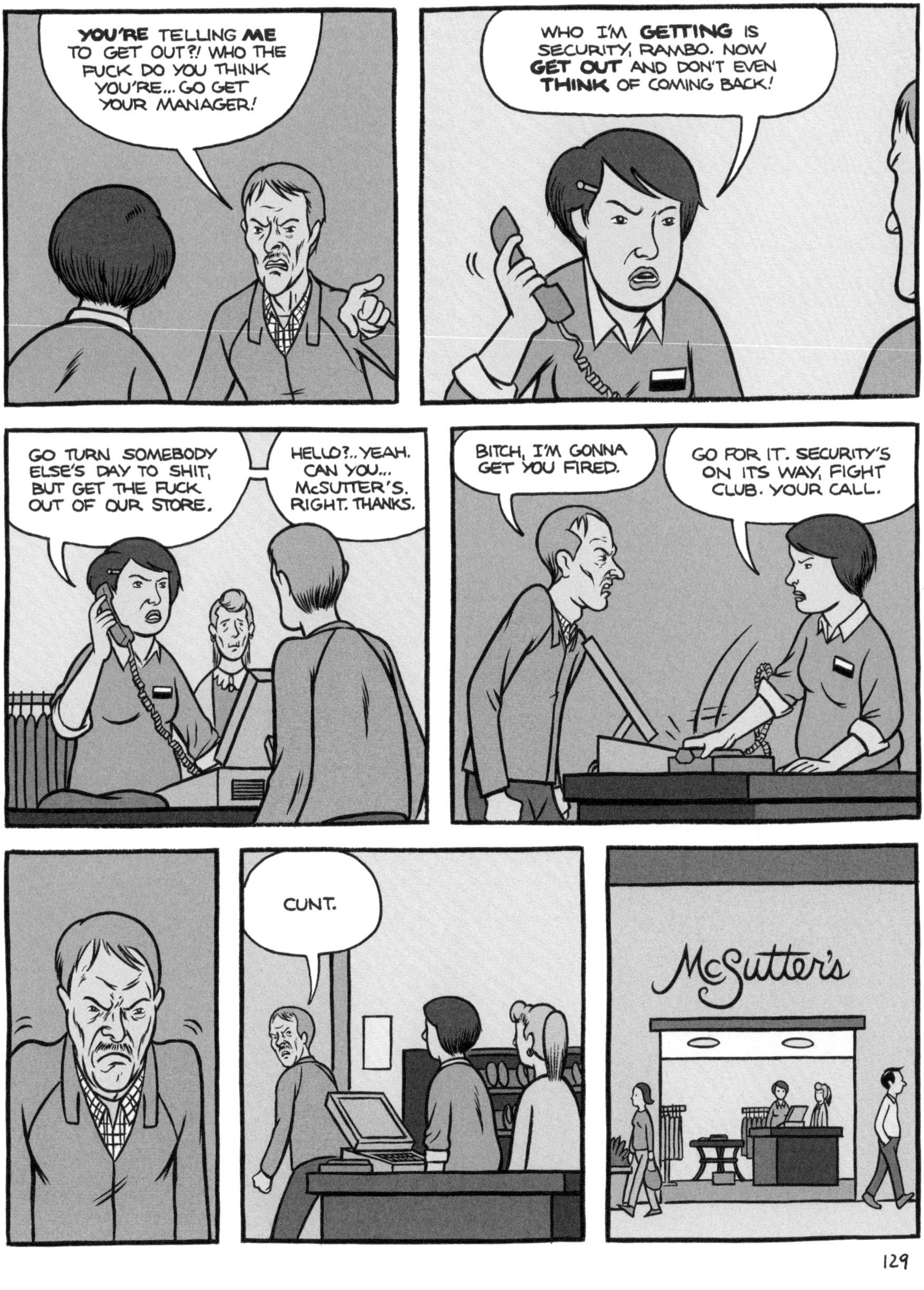
YOU'RE TELLING ME TO GET OUT?! WHO THE FUCK DO YOU THINK YOU'RE... GO GET YOUR MANAGER!
WHO I'M GETTING IS SECURITY, RAMBO. NOW GET OUT AND DON'T EVEN THINK OF COMING BACK!
GO TURN SOMEBODY ELSE'S DAY TO SHIT, BUT GET THE FUCK OUT OF OUR STORE.
HELLO?.. YEAH. CAN YOU... McSUTTER'S. RIGHT. THANKS.
BITCH, I'M GONNA GET YOU FIRED.
GO FOR IT. SECURITY'S ON ITS WAY, FIGHT CLUB. YOUR CALL.
CUNT.
McSutter's

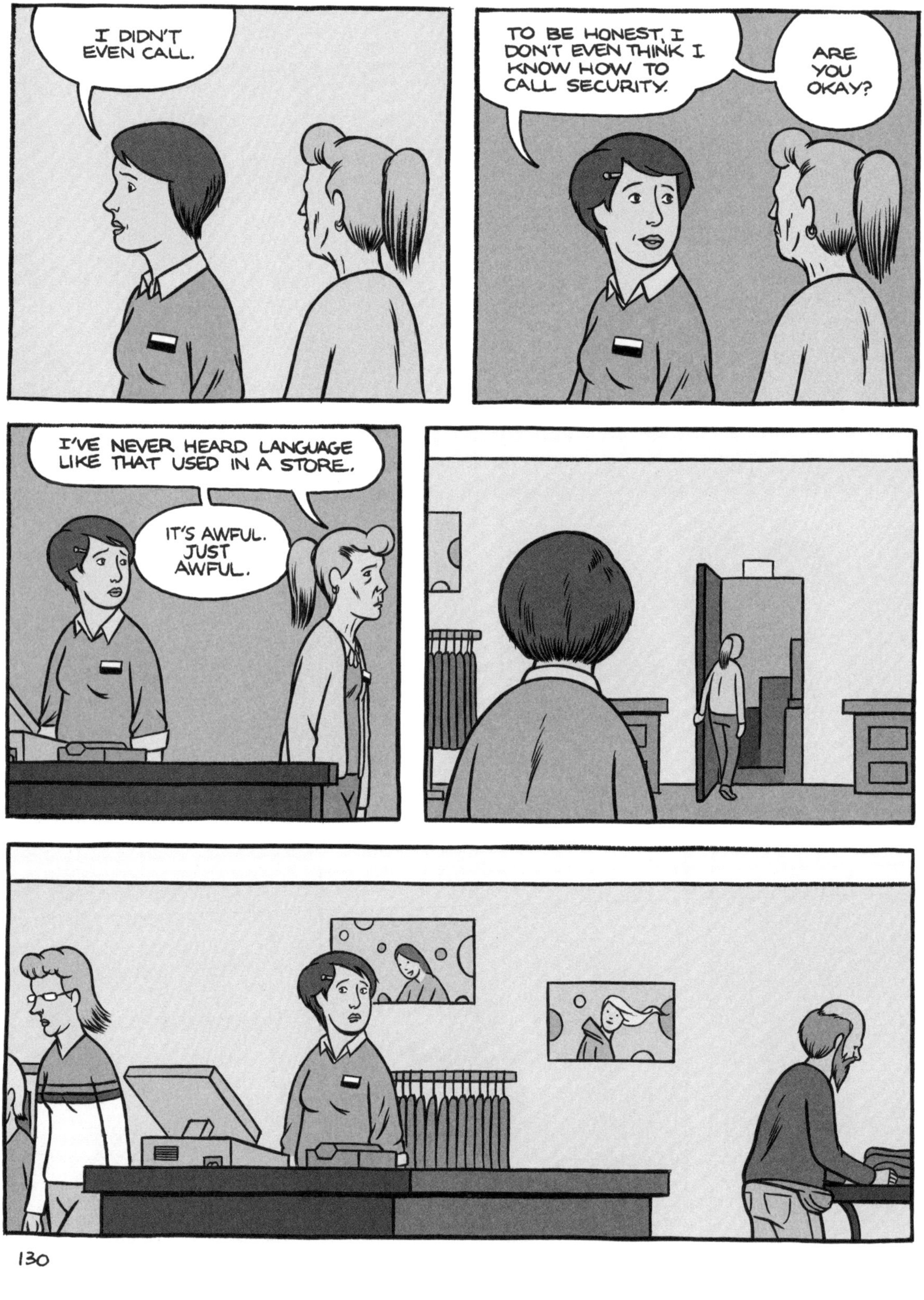
I DIDN'T EVEN CALL.
TO BE HONEST, I DON'T EVEN THINK I KNOW HOW TO CALL SECURITY.
ARE YOU OKAY?
I'VE NEVER HEARD LANGUAGE LIKE THAT USED IN A STORE.
IT'S AWFUL. JUST AWFUL.

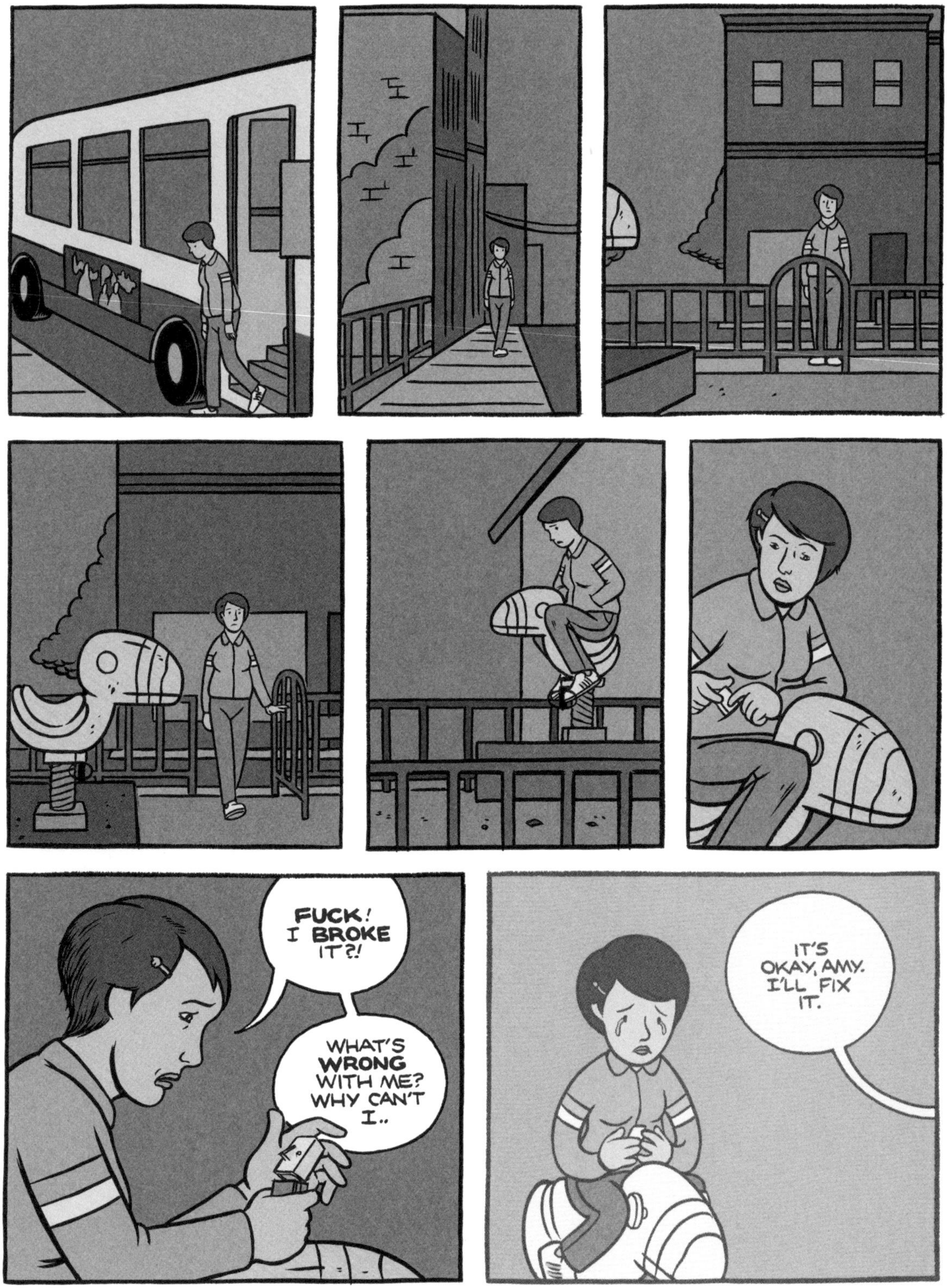
FUCK! I BROKE IT?!
WHAT'S WRONG WITH ME? WHY CAN'T I..
IT'S OKAY, AMY. I'LL FIX IT.

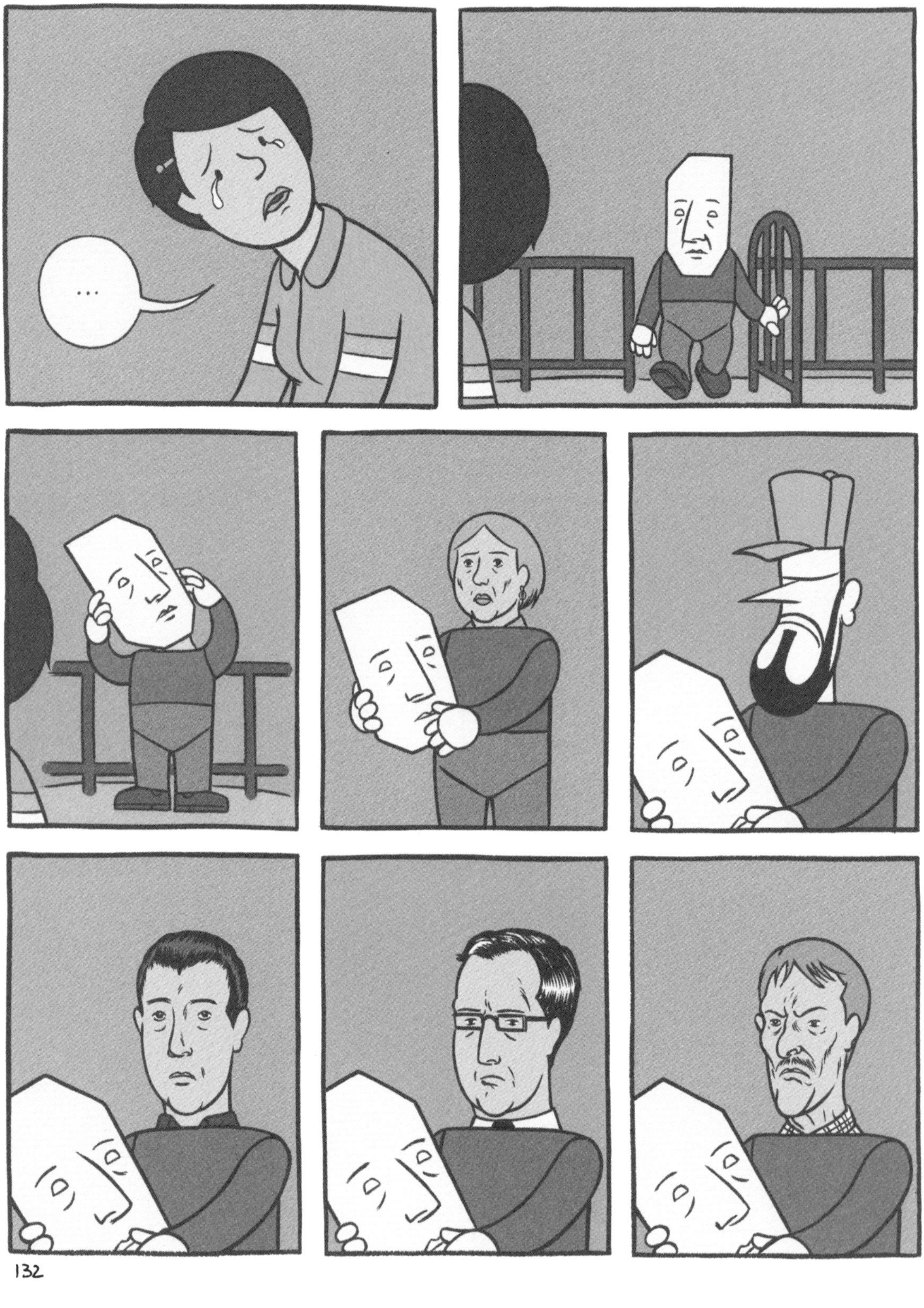
...

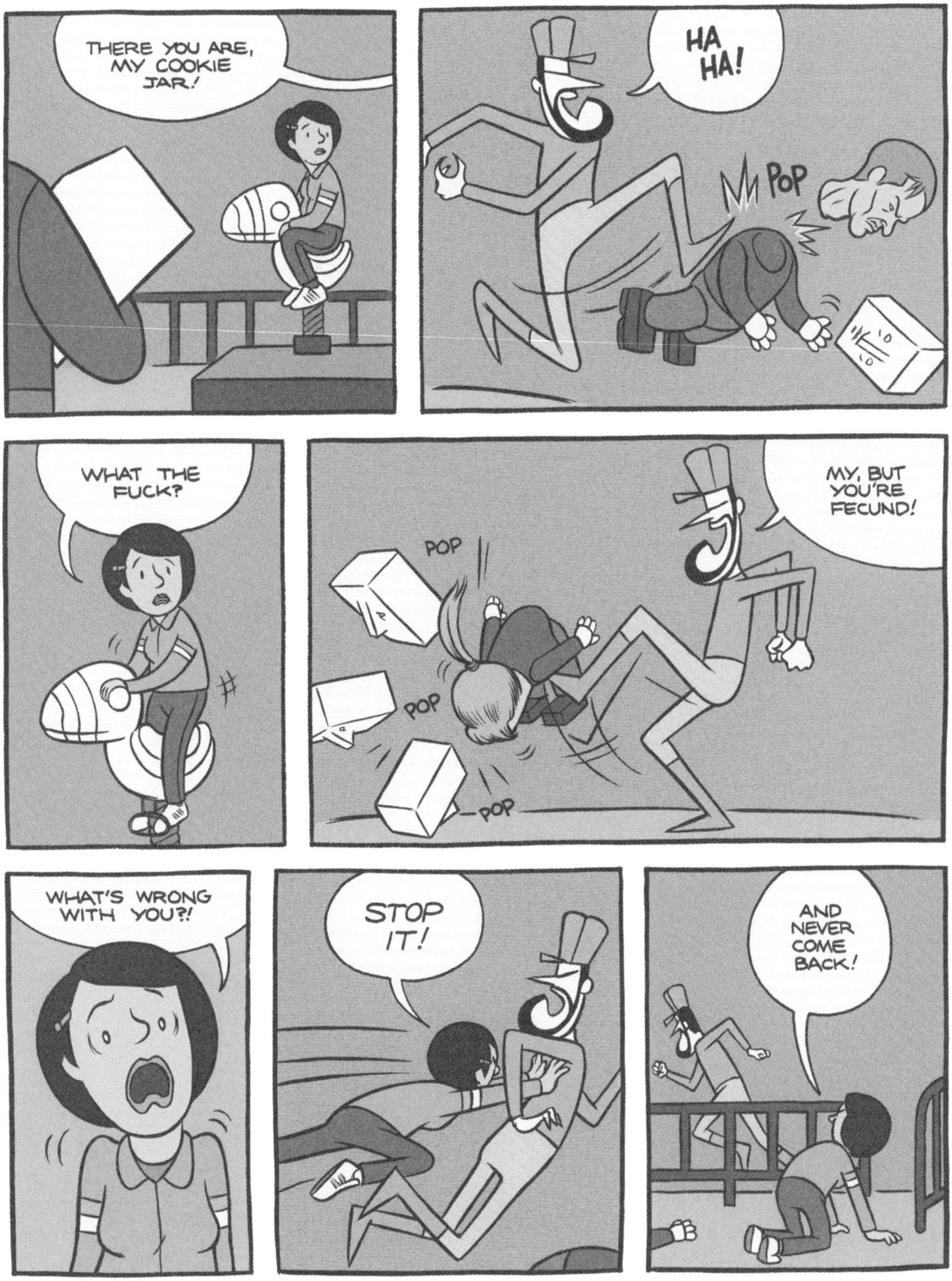
THERE YOU ARE, MY COOKIE JAR!
HA HA!
POP
WHAT THE FUCK?
MY, BUT YOU'RE FECUND!
POP
POP
POP
WHAT'S WRONG WITH YOU?!
STOP IT!
AND NEVER COME BACK!

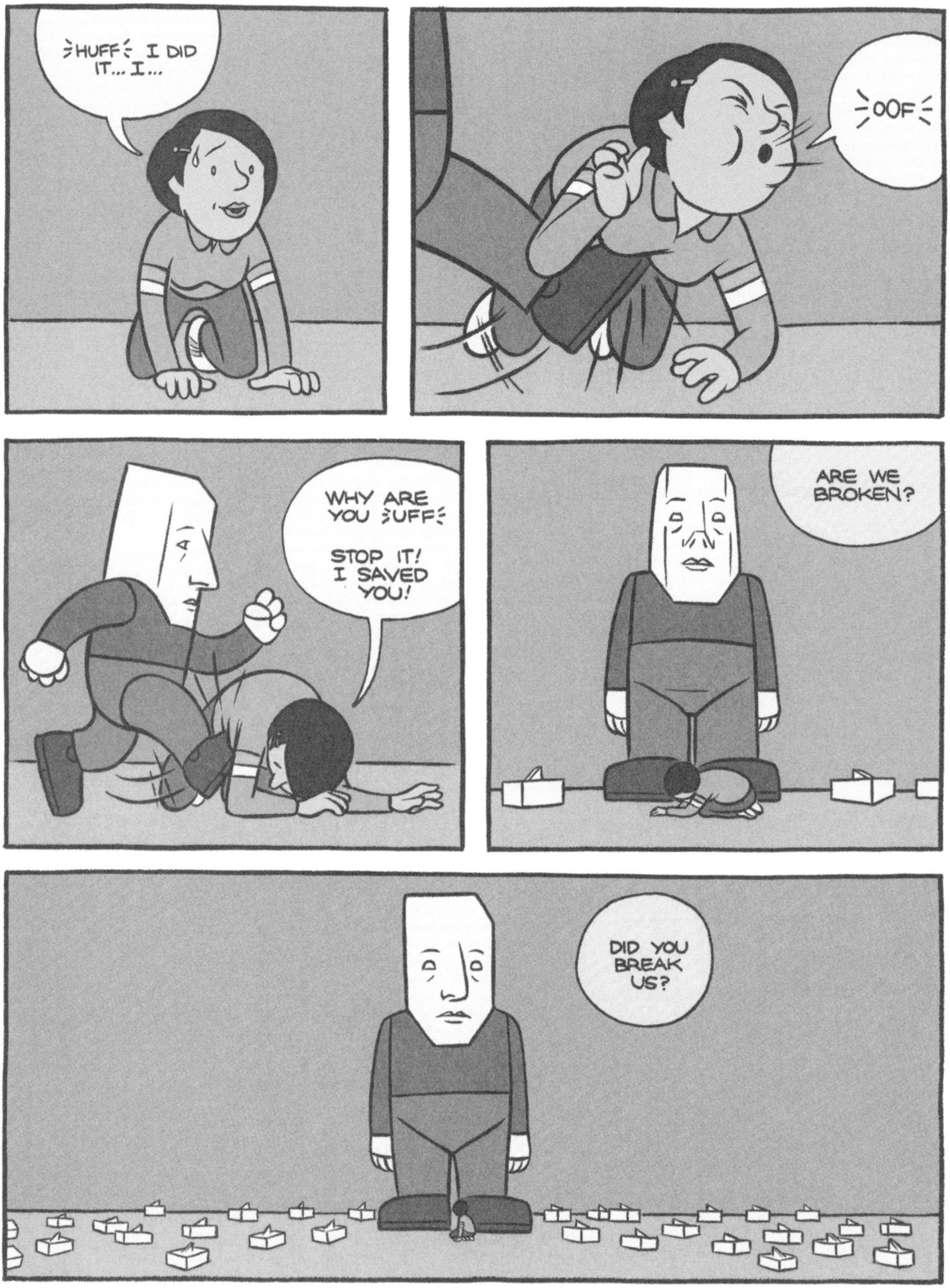
HUFF I DID IT... I...
OOF
WHY ARE YOU UFF
STOP IT! I SAVED YOU!
ARE WE BROKEN?
DID YOU BREAK US?

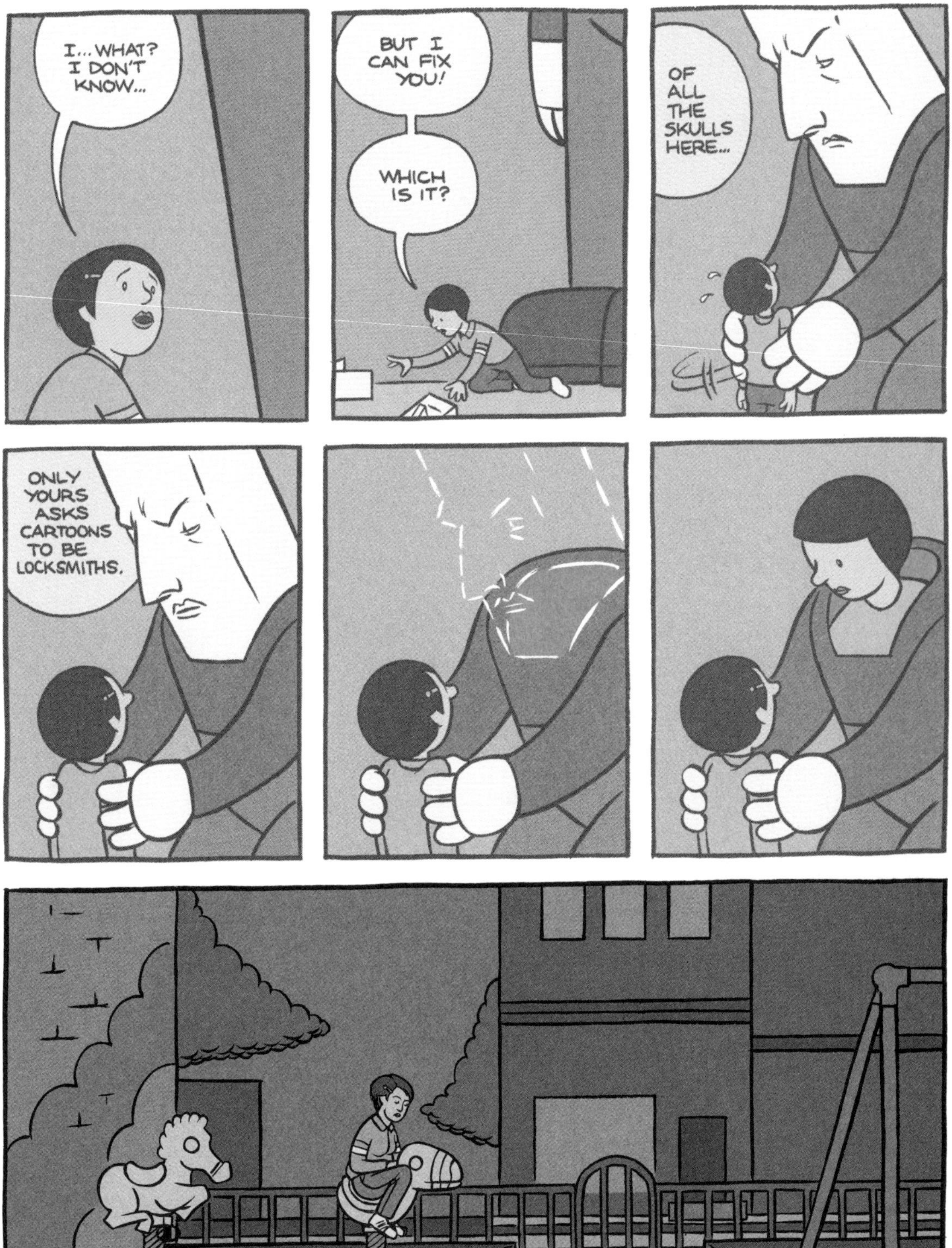
I... WHAT? I DON'T KNOW...
BUT I CAN FIX YOU!
WHICH IS IT?
OF ALL THE SKULLS HERE...
ONLY YOURS ASKS CARTOONS TO BE LOCKSMITHS.

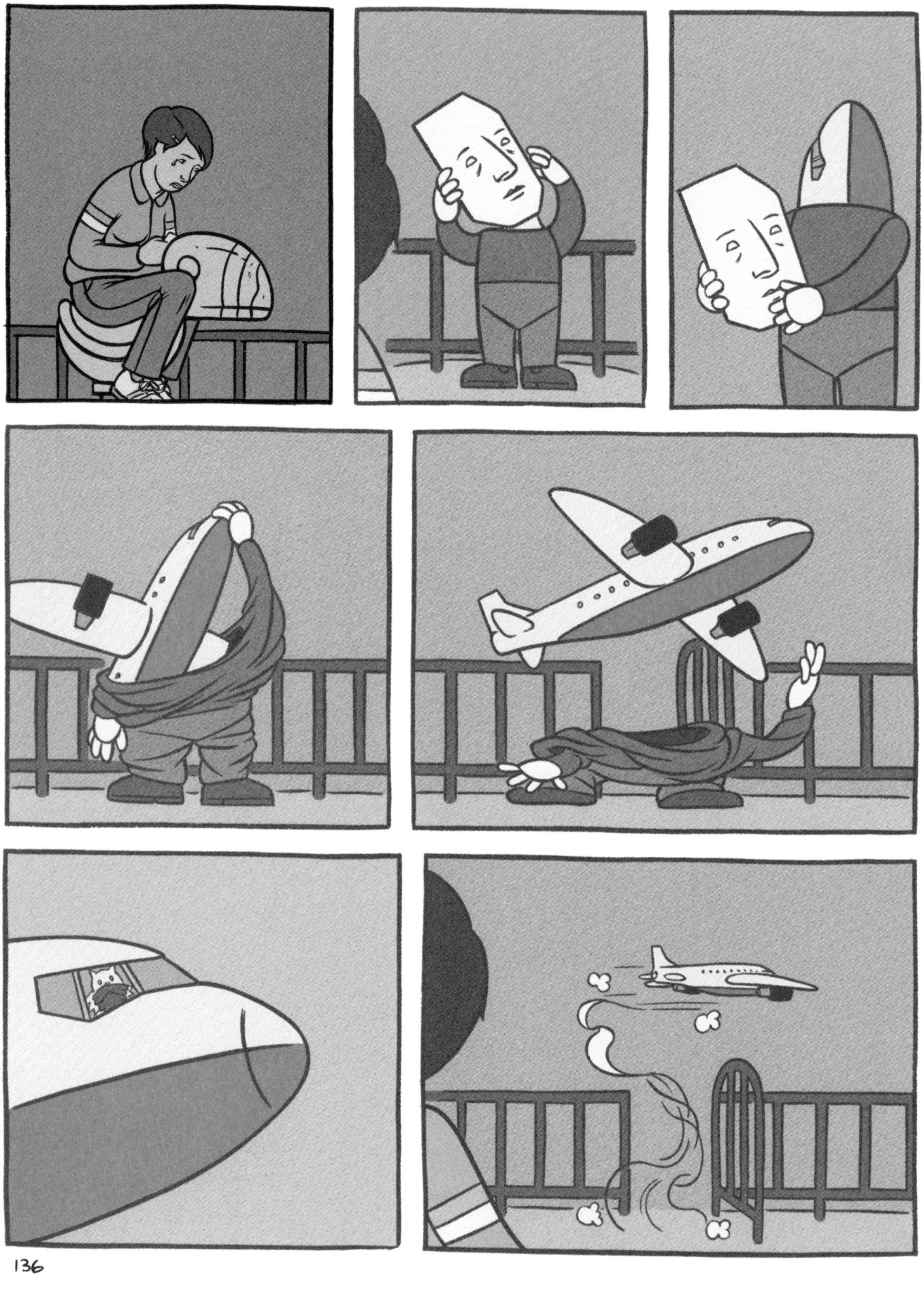

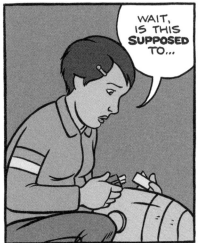

WAIT, IS THIS **SUPPOSED** TO...

Whatever it is, it's always better figuring it out with you.
I miss you, Amy.
Happy birthday.

With all my love,
Michael

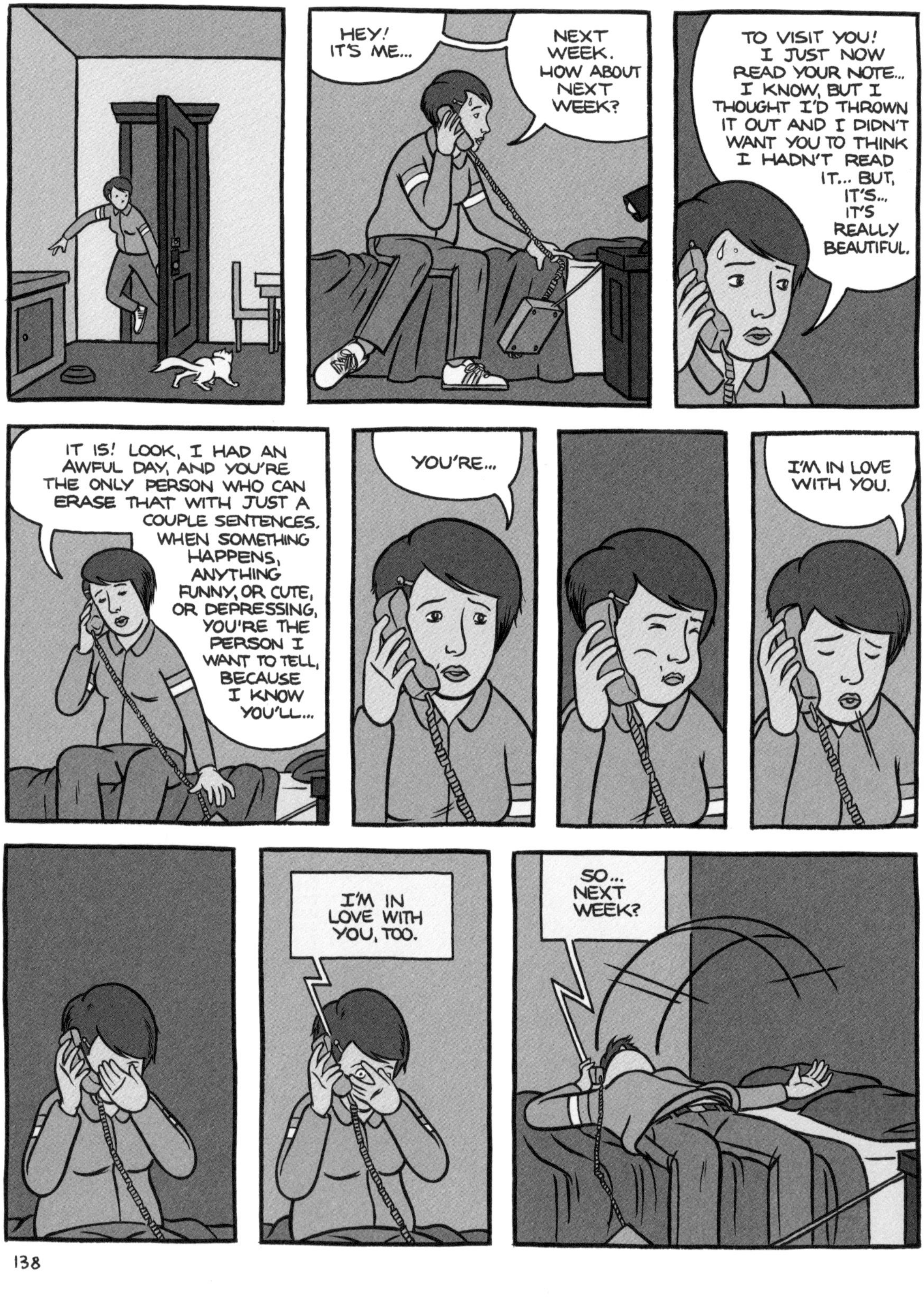
HEY! IT'S ME...
NEXT WEEK. HOW ABOUT NEXT WEEK?
TO VISIT YOU! I JUST NOW READ YOUR NOTE... I KNOW, BUT I THOUGHT I'D THROWN IT OUT AND I DIDN'T WANT YOU TO THINK I HADN'T READ IT... BUT, IT'S... IT'S REALLY BEAUTIFUL.
IT IS! LOOK, I HAD AN AWFUL DAY, AND YOU'RE THE ONLY PERSON WHO CAN ERASE THAT WITH JUST A COUPLE SENTENCES. WHEN SOMETHING HAPPENS, ANYTHING FUNNY, OR CUTE, OR DEPRESSING, YOU'RE THE PERSON I WANT TO TELL, BECAUSE I KNOW YOU'LL...
YOU'RE...
I'M IN LOVE WITH YOU.
I'M IN LOVE WITH YOU, TOO.
SO... NEXT WEEK?

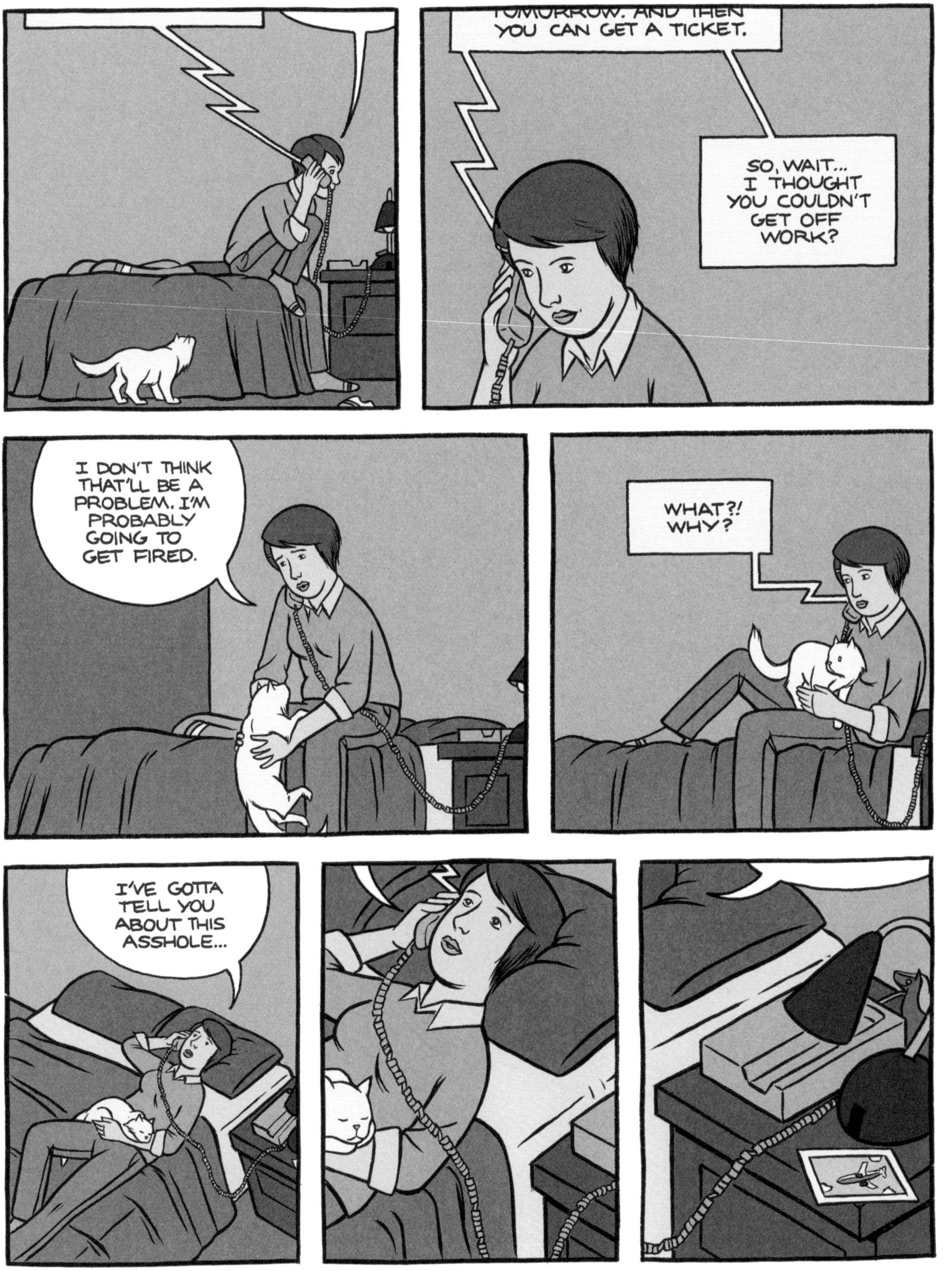
YOU CAN GET A TICKET.
SO, WAIT... I THOUGHT YOU COULDN'T GET OFF WORK?
I DON'T THINK THAT'LL BE A PROBLEM. I'M PROBABLY GOING TO GET FIRED.
WHAT?! WHY?
I'VE GOTTA TELL YOU ABOUT THIS ASSHOLE...

14
The I in Team

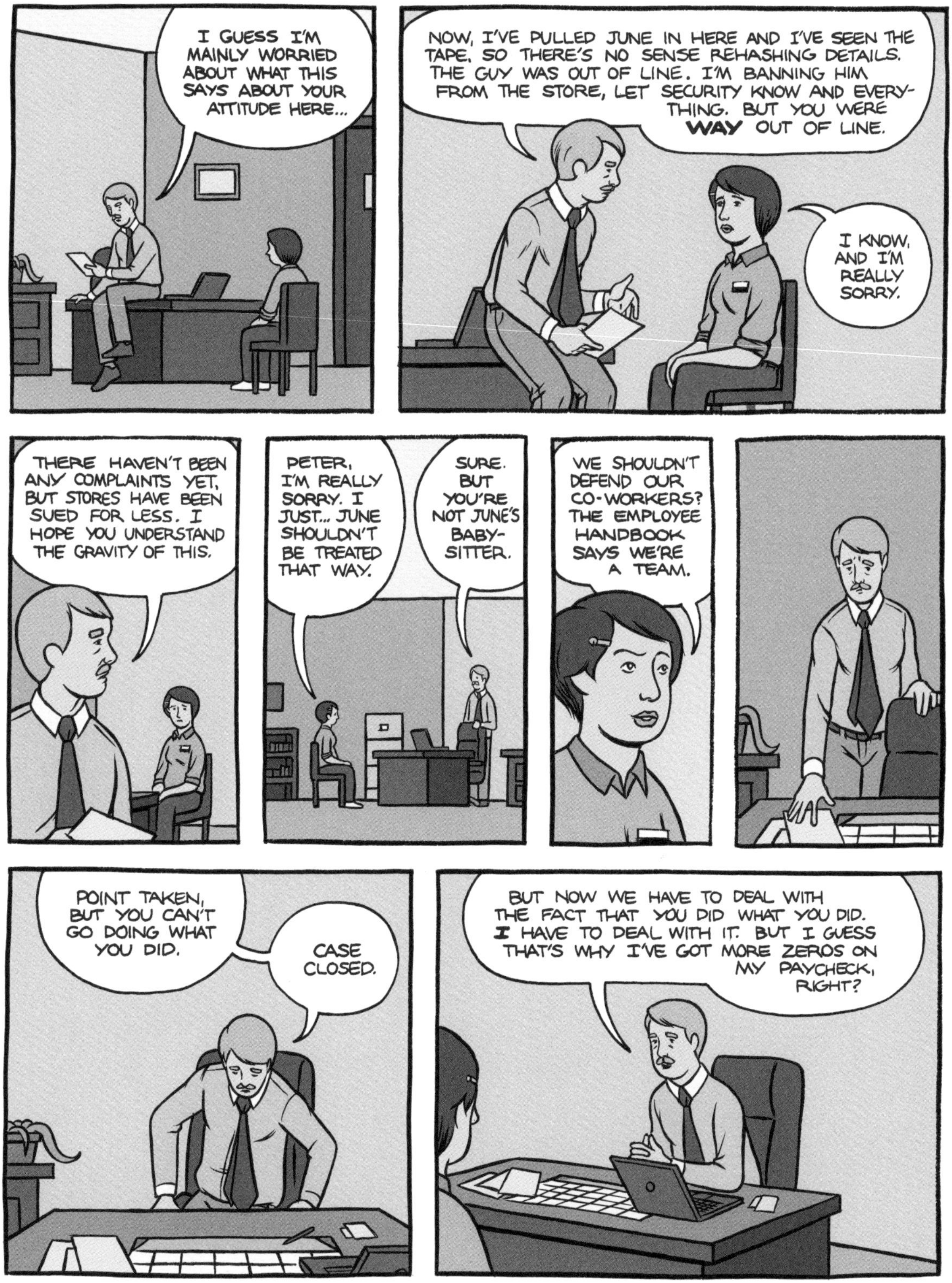
I GUESS I'M MAINLY WORRIED ABOUT WHAT THIS SAYS ABOUT YOUR ATTITUDE HERE...
NOW, I'VE PULLED JUNE IN HERE AND I'VE SEEN THE TAPE, SO THERE'S NO SENSE REHASHING DETAILS. THE GUY WAS OUT OF LINE. I'M BANNING HIM FROM THE STORE, LET SECURITY KNOW AND EVERYTHING. BUT YOU WERE **WAY** OUT OF LINE.
I KNOW, AND I'M REALLY SORRY.
THERE HAVEN'T BEEN ANY COMPLAINTS YET, BUT STORES HAVE BEEN SUED FOR LESS. I HOPE YOU UNDERSTAND THE GRAVITY OF THIS.
PETER, I'M REALLY SORRY. I JUST... JUNE SHOULDN'T BE TREATED THAT WAY.
SURE. BUT YOU'RE NOT JUNE'S BABY-SITTER.
WE SHOULDN'T DEFEND OUR CO-WORKERS? THE EMPLOYEE HANDBOOK SAYS WE'RE A TEAM.
POINT TAKEN, BUT YOU CAN'T GO DOING WHAT YOU DID.
CASE CLOSED.
BUT NOW WE HAVE TO DEAL WITH THE FACT THAT YOU DID WHAT YOU DID. **I** HAVE TO DEAL WITH IT. BUT I GUESS THAT'S WHY I'VE GOT MORE ZEROS ON MY PAYCHECK, RIGHT?

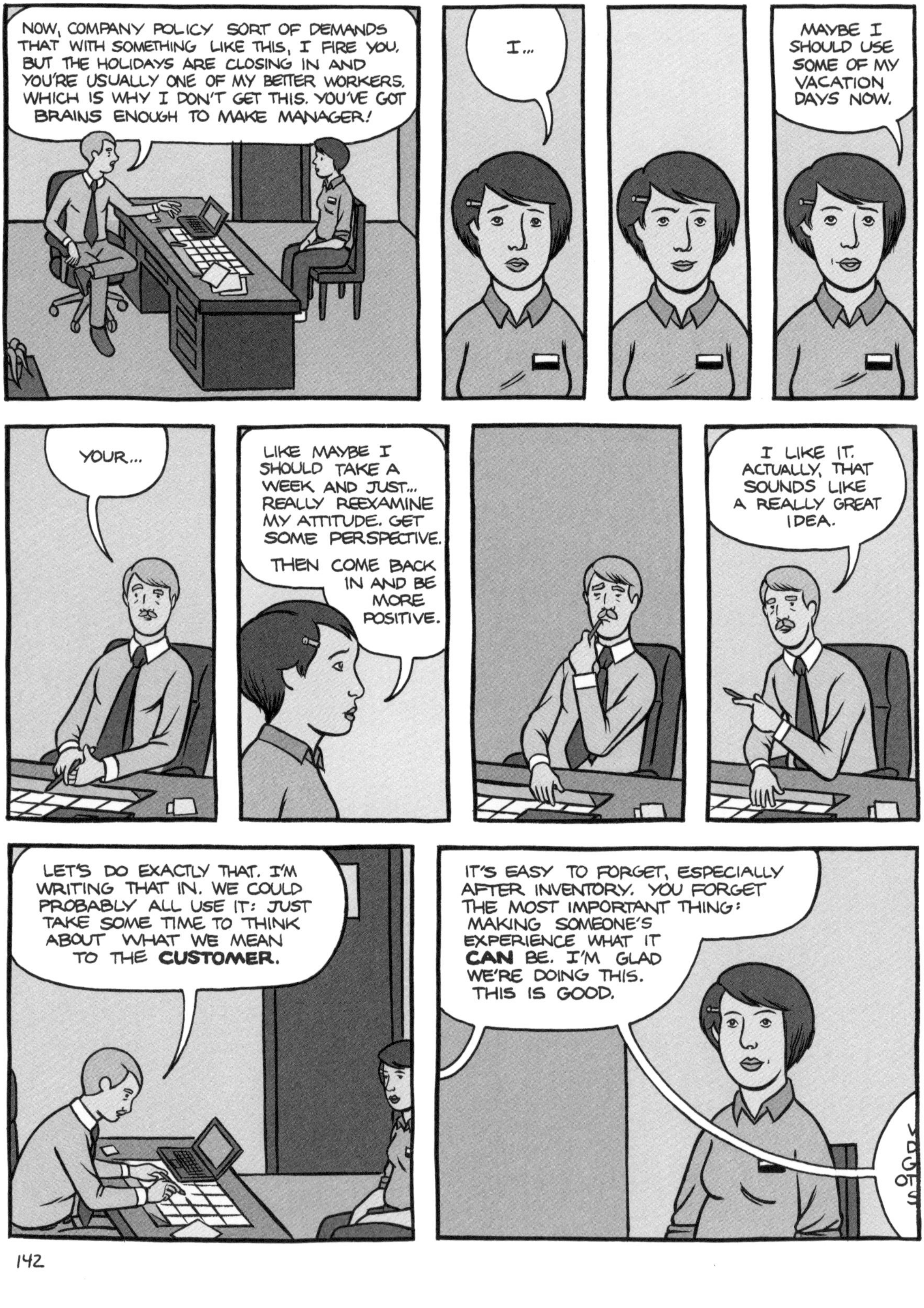
NOW, COMPANY POLICY SORT OF DEMANDS THAT WITH SOMETHING LIKE THIS, I FIRE YOU. BUT THE HOLIDAYS ARE CLOSING IN AND YOU'RE USUALLY ONE OF MY BETTER WORKERS. WHICH IS WHY I DON'T GET THIS. YOU'VE GOT BRAINS ENOUGH TO MAKE MANAGER!
I...
MAYBE I SHOULD USE SOME OF MY VACATION DAYS NOW.
YOUR...
LIKE MAYBE I SHOULD TAKE A WEEK AND JUST... REALLY REEXAMINE MY ATTITUDE. GET SOME PERSPECTIVE.
THEN COME BACK IN AND BE MORE POSITIVE.
I LIKE IT. ACTUALLY, THAT SOUNDS LIKE A REALLY GREAT IDEA.
LET'S DO EXACTLY THAT. I'M WRITING THAT IN. WE COULD PROBABLY ALL USE IT: JUST TAKE SOME TIME TO THINK ABOUT WHAT WE MEAN TO THE **CUSTOMER**.
IT'S EASY TO FORGET, ESPECIALLY AFTER INVENTORY. YOU FORGET THE MOST IMPORTANT THING: MAKING SOMEONE'S EXPERIENCE WHAT IT **CAN** BE. I'M GLAD WE'RE DOING THIS. THIS IS GOOD.

15
Essential Items

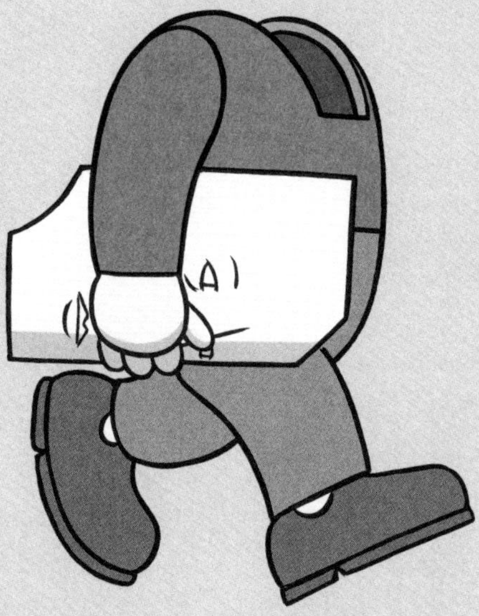

(A)
(B

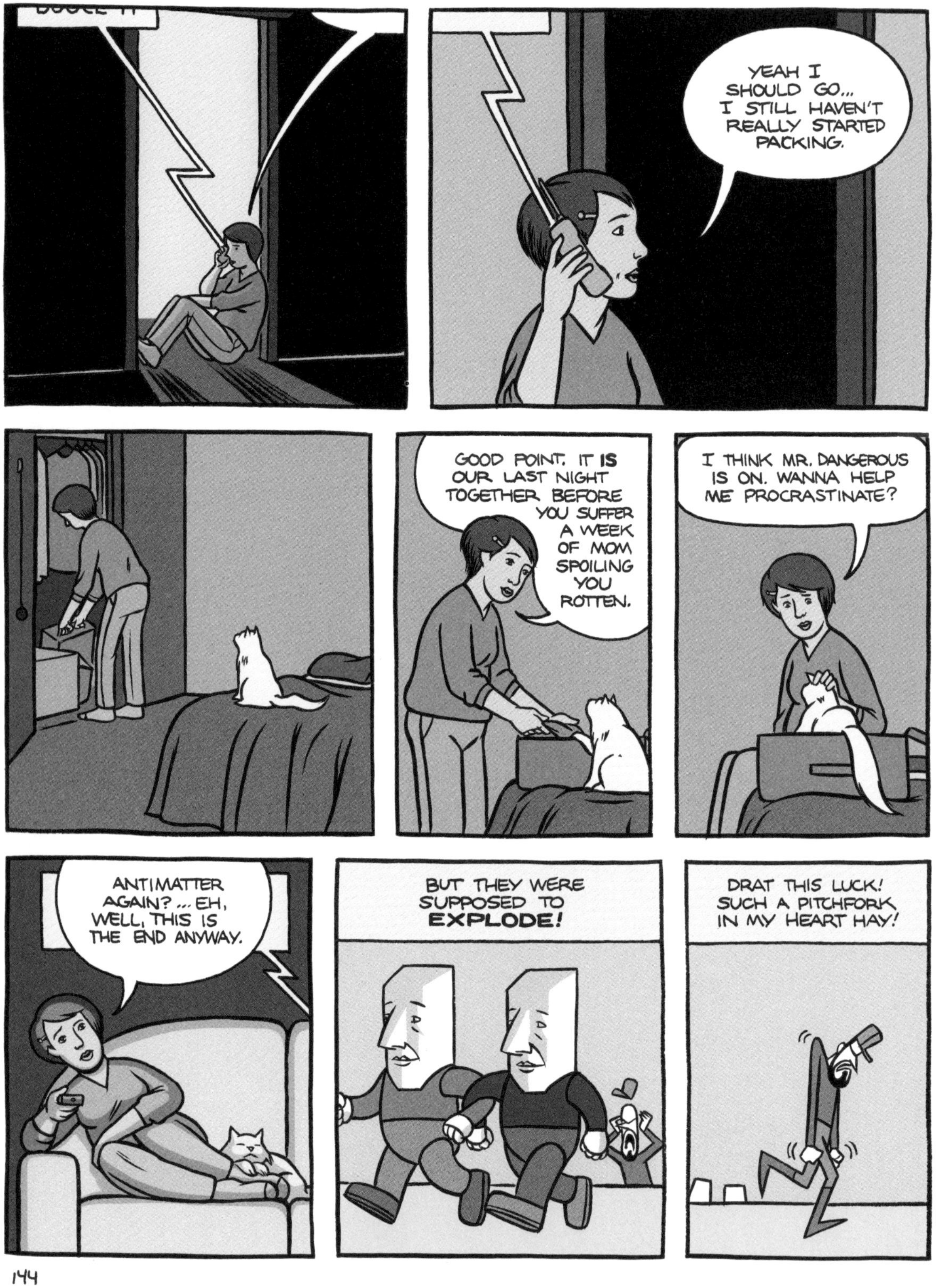
YEAH I SHOULD GO... I STILL HAVEN'T REALLY STARTED PACKING.
GOOD POINT. IT IS OUR LAST NIGHT TOGETHER BEFORE YOU SUFFER A WEEK OF MOM SPOILING YOU ROTTEN.
I THINK MR. DANGEROUS IS ON. WANNA HELP ME PROCRASTINATE?
ANTIMATTER AGAIN? ... EH, WELL, THIS IS THE END ANYWAY.
BUT THEY WERE SUPPOSED TO EXPLODE!
DRAT THIS LUCK! SUCH A PITCHFORK IN MY HEART HAY!

HUH. MAYBE I'VE NEVER EVEN SEEN THE END... I'VE TURNED THIS OFF SO MANY TIMES, I FORGET THIS PART.

YOU'RE MUTE, AREN'T YOU?

AND US BEING OPPOSITES, I SUPPOSE THAT MEANS I CAN TALK.

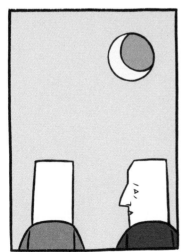

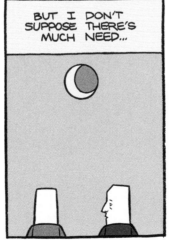

BUT I DON'T SUPPOSE THERE'S MUCH NEED...

.EMORDNILAP A ERA ENIM DNA STHGUOHT RUOY

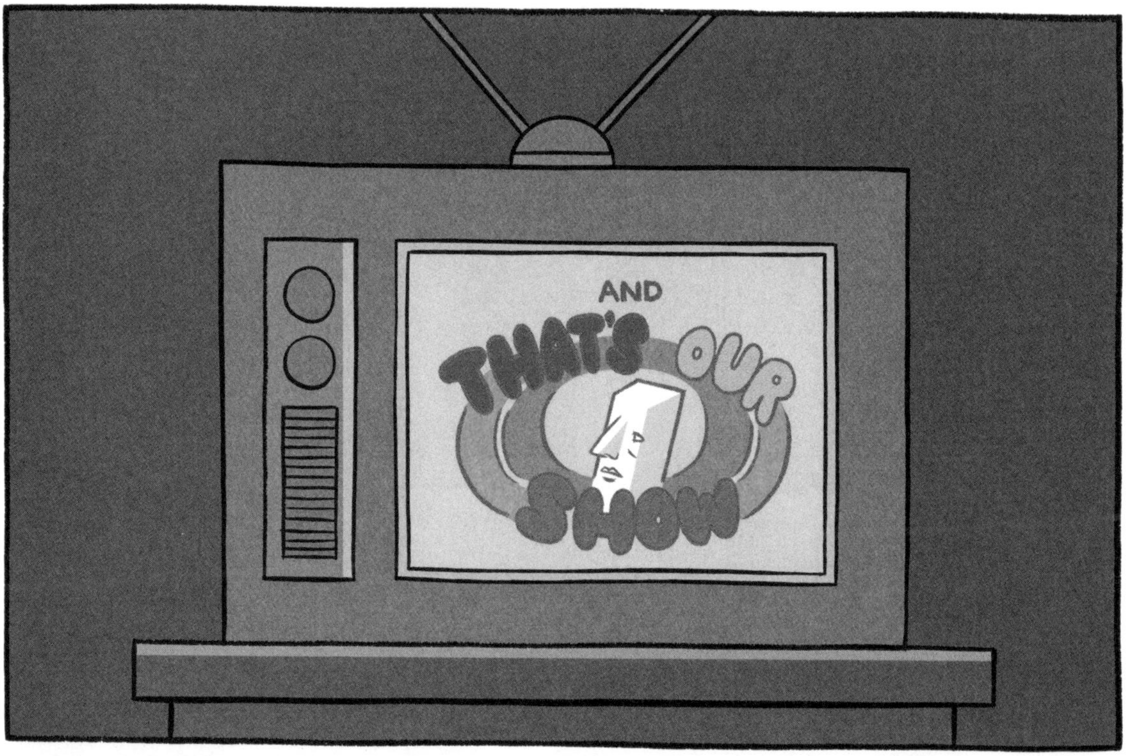
AND
THAT'S OUR SHOW
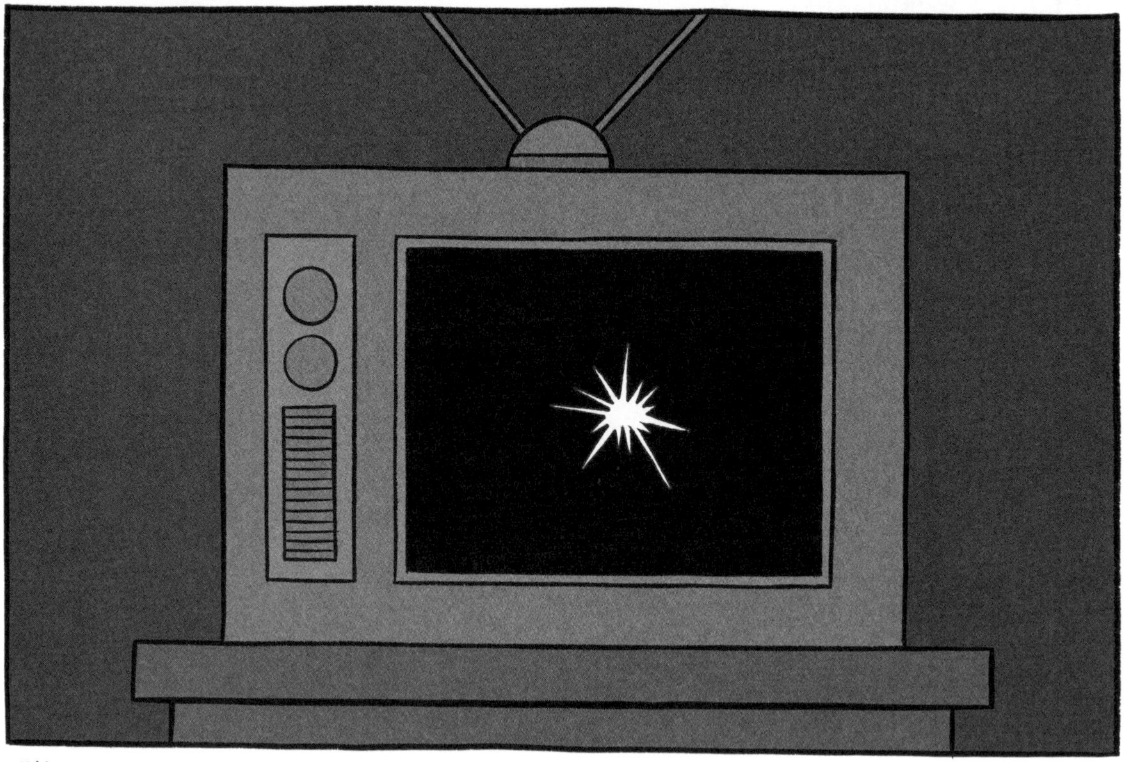

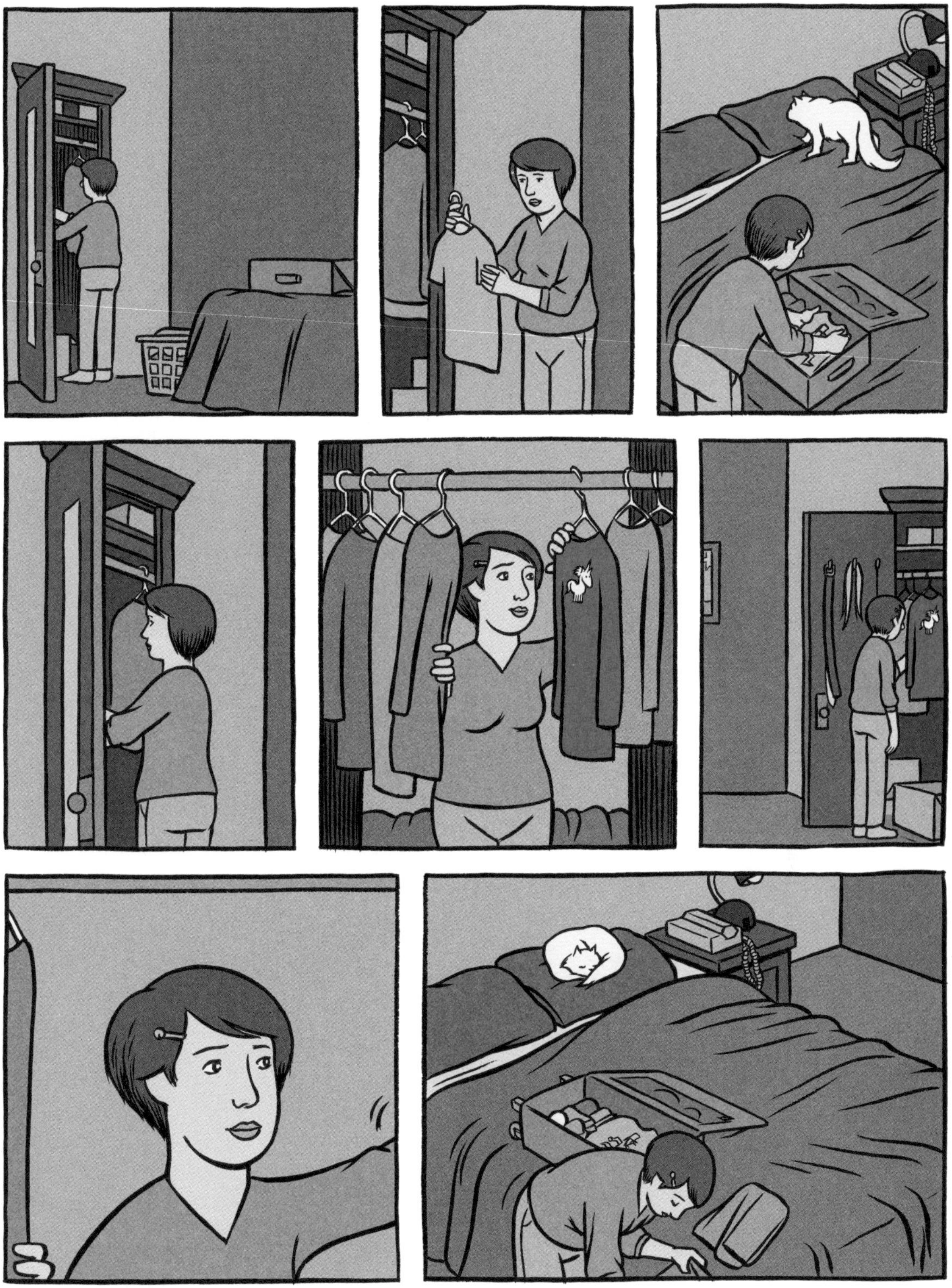

16
The New Adventures
of Smiley Trotter

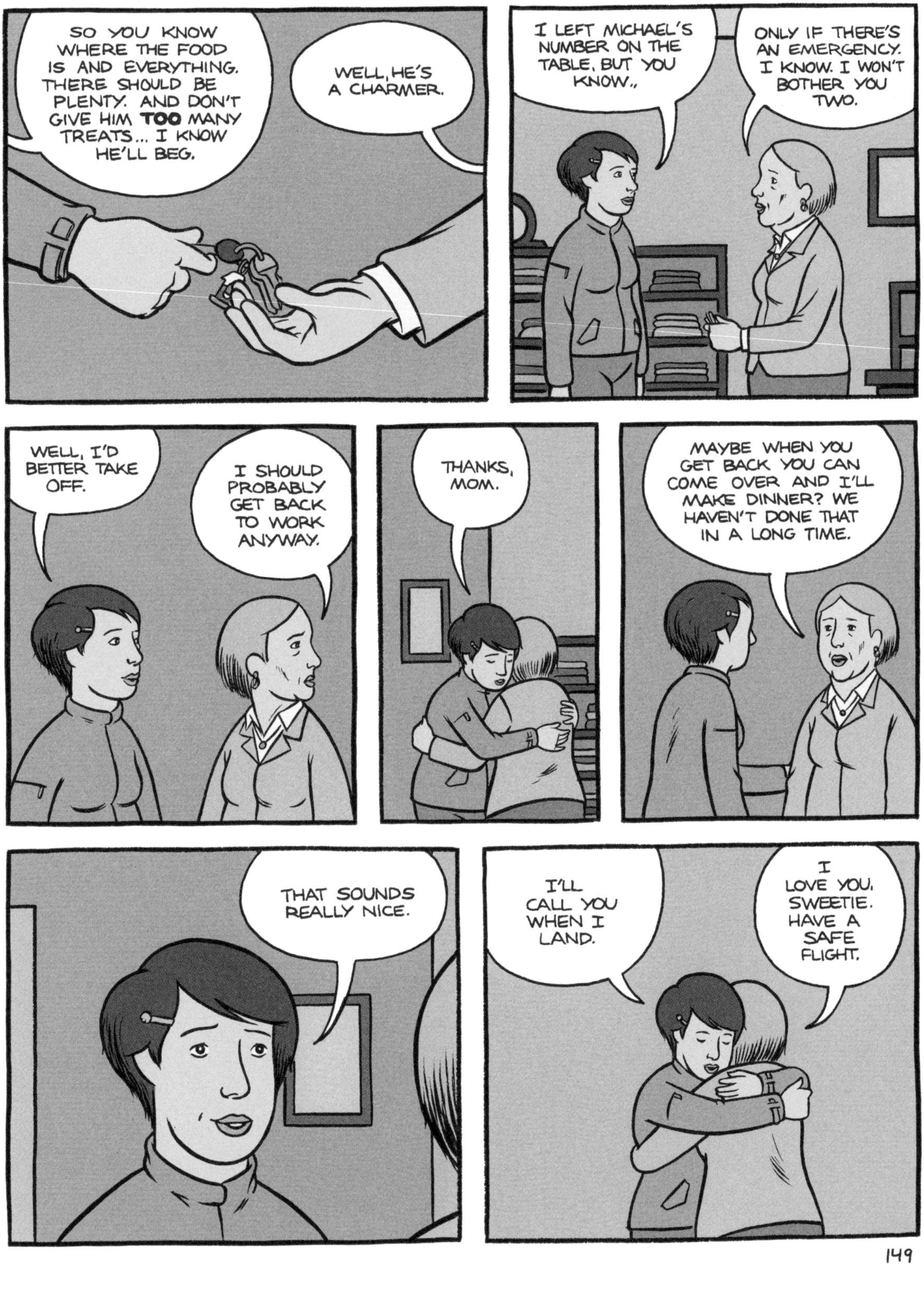
SO YOU KNOW WHERE THE FOOD IS AND EVERYTHING. THERE SHOULD BE PLENTY. AND DON'T GIVE HIM **TOO** MANY TREATS... I KNOW HE'LL BEG.
WELL, HE'S A CHARMER.
I LEFT MICHAEL'S NUMBER ON THE TABLE, BUT YOU KNOW..
ONLY IF THERE'S AN EMERGENCY. I KNOW. I WON'T BOTHER YOU TWO.
WELL, I'D BETTER TAKE OFF.
I SHOULD PROBABLY GET BACK TO WORK ANYWAY.
THANKS, MOM.
MAYBE WHEN YOU GET BACK YOU CAN COME OVER AND I'LL MAKE DINNER? WE HAVEN'T DONE THAT IN A LONG TIME.
THAT SOUNDS REALLY NICE.
I'LL CALL YOU WHEN I LAND.
I LOVE YOU, SWEETIE. HAVE A SAFE FLIGHT.

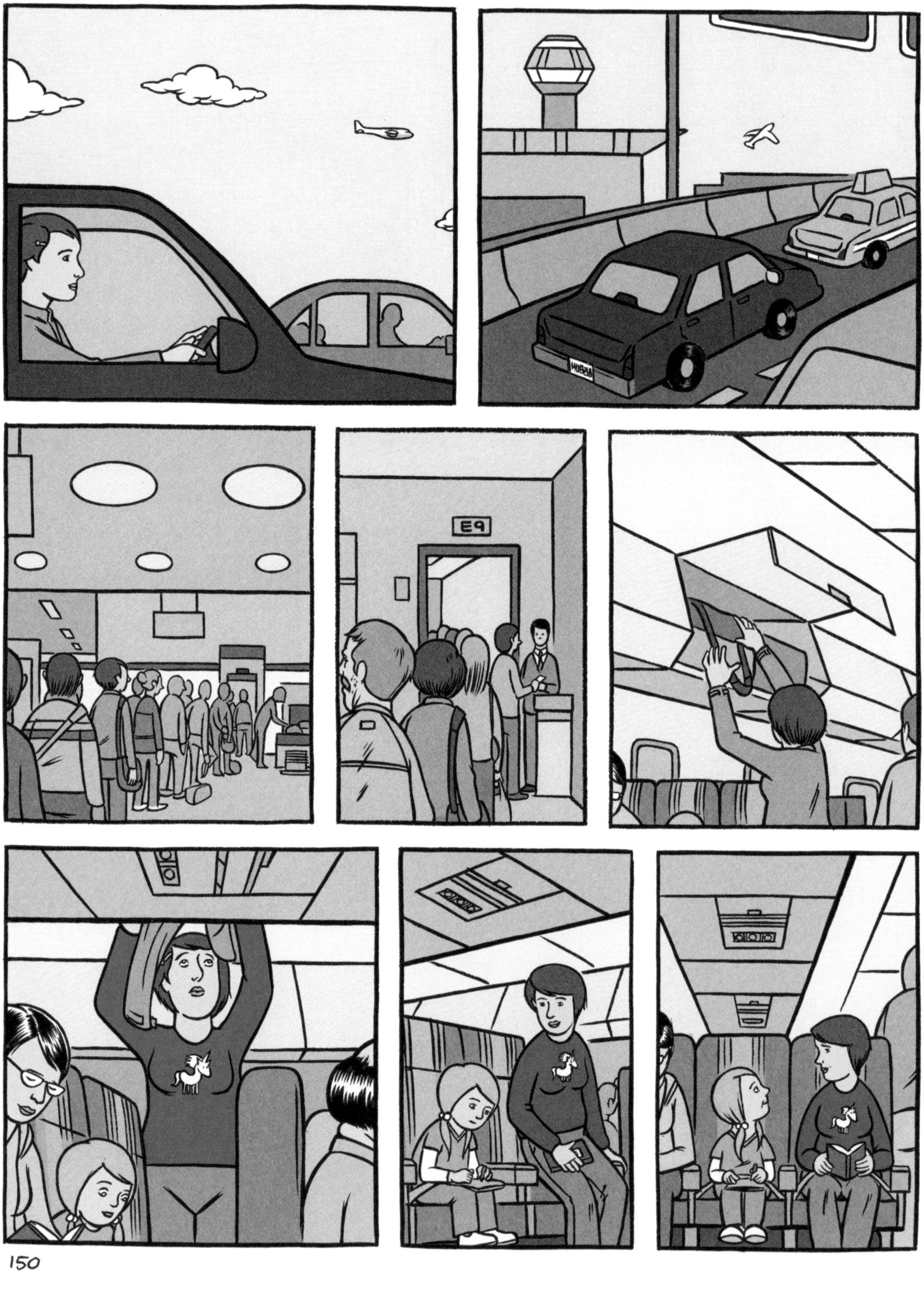
E9

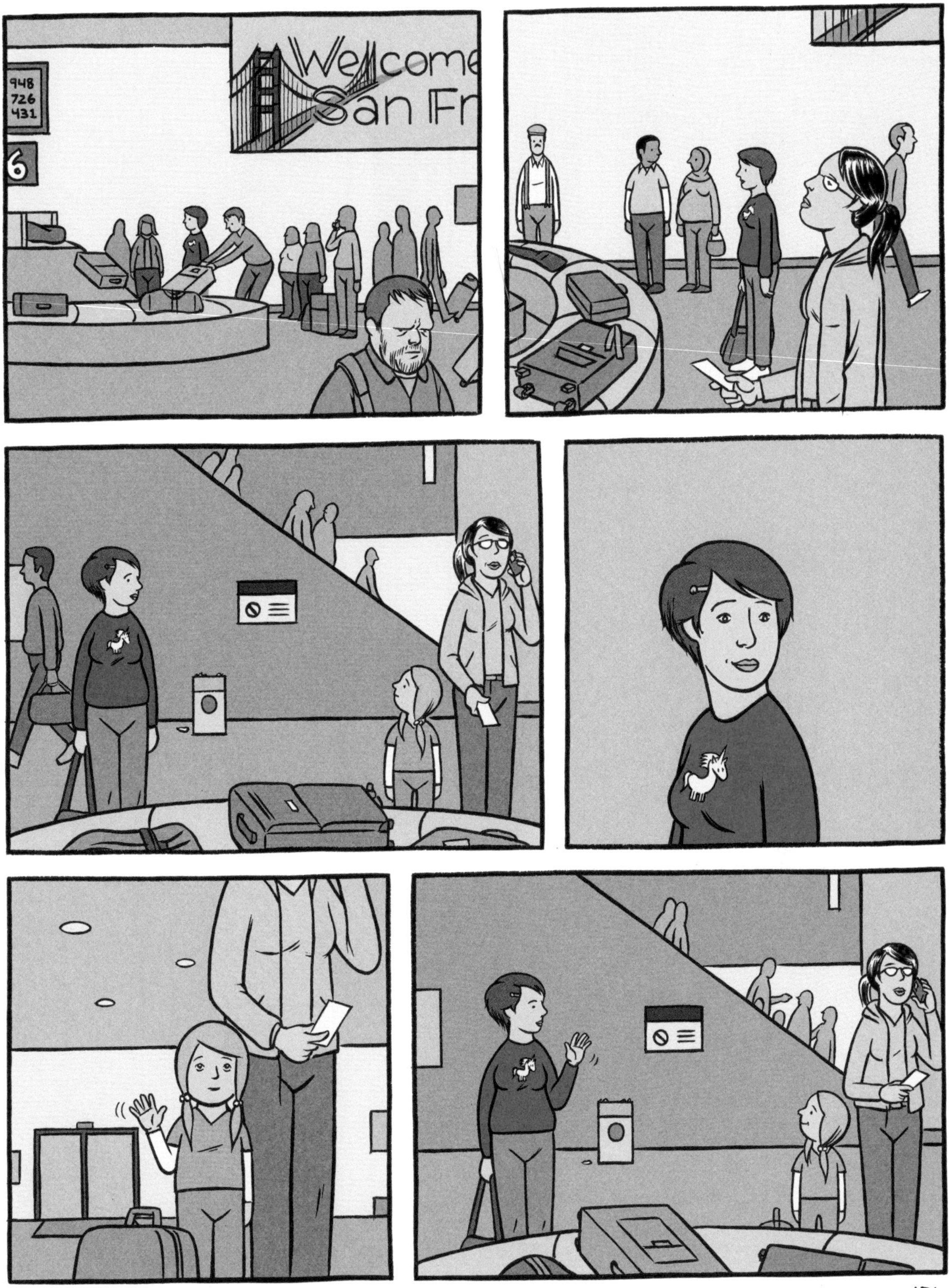
948
726
431
6
Welcome
San Fr

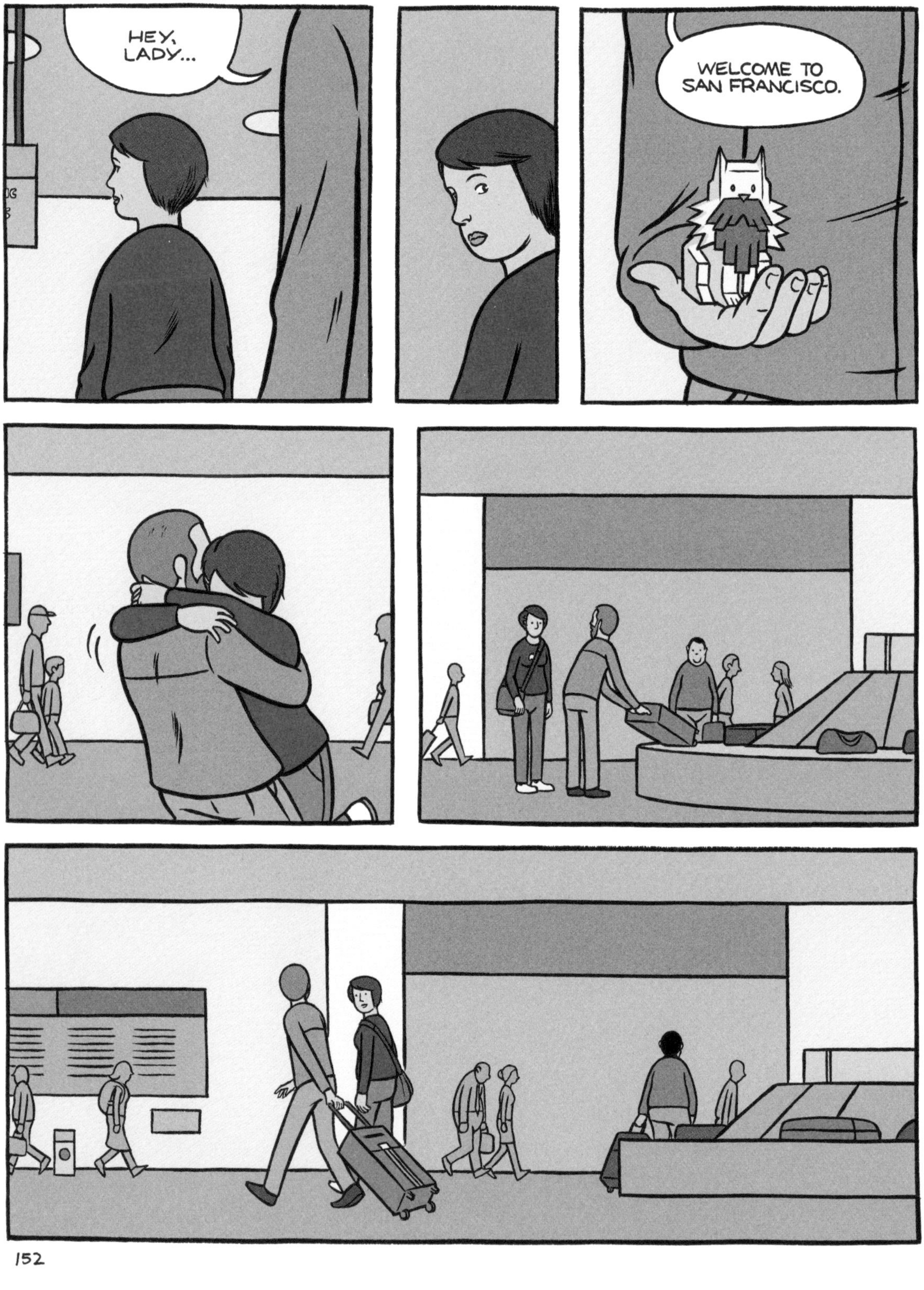
HEY, LADY...
WELCOME TO SAN FRANCISCO.

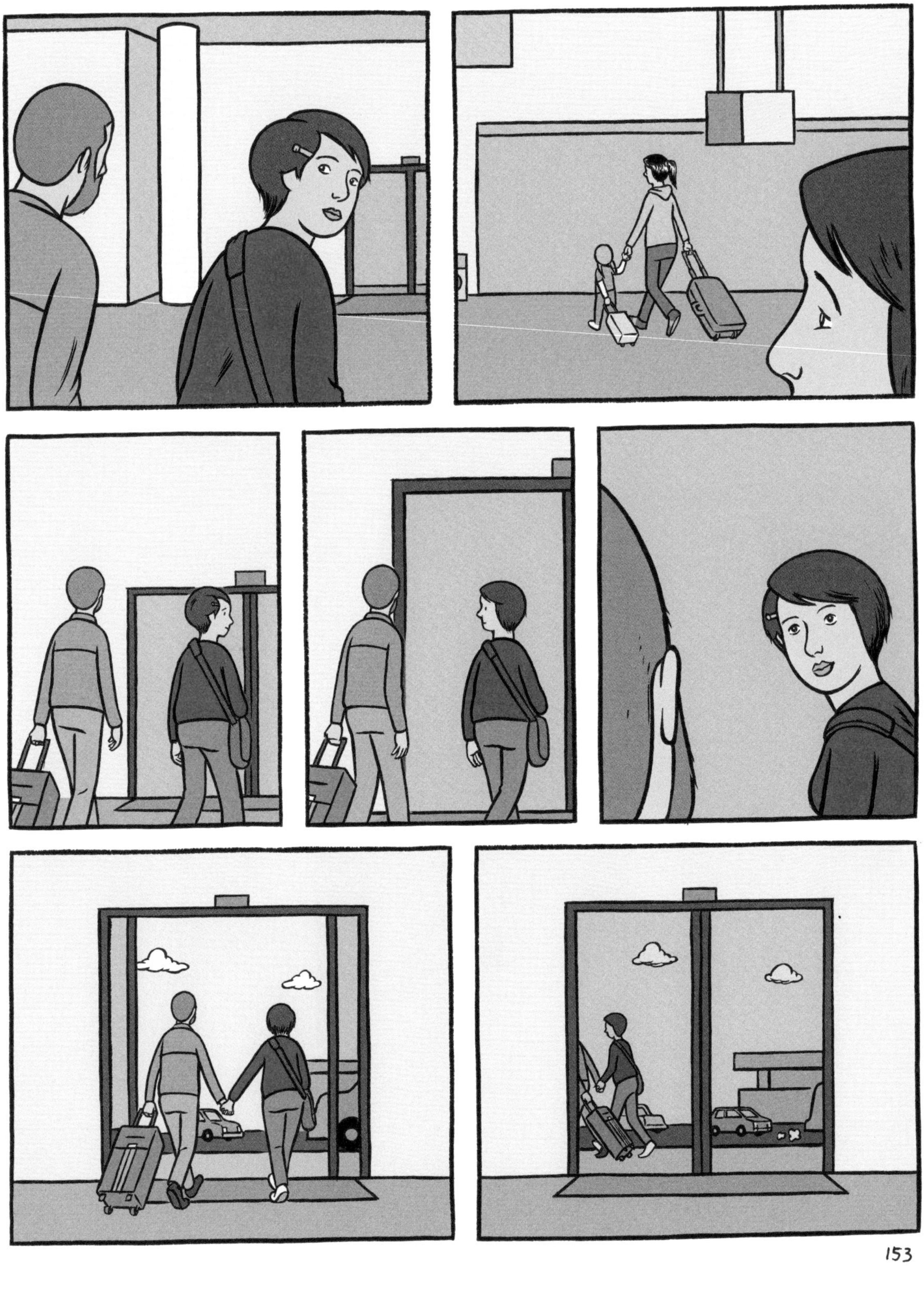

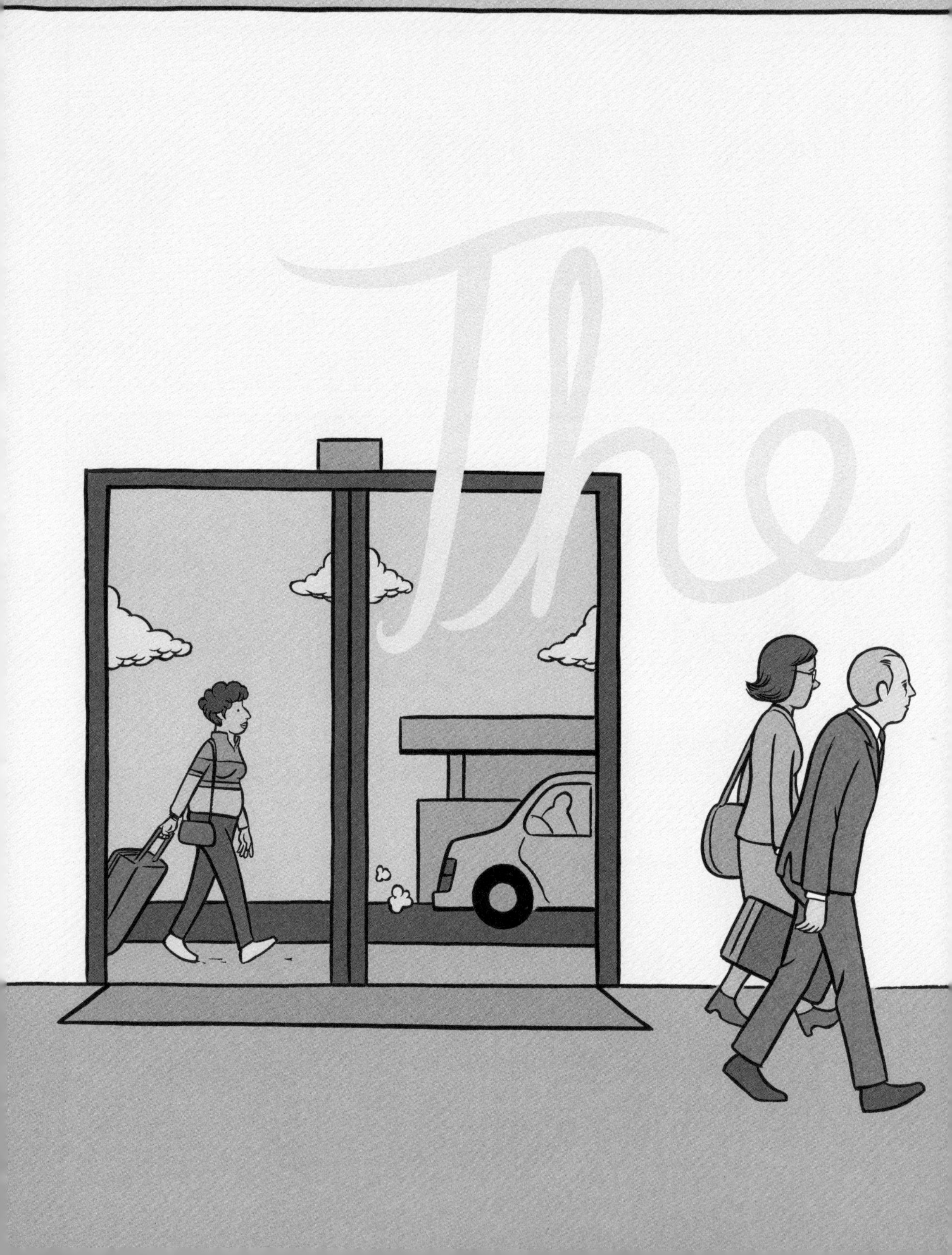
The

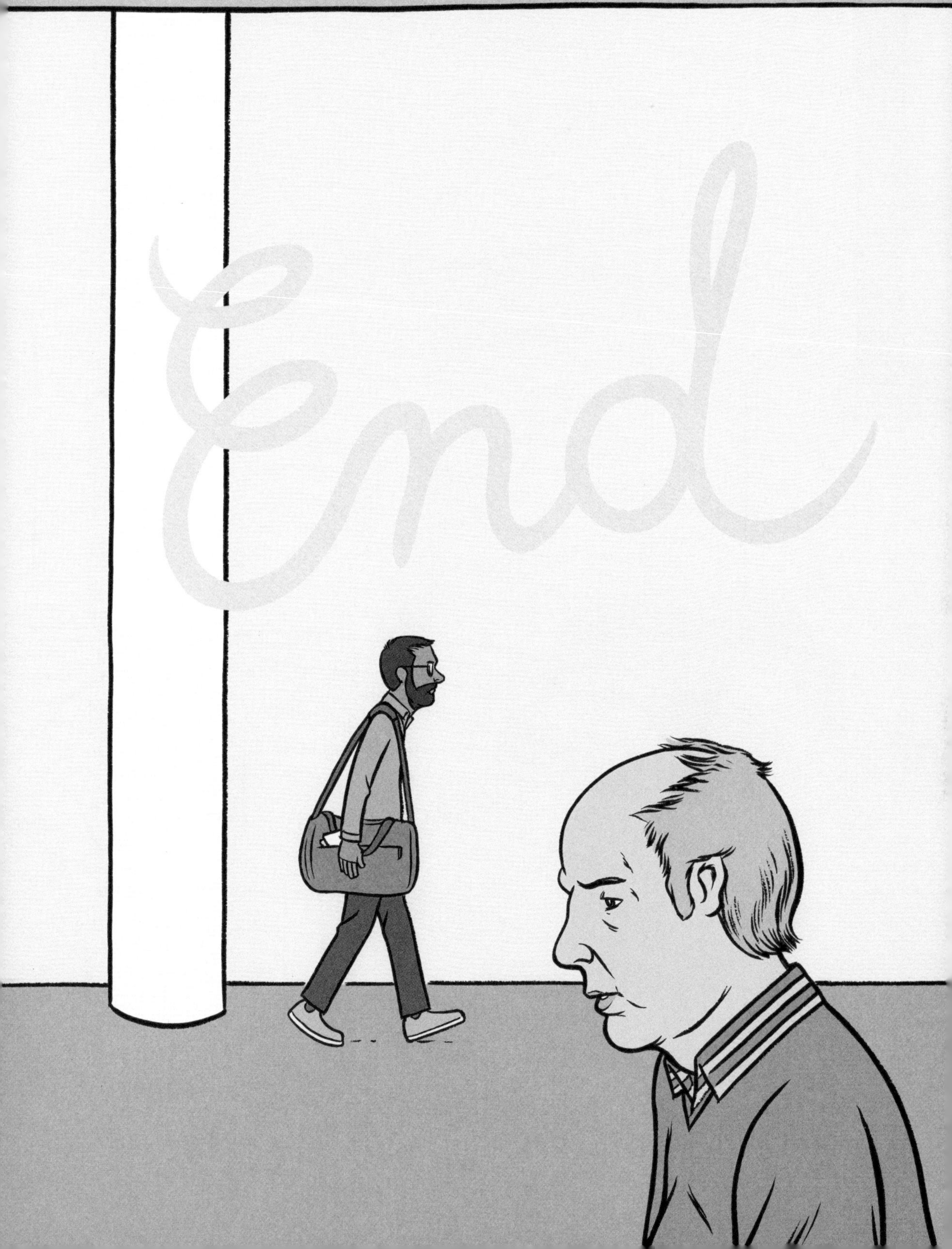
End

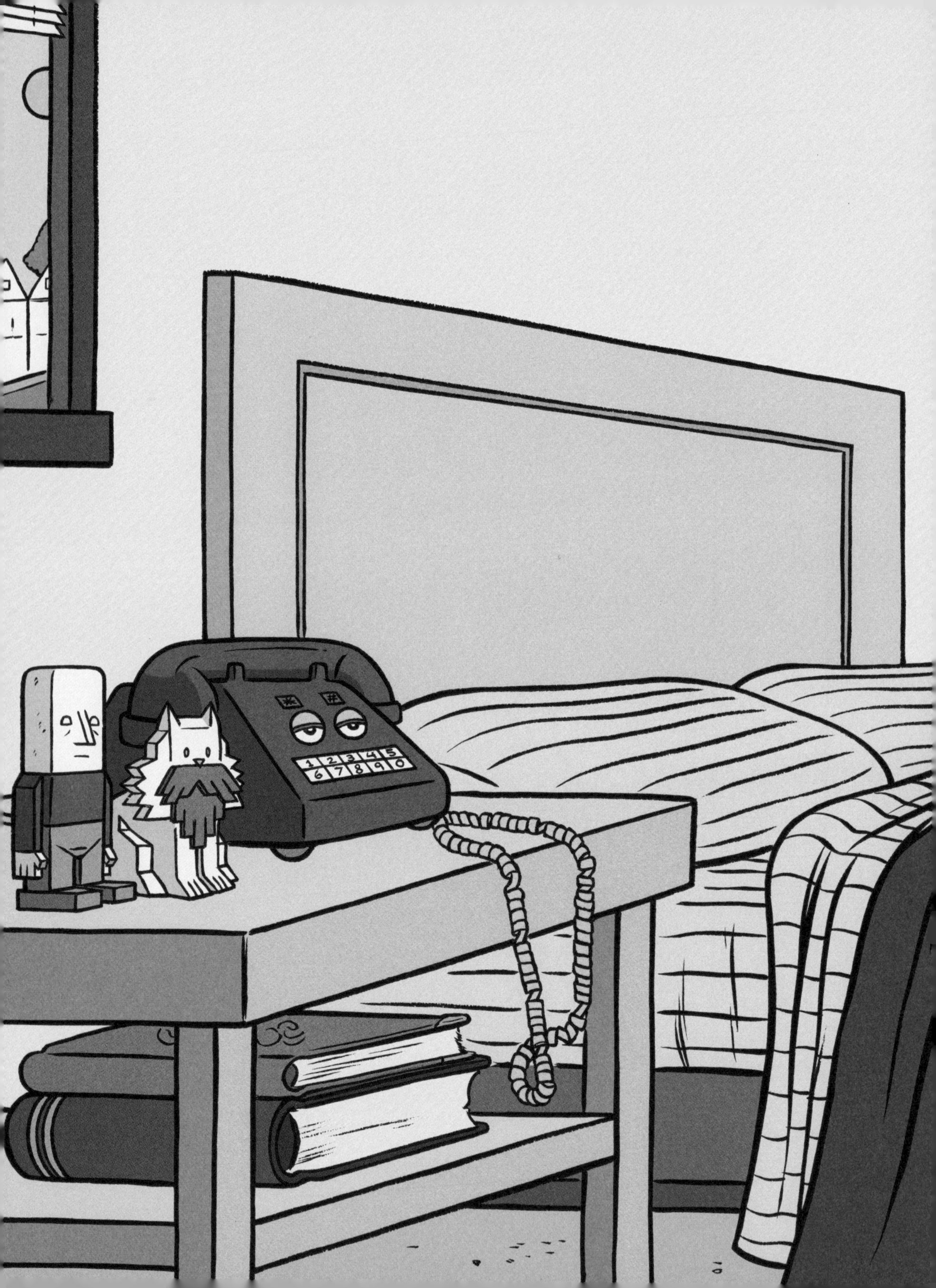

Thanks

A MILLION THANKS TO MY WIFE, EMILY, FOR HER ENDURING
EAR AND LAUGH. WITHOUT HER PATIENCE, LISTENING, AND
EXCITEMENT, LIFE WOULD BE INFINITELY MORE PALE.

TO MARGO, MY BEST FRIEND AND STUDIO MATE FOR THE PAST
DECADE. YOU ARE MISSED DAILY.

TO CHRIS SCHLUEP FOR HIS TENACITY AND CONVERSATION.
TO DANIEL GREENBERG, BETH FISHER, AND EVERYONE AT
LEVINE GREENBERG FOR ALL THEIR SUPPORT. TO ERIC
REYNOLDS, GARY GROTH, KIM THOMPSON, THE STAFF OF
FANTAGRAPHICS, AND ALL THE ARTISTS OF *MOME* FOR MY
TENURE THERE.

TO JULIANE GRAF FOR ALL HER INSPIRATION THROUGH
THE FORMATION OF THIS STORY AND MANY OTHERS.
FROM CEREAL BOX *SPASS* TO CASTLE CLIMBING, THANK YOU.

TO CHARLES HARTMAN FOR HIS DILIGENCE AND BELIEF.

AND THANK YOU TO ALL MY FRIENDS AND FAMILY WHO
READ AND LISTENED ALONG THE WAY.

AND TO YOU.
INSERT YOUR NAME HERE:

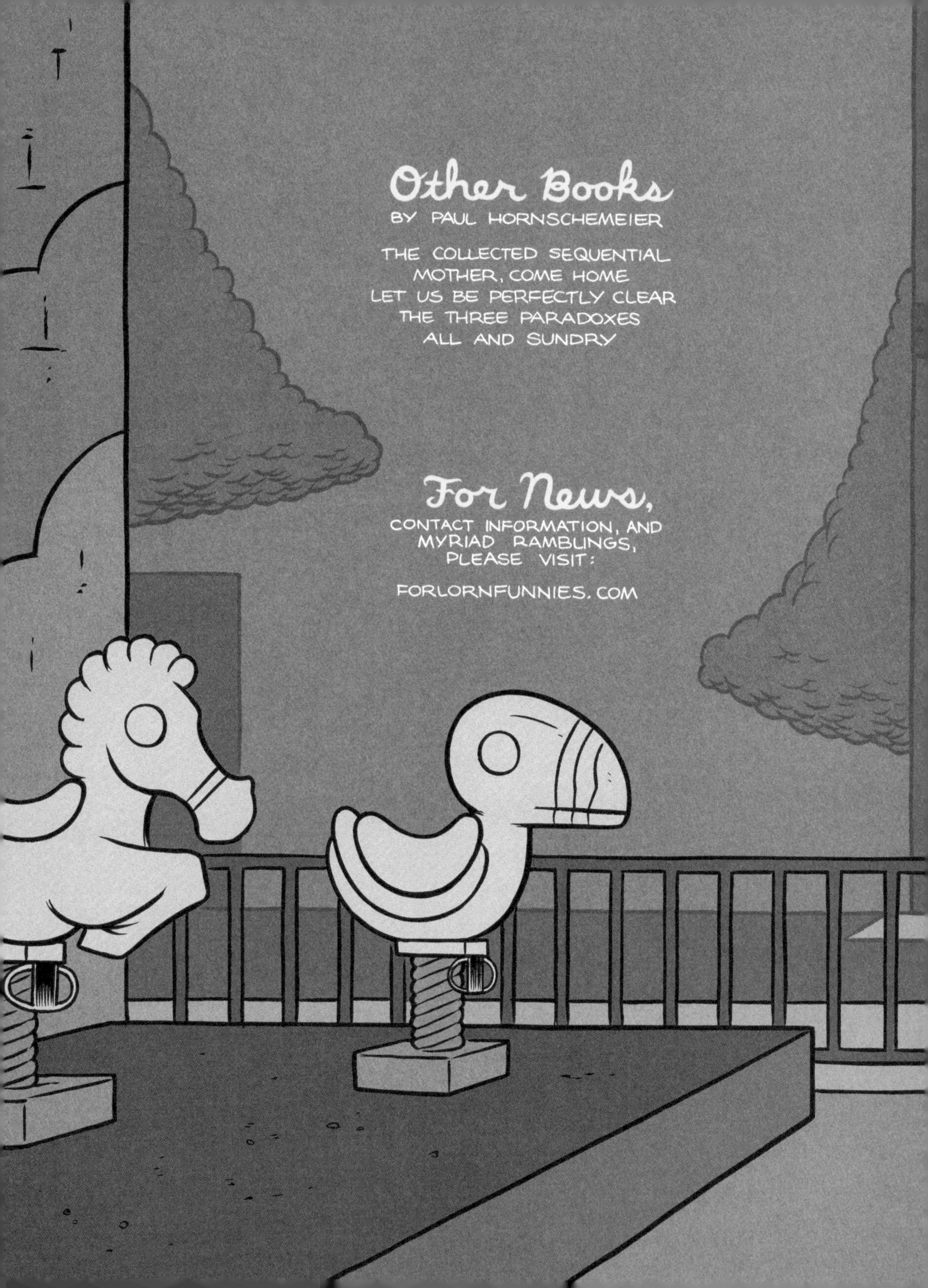

Other Books

BY PAUL HORNSCHEMEIER

THE COLLECTED SEQUENTIAL
MOTHER, COME HOME
LET US BE PERFECTLY CLEAR
THE THREE PARADOXES
ALL AND SUNDRY

For News,

CONTACT INFORMATION, AND MYRIAD RAMBLINGS, PLEASE VISIT:

FORLORNFUNNIES.COM

About the Author

PAUL HORNSCHEMEIER WAS BORN IN 1977 TO TWO CINCINNATI ATTORNEYS WHO OPTED TO REAR HIM AND HIS TWO SISTERS IN A SOUTHERN OHIO FARM TOWN. HE RECEIVED HIS FIRST COMIC BOOK FROM HIS DENTIST. HE CURRENTLY EATS TOO MANY SWEETS, A HABIT POSSIBLY ORIGINATING IN A CHILDHOOD DEPRIVATION OF SUGAR BY THE OTHERWISE WELL-MEANING AFOREMENTIONED ATTORNEYS. HIS WORK HAS BEEN TRANSLATED INTO MULTIPLE LANGUAGES AND HAS GARNERED ACCLAIM AND AWARDS AROUND THE WORLD. HE CURRENTLY LIVES IN EVANSTON, ILLINOIS WITH HIS WIFE. AS HE WRITES THIS ABOUT HIMSELF, A DISCARDED CHRISTMAS TREE RESTS ON ITS SIDE, WAITING BY THE CURB OUTSIDE HIS WINDOW, TO BE PICKED UP AS TRASH, BREEDING SIMULTANEOUS AND OFT-COUPLED PANGS OF NOSTALGIA AND DEPRESSION. THEN A DOG WALKS BY.

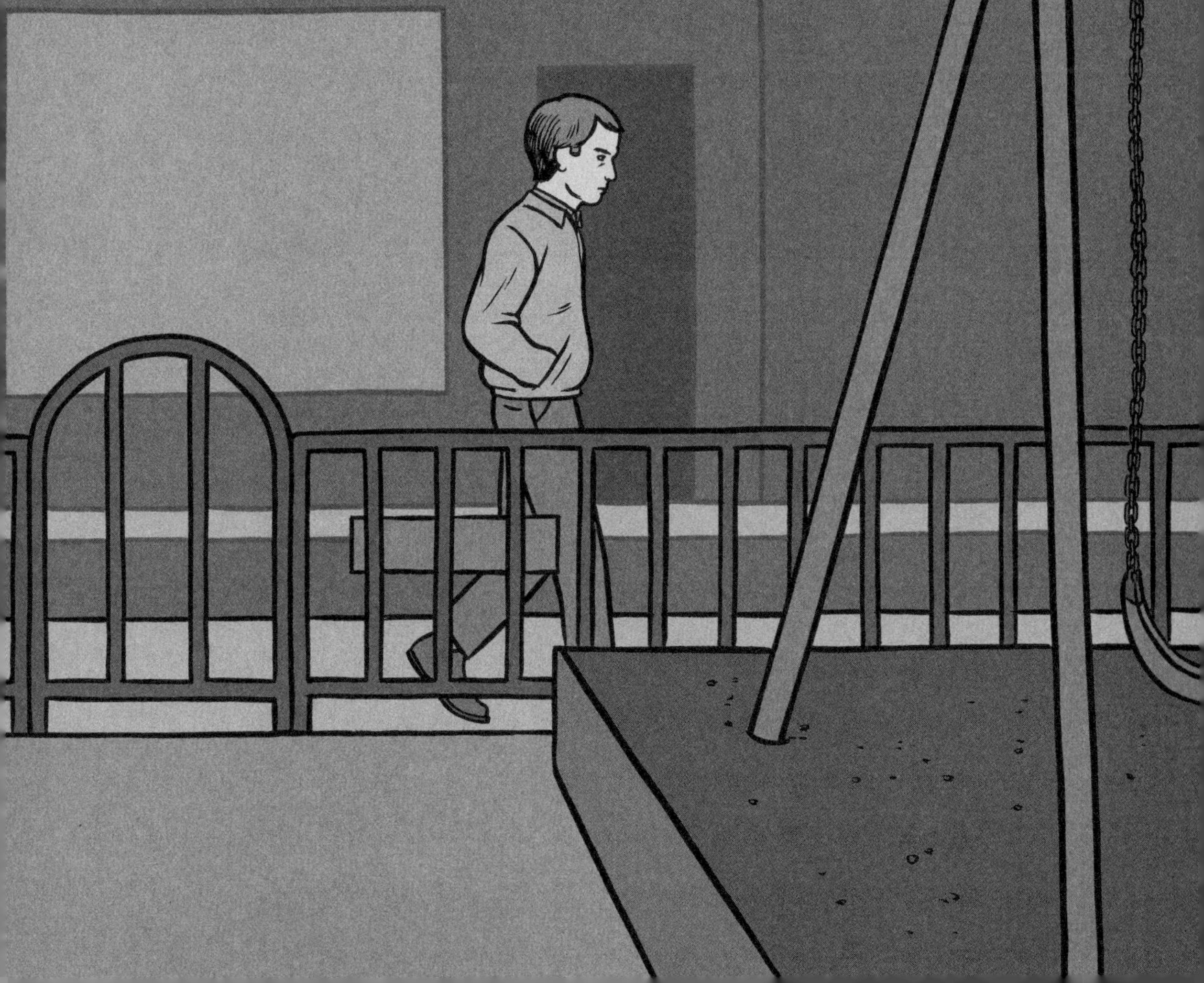

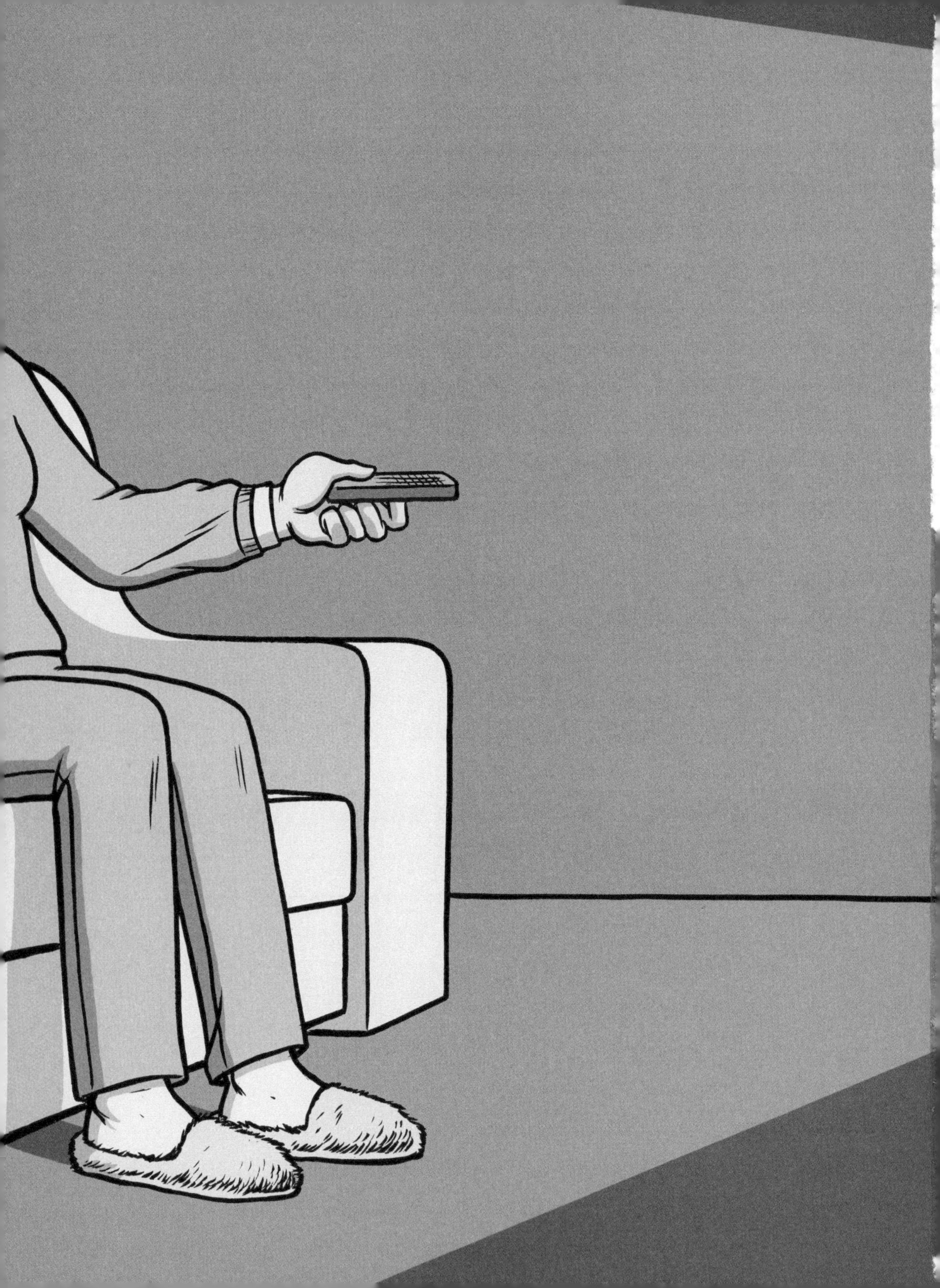